the GROSS

Also by Peter Bart

Fiction

Destinies

Thy Kingdom Come

Nonfiction

FADEOUT: The Calamitous Final Days of MGM

the GROSS

The Hits, the Flops—the Summer That Ate Hollywood

Peter Bart

St. Martin's Griffin ⚮ New York

Book Design by Gretchen Achilles

ISBN 0-312-25391-5

First St. Martin's Griffin Edition: February 2000

10 9 8 7 6 5 3 2 1

Contents

The GROSS

Introduction

When I opened the steel door leading to the sound stage, a rush of noxious air greeted me, as though I had pried open a long-abandoned cellar. The air smelled at once moldy and metallic, and stepping inside only reinforced a sense of the ominous. The grinding noise of large equipment being moved into place and the voices of men shouting could be heard. At the center of this vast stage was a giant polyurethane asteroid, a grotesque object whose bilious hues of green and gray made it look diseased and alien. The object was so huge that there was scant room for the men and machines to maneuver around it.

For some ninety days a crew of seventy-five artisans had labored over this plastic blob, shooting some three thousand takes of men in space suits crawling around and through it. On two occasions the crew, including the director, had become ill from the mold and foul smell, and the set had to be shut down. But now there was a growing realization that the time had come to nuke the damned thing—literally—and be done with it. The actors, hot and steamy inside their helmets and space suits, had had enough of the set. So had Michael Bay, the temperamental young director who presided over the asteroid like a relentless tyrant, barking orders into his walkie-talkie.

"Why aren't you ready down there?" Bay demanded, aiming his remarks at a cluster of technicians preparing the detonation in the bowels of the asteroid. This was the sort of prodding normally made by the assistant director, but Bay was inclined to forgo the customary channels. Slim and hawk-faced, with eyes like a bird of prey, Bay ran his own set and barked his own instructions.

The technicians replied they still had to prepare a few more safeguards and would be ready shortly. Bay rolled his eyes—there were always delays to be dealt with, and he was not a patient man. This was a complex set and it smelled awful, but at least there were real actors on hand and they were shooting a real scene. He had spent several weeks on sound stages working with actors who were effectively talking to themselves in front of a blue screen. In the final movie, of course, an audience would see them interacting with some morphed creature or perhaps with a computer-generated spacecraft. So much of moviemaking now consisted of spouting lines on empty sets and catering to the tyranny of special-effects wizards.

What was about to happen on the set of *Armageddon* was of no small import, to be sure. A nuclear device was about to be buried in the asteroid and, by blowing it up and getting blown up with it, Bruce Willis would save the world. Cameras had been positioned all over the stage to record this historic event, including one sticking out of the end of a tall Chapman crane.

"Just another day at Disney," Jerry Bruckheimer, the steely producer, shrugged. "We're out here saving the world, and sucking up this moldy air as our just reward." A slender man with a poker player's wary eyes, Bruckheimer wore a sports jacket and monogrammed shirt that contrasted with the combat gear of his youthful crew.

Moments later there was a blast, followed by a plume of smoke. Men around the stage chattered away on their walkie-talkies, assessing the detonation with a high solemnity suggesting they had just bombed terrorist bases in the Middle East. Michael Bay looked over to me. "That one was a success, which means we're gonna do it again anyway," he said dryly, and proceeded to bark the order for the next take.

A day on the set of *Armageddon* was an appropriate welcome to moviemaking at the end of the century. In a quiet, insidious way, just about everything has changed over the last several years in the way movies are created, edited, and marketed. In the old days, when you wandered onto a sound stage actors would be playing a scene for the camera with the director looking on. It was a bit like shooting a play.

It doesn't happen that way anymore. On the sound stages you're more likely to see a single actor reciting his lines against a blank background—lines that will be reacted to by something or someone that the computer graphics mavens will conjure up. The setup that the director sees through his viewfinder may bear no relation to what the moviegoer ultimately will see. The images will be massaged, morphed, and digitally hyped until an entirely different vision emerges; then that material is fed into electronic editing machines to be mixed and matched, sliced and diced so that the finished film can be propelled into theaters in record time. The *auteur* of the movie is as much the techie as the director.

Indeed, the entire process has been so digitally accelerated that movies often find their way into theaters before the filmmakers themselves can ruminate over what they have wrought and before the studios can properly test and temper their product.

And if the modus operandi is changing fast on the sound stages and in the editing rooms, the pace is even more bewildering in the arenas of marketing and distribution.

A mere twenty years ago, it was common practice to open a movie in a few theaters across the country, build word of mouth, adjust advertising strategies to audience response, and then slowly expand to an ever broader audience. Today a movie is unveiled, not with a quietly orchestrated build, but with a cosmic paroxysm, a global spasm of hype involving giant marketing partners like McDonald's and profligate network ad buys on the Super Bowl or the Olympics. A new film is thus machine-tooled to become either an instant blockbuster or an overnight flop. There is no room for adjustment or strategic change. There is no shelf life available for the weak or infirm in the bold new Darwinian economics of the nineties.

Summer is crunch time for the movie industry—a time when egos are on the line, when careers rise and fall, when the specter of failure looms large. The summer months are responsible for roughly 40 percent of Hollywood's box office revenues, and the race for dominance continually grows ever more feverish—and expensive. Each year studios spend exponentially more money on their effects-laden blockbusters, and the spoils of victory grow more enticing. Vast riches in the form of bonuses, gross percentages, and other perks rain down upon the stars and filmmakers who gamble wisely. More important, those who figure in the hits of summer come away with the power to squander untold millions on their future projects—the chance to compete yet again in the next summer crunch time. And for the losers, dreams are dashed, careers blown away.

No previous summer spotlighted these forces more vividly than the summer of 1998. It was a summer of the unexpected.

Summer '98 was supposed to belong to *Godzilla* and *Armageddon,* the two most extravagantly hyped movies in the history of the movies. But it didn't happen that way. Instead, summer '98 was memorable because of several movies of the sort that are never supposed to open in summer—*Saving Private Ryan, The Truman Show,* and *Bulworth* among them.

And there were myriad other surprises. A cheaply made gross-out comedy generated twice the revenues of a Steven Spielberg high-concept adventure; two pricey asteroid films collided, yet neither suffered damage; Jim Carrey made a hit movie that didn't offer a single laugh; Eddie Murphy buried his hard edge long enough to create two successful, warm-and-cuddly family films; Harrison Ford made a love story playing opposite a self-avowed lesbian; and finally, defying the mythology of the "youth demos," two stars in their sixties, Robert Redford and Warren Beatty, enjoyed yet another warm moment in the sun.

While everyone was talking about these surprises, however, summer '98 marked another milestone that few in the industry were eager to acknowledge. In a curious sort of public confession, the corporate chiefs who controlled the movie industry stepped forward, one after the other, to admit that they really didn't want to be in the business of making films after all. The economics of moviemaking were out of control, they declared. Profit margins had all but disappeared. While product was needed to fill the distribution pipelines of their vast multinational corporations, the suits acknowledged publicly that they wished someone else would come along to help share the risk.

In stating this, of course, they were tacitly admitting their own failure. Over the last generation, control of the studios had passed from professional movie people to the CEOs of multinational corporations, whose main interest was in distribution, not production. And as the corporations grew bigger, and management more lax, the fundamental equations of moviemaking no longer applied. In a business dependent on risk-taking, the inordinate increase in production and marketing costs had rendered the risks prohibitive.

As the production chief of one major studio told me in June of 1998, "People look at the strong grosses and ask me why the business seems to be in a state of depression. I'll tell them why: When I inform my boss and the board of directors about the movies I am making, they all look like they're passing a kidney stone. They don't really believe in movies, and that negativity gets subtly passed down the line until it poisons an entire company."

Paradoxically, when the box office receipts of summer '98 were added up, they set a season record. Moviegoers rallied to support their favorites. Grosses surpassed all expectations. But by summer's end, the mood of Rupert Murdoch, Sumner Redstone, Edgar Bronfman Jr., and other corporate chieftains remained the same. They may have survived another summer, but they were looking even more hungrily for someone else to foot the bill. Sure, the movie business was glamorous and exciting; they just wished they weren't in it.

The dysfunctional economics of the movie industry will make itself felt in many ways as this book wends its way through the melodramas of summer '98. I will focus not only on the "suits," but also on the people who actually wrote, directed, produced, and starred in the movies of summer. My purpose is to reveal why particular films got made, who was responsible for their creation, and who were the true heroes and villains—not only in the making of the films, but also in their marketing and distribution.

But the overriding question to be examined relates to the system itself, to the way it inhibits the true innovators and encourages the mediocre. For summer '98 served up a much-needed reminder of Hollywood's true potential to create movies that offer a glimpse of truth, not merely a splash of effect-laden fantasy. With all of its false moves and stubbed toes the summer of '98 was a wake-up call.

A brief note about point of view: I have lived a split-level life in Hollywood. Half of my years here have been devoted to journalism, first as a reporter for the *New York Times,* then as editor-in-chief of *Variety* and *Daily Variety,* the Los Angeles–based newspapers that cover the media and entertainment industries. Sandwiched between these two stints was a seventeen-year career as a production executive at Paramount, Lorimar, and MGM/UA. It was a career that was at times exciting, at others utterly exasperating. Along the way, I held titles ranging from vice president to president, and there was usually an inverse correlation between the weight of the title and the satisfaction of the job.

As a result, I admit to a sort of two-edged perspective about the movie business, and about the annual siege of summer pictures in particular. As a journalist, I have sat at screenings and said to myself, "How could they have made this movie? What were they thinking?" As a member of the team that helped shape these movies, I remember saying to myself, "How could this great idea have turned out so lousy?" Or, more rarely, I would think, "This movie is so damned good I already feel the elbows of people maneuvering to grab credit."

As a neophyte in the film business, I lived through summers at Paramount that seemed surreal, and, from the perspective of history, that was an accurate impression. I remember a preview of an absolutely wretched Julie Andrews musical called *Darling Lili* in summer '70 which featured a uniquely nonerotic love scene between Julie and Rock Hudson—the only movie love scene I ever saw that elicited boos from the audience. By the end of the screening, it seemed as if the entire theater had fallen into a bored stupor, too groggy even to fill out preview cards. Shortly thereafter, a pricey Italian import called *Red Tent* also was previewed, to even more devastating results. By the time the movie ended, the entire audience had fled, leaving no one in the theater but the crestfallen producer and studio executives.

I had nothing to do with the decision to make either of these movies, but I could never shake the creepy-crawly feeling that comes with disaster. Happily, subsequent summers brought more highs than lows. I learned there were few experiences more exhilarating than watching a hit movie for the first time with an audience, sensing the emotion, hearing the laughs, watching hankies come out to dab the eyes. The first screenings of *The Godfather* provided that sort of high, though even as audiences loved the movie, the studio marketing chiefs still shook their heads, predicting failure. At times like that you come to understand the almost mystical power of film, the potential to surprise and to manipulate, to entertain, and even, now and then, to inform.

As a journalist, you sense all this, but studiously remain above the fray. You are one step removed from the anguish and frustration, from the politics and greed. You understand what's at stake in terms of money; you cannot, however, grasp the emotional investment—the ambitions dashed, the egos fractured. Viewed from this perspective, Hollywood provides a never-ending cavalcade of intrigue and adventure. The business of entertainment is itself marvelously entertaining.

GENESIS

The Strategy

Before leading his troops into battle in World War II, George S. Patton, the brave and bizarre general, always paused to study military history. A believer in reincarnation, Patton was persuaded not only that history repeated itself, but that he personally had played a role in the great campaigns of antiquity.

Hollywood's top generals also tried to assimilate the lessons of the past before determining their profligate strategies for the summer of 1998. Specifically, they grappled with the message, or mixed messages, of the summer before—the baffling summer of 1997. Not surprisingly, they came away with divergent conclusions.

To Bill Mechanic, who held the title of chairman of filmed entertainment at Twentieth Century Fox, the lesson of 1997 was one of caution. Formerly the top video executive at Disney but a relative newcomer to the front lines of the movie business, the soft-spoken Mechanic had emerged from 1997 feeling bruised. Having survived enormously expensive movies like *Titanic* and *Speed 2*, he decreed that there would be no more $100 million extravaganzas. Every Fox release would be designed for a specific demographic group—a sort of built-in safety net—with the hope that one or two would gain the momentum to reach a wider audience.

Disney's steely, silvery-haired studio chief, Joe Roth, meanwhile, came to the opposite conclusion. Having formerly occupied Mechanic's post at Fox, Roth had observed many cyclical swings over the years and had decided that this season represented not a threat but an opportunity. "Since most of my competitors got beat up pretty bad in summer '97, I figured they'd be pulling in their horns," he told me in late September 1997, "so I told myself, let's go for it." For the Disney studio, this would translate into $100 million–plus gambles like *Mulan* and *Armageddon* as well as far heavier ad spending on all projects. The time had come to spread the chips across the table.

What untoward events had occurred the year before to produce such contrasting strategies?

Basically, summer '97 was a study in Hollywood hubris, a season when every studio seemed caught up in the mythology of the blockbuster. Backed by massive fusillades of advertising, some thirty-five movies were slated to open nationwide, at least ten of which would cost over $100 million. To be sure, many seemed like safe bets— sequels to such hits as *Batman, Jurassic Park,* and *Speed,* for example. The path to success looked clear enough—lavish millions on TV campaigns, mobilize a few free-spending promotion partners such as fast-food chains and toy companies, and then spread the movies across every available screen at every multiplex and megaplex one could find.

Certainly *Independence Day,* the unexpected megahit of summer '96, had reinforced this strategy, becoming Hollywood's first billion-dollar blockbuster. *ID4,* as it came to be known, demonstrated more convincingly than ever the studios' apparent ability to create action-oriented, effects-laden entertainments that would seize the imagination of audiences worldwide, spewing forth vast revenues not only at the box office but from music, TV, theme parks, video, and myriad other tie-ins. If Hollywood had a lock on the blockbuster, then the brave new world of computer graphics had only enhanced this amazing franchise. With this sense of invincibility, Hollywood marched into summer '97.

The heady mood was quickly punctured. Starting around Memorial Day, Hollywood found itself launching one projectile after another, only to see it fizzle and fall to earth.

The first studio to start wringing its hands was Warner Bros., led for almost two decades by the imperiously self-confident team of Robert Daly and Terry Semel. Rarely straying from safe, formulaic super-star projects, Daly and Semel started their summer with a formula comedy, *Father's Day*, starring Billy Crystal and Robin Williams, and the fourth iteration of their *Batman* franchise, *Batman and Robin*. Hoping for a respectable opening weekend of about $12 million, *Father's Day* debuted instead to a tepid $8.8 million. As its grizzled distribution chief, Barry Reardon, put it, "The audience simply rejected the concept." (The movie ultimately did a paltry $36.4 million worldwide.)

Batman and Robin, too, opened to the weakest numbers of any *Batman* sequel. Disney's animated entry, *Hercules*, did respectable business, but its audience was disappointing compared with its triumphant predecessor, *The Lion King*. Twentieth Century Fox trotted out a big disaster picture called *Volcano*, but whatever anticipation may have existed had been drained off by *Dante's Peak*, another volcano epic released four months earlier.

There was a bright spot, to be sure. The ever-dependable Steven Spielberg delivered yet another major hit in *Jurassic Park: The Lost World*. Indeed, so sure were rival filmmakers that Spielberg still held the magic formula that they waged a furious battle for the right to attach their previews, called trailers, to his print. All told, some eleven movies jostled for the vaunted "*Jurassic* slot," including two projects which, as it would turn out, didn't need it—Sony's *Men in Black* and the Fox-Paramount co-venture, *Titanic*, which was originally slated as a summer picture, but had been pushed back to winter due to production delays.

But if Spielberg had mastered the formula, his rivals had not. It was Fox's sequel to *Speed*, called *Speed 2: Cruise Control*, that provided the most devastating evidence. The first *Speed*, released in 1996, had cost a mere $37 million and grossed $125 million in the U.S. alone. Confident that it had uncovered a new franchise, Fox poured some $140 million into the sequel, even though Keanu Reeves, who had costarred with Sandra Bullock in the original, had bowed out of *Speed 2* and been replaced by an inert actor, Jason

Patric. Opening amid an extravagant promotional blast, *Speed 2* registered a respectable $16.2 million at 2,600 theaters, but then sank beneath the radar; the film ultimately grossed a mere $48.6 million in the U.S. but partially recouped with $105.2 million overseas.

The failure of *Speed 2* came as a particular shock because it contradicted the notion that special-effects movies were the new opiate of the mass market. When *Twister* became a big hit in 1996, Hollywood felt sure that digital magic could compensate for the absence of credible story and character. Not so for *Speed 2*, which featured arguably the most expensive special-effects stunt yet attempted. Audiences would supposedly be riveted by the sight of a giant cruise ship smashing into a coastal resort, literally sailing through the middle of town. "The audience thought it was blah," reported Bill Mechanic in disbelief after seeing a preview. "Fun rides aren't enough anymore."

By the beginning of July 1997, a palpable gloom had settled over the studios. Executives wore long faces; even the lunchtime crowds in the commissaries seemed subdued. Summer had reached its halfway point by Hollywood's calendar and, as *Variety* intoned, "few expect that a second-half upturn will bring the numbers up to the '96 level." It wasn't merely that the summer movies were misfiring; they all seemed alarmingly similar. "The audience feels they've already seen most of the new movies," observed Howard Lichtman, executive vice president of the Cineplex chain.

And the losses kept mounting. While the studios tried to keep budget figures secret, the whole town seemed to be whispering that *Speed 2* and *Batman and Robin* both had approached $150 million in cost, and there was a growing buzz about James Cameron's runaway project shooting in Mexico—a movie called *Titanic* that would become history's most expensive epic. *Titanic* had been scheduled to be the centerpiece of Fox's summer, but production delays now ruled out that possibility. Given its complex special effects, *Titanic* would be iffy even for Christmas.

Just at the time when insiders were concluding that there would be no sleepers—surprise hits—to rescue the summer, along came the ultimate sleeper. It was called *Men in Black* and it opened, ironically, on Independence Day.

Men in Black did not exactly come out of the blue. Early tracking studies—Hollywood's name for audience research—had suggested a strong "want-to-see," especially among young moviegoers, but Sony, a jinxed studio for several years, had held its breath, afraid of its own projections. Certainly there were reasons for skepticism. The movie lacked a major star. Its skimpy story blatantly reflected its comic book origins. And in an era when movies dawdled well past two-and-a-half hours, *Men in Black* clocked in at ninety-eight minutes, with credits.

As the old pros like to put it, however, *Men in Black* didn't open—it exploded. The picture generated $51 million at the box office during its initial three-day weekend. By mid-July it had already grossed close to $140 million and was being heralded as the hit of the summer.

And suddenly, everyone seemed to be getting lucky. Disney's eccentric little comedy, *George of the Jungle*, was packing in the kids—its success enhanced considerably by a massive injection of McDonald's promotion money. Sony's comedy *My Best Friend's Wedding* struck a chord with the female audience as a welcome bit of counterprogramming. *Air Force One*, starring Harrison Ford as a sort of presidential last-action hero, also rolled up astonishing box office numbers, ultimately grossing almost $300 million worldwide.

Suddenly "the summer that wasn't" seemed like a ringing success, and the momentum continued into the fall. First came a couple of low-profile sleepers, *Bean* and *The Full Monty*, both of which arrived in the U.S. with rave notices from abroad. By year's end, *Bean* had grossed a formidable $217 million, *The Full Monty* not far behind with $167 million—the most profitable movies of the year by far relative to their modest cost.

But the defining moment of 1997 was to occur in December when Twentieth Century Fox and Paramount jointly delivered their much-delayed, much-maligned Christmas present—*Titanic*. Costing be-

tween $220 million and $240 million (depending on which accounting methods are used), *Titanic* was too long, too expensive, and too
accident-prone. By year's end it already had grossed $134 million, on
its way to $1.3 billion worldwide.

The very executives who had earlier scaled back their spending
and their expectations were now even more perplexed. Final numbers
revealed that the industry had rolled up an impressive 8.3 percent
gain in total box office, the highest jump of the decade. Moreover,
admissions had climbed to 1.31 billion, the loftiest level since 1966,
when the rapid rise of television all but decimated the moviegoing
audience. Some twelve Hollywood movies had grossed more than
$100 million in the U.S. alone, while seventeen did so internation-
ally—numbers that seemed to validate the idea of the $100 million
movie.

Yet some of the year-end data was troubling. For one thing, the
largesse was divided up disproportionately, with Sony and Disney
having the lion's share while other companies—especially Warner—
had lean pickings. Moreover, the amount of money being lavished on
producing and marketing had clearly escalated to daunting levels.
According to figures released by the Motion Picture Association of
America, the average studio movie cost over $75 million in terms of
combined production and advertising expenditures. This meant that
the typical Hollywood movie essentially had to achieve blockbuster-
level revenues in order to recoup its investment—something that
clearly was not taking place.

Apart from cost, there was an even bigger issue of content. A
curious weightlessness characterized even the hit movies of summer
'97, almost as though they had been designed to be instantly forgotten.
The much-ballyhooed sequels, whether to *Batman* or *Speed,* somehow
emerged more like products off an industrial assembly line that had
been machine-tooled rather than crafted. Comedies like *Father's Day*
seemed oddly flat; *George of the Jungle* was almost too obviously tailored for McDonald's cross-promotions. Even the clever *Men in Black*
was oddly derivative, a spoof without a target, an empty vessel de-

signed to sell goods, yet ridiculing the very act of commerce. It represented a new genre—as critic David Denby termed it: corporate irony.

In the end, Hollywood had escaped what at the outset had seemed like looming disaster. It nonetheless sustained a bad scare. If summer '97 was a success, it was a hairy success—something no one wanted to relive.

Yet, even as the 1998 summer releases were being hammered into place, there was a lingering suspicion among many that things would not be that different, that irrevocable forces had been put in place that could not easily be reversed. "Going into the summer I felt that the trains were already on the track, that they were rumbling my way and that all I could do was jump out of the way and watch the pileup," said Michelle Manning, president of production at Paramount and one of the sharper young executives in town.

Indeed, more and more of the young executives, like Manning, approached the rites of summer with a certain foreboding. To them, October and February represented the more challenging niches on the schedule—times when studios could launch their more artistically ambitious projects, without massive TV fusillades. Summer, like Christmas, meant go-for-broke, when the big moviegoing audiences were out there, wallets in hand. Summer was blockbuster time.

Most of the movies that would be released in summer '98 had been in the works for years—a glimmer in a filmmaker's eye. Starting in the fall of 1997, the studios had begun the process of lining up their likely summer candidates. The process had accelerated through winter and into the spring, when the final slates had been agreed upon.

At each studio, the process had taken a different shape, reflecting the personality of the studio chief as well as the financial condition and strategic objectives of the company itself.

At Disney's well-oiled machine, preparations for summer seemed almost like a paramilitary operation. Both the officers and the enlisted men had been through all this many times before. They appeared ready for whatever eventualities they might face.

At Universal, a certain skittishness was in evidence. A new management was in place and some exasperating eleventh-hour decisions had to be made—decisions that would resonate with import as the company's future plans took shape.

At Warner Bros., a studio caught in a desperate downward spiral, a palpable crisis mentality gripped the studio as executives cobbled together a summer program of pictures to fill what had suddenly appeared to be an ominous void.

The days of reckoning were at hand.

The Studios

Paramount

The executive team at Paramount was feeling a strong sense of vindication with the approach of summer '98. The studio had been the first to systematically demand financial partners for its more expensive movies, and at first had been denigrated by rivals and Hollywood pundits. Because of its rigid insistence on "passing the hat," critics said, Paramount had lost out on many profitable projects and had given away much of its upside on those movies it had decided to make.

The cofinancing schemes were especially frustrating to the studio's own production staff, which frequently had to tell agents, "We like your movie, now bring us half the money." According to the second-guessers, Paramount should have owned all rights to hits like *Face/Off* instead of settling for half the action. The studio had developed *Saving Private Ryan*, but nonetheless ended up with a split-rights deal with DreamWorks.

The rationale for this policy, as implemented by Sherry Lansing, president of production, and Jonathan Dolgen, who looked after the business side, was to make the studio's dollars go further and reduce the risk. Look how the policy had worked on *Titanic*, they argued. Paramount and Twentieth Century Fox had cofunded the movie, but Paramount's contribution was capped at $65 million and the movie ended up costing around $300 million to produce and market. Thus Paramount ended up making millions without experiencing either the risk or the pain of the troubled but hugely successful production.

Indeed, going into summer, the studio was way ahead of the pack in market share, thanks to the success of *Titanic*, and Lansing and Dolgen both felt confident that their summer projects would keep them there. *Deep Impact*, a coproduction with DreamWorks, had been tracking excellently and, slated to open earlier than *Armageddon*, could claim first place in the asteroid derby. *The Truman Show*, starring Jim Carrey, had been shown to influential critics throughout the spring and was receiving ecstatic responses. There also were high hopes for *Snake Eyes*, a thriller directed by Brian De Palma starring Nicolas Cage.

And then there was *Saving Private Ryan*. Several of the bright young production executives at the studio felt that this was one of the best screenplays developed by any company in years. Don Granger, an executive vice president, had hired Robert Rodat to develop the script from an original idea. When Steven Spielberg shocked everyone by saying he wanted to direct the film, suddenly *Saving Private Ryan* became a DreamWorks-Paramount project. To some unhappy Paramount executives, this meant that DreamWorks would get all the credit, not to mention glean half the revenues.

Ever the shrewd politician, Sherry Lansing managed to deflect much of the criticism. A onetime teacher who had worked briefly as an actress, the fifty-six-year-old Lansing had been Hollywood's first woman studio chief, starting at Fox in 1980, and few had greater insight into the workings of Hollywood's power pyramid. While her counterparts at rival studios—Joe Roth at Disney and John Calley at Sony, for example—avoided the social circuit, Lansing was constantly in motion. Cheerful and exuberant, she would work the room at industry functions like an elected official, piping her familiar "Hi, honey" greeting to all.

Lansing's supporters pointed to her solidly mainstream commercial tastes and to her popularity in the creative community. Critics, on the other hand, argued that Lansing had become so wealthy, and had been at the top so long, that she was no longer motivated to do the really hard work of a studio executive—meeting young talent and scouting out intriguing new movies. "I really like Sherry, but whenever we're in a meeting, I honestly feel she'd prefer to be shopping at Neiman's," said one top director who had worked at Paramount.

Behind her smiling exterior, Lansing could be tough on colleagues. "She's as iron-willed as any guy in the business," insisted one of her top employees. "The smile can vanish in a nanosecond."

Her partner, Jonathan Dolgen, who held the title of chairman, Viacom Entertainment Group, also knew the town well, having worked at Fox and Columbia. A heavy-set man with fierce blue eyes, the fifty-four-year-old Dolgen knew how to mobilize the power of a studio to implement his policies. A jazz lover, Dolgen could put his feet up and talk about music for hours in the middle of a hectic business day. He was also a tough—and, some say, unnecessarily combative—negotiator.

Lansing and Dolgen had their doubters when they took office in 1994. But despite all the naysayers, the studio had been a consistent performer over the years, and its pass-the-hat policy was now accepted gospel at virtually every studio. Far from criticizing Paramount's deals, other studios suddenly were emulating them.

Paramount, too, had weathered the tough times of the parent company, Viacom, controlled by a seventy-five-year-old former film exhibitor from Boston, Sumner Redstone. Despite a booming stock market, Viacom shares had been inert over the last couple of years, principally in reaction to what had become known as the "Blockbuster problem." In acquiring the vast video chain in 1994, Viacom had expected to benefit from its huge revenues—Blockbuster was considered a cash machine at the time. But shortly after the purchase, the video rental business slumped.

Finally, between November 1997 and May 1998, Wall Street's analysts revised their estimates upward and Viacom stock doubled in value, only to hit another pothole, dropping about 6 percent just around the time that *Deep Impact* and *The Truman Show* both experienced excellent openings. All this served as a reminder that, given the size and diversity of global entertainment conglomerates, the performance of individual movies no longer impacted share prices.

Yet Viacom as a whole seemed in solid shape as summer '98 drew near. The MTV networks were a strong franchise, Nickelodeon was immensely healthy, and a greater than predicted $4.6 billion sale of Viacom's book publishing unit had been completed. And last, there was Paramount, which had suddenly emerged as Viacom's fastest-growing division—fastest, that is, if summer '98 could live up to expectations.

Twentieth Century Fox

Throughout the spring of '98, the behavior of the senior executives at Fox was akin to that of a weekend gambler who, having finally hit the jackpot, was determined never again to blow his winnings. Even though *Titanic* had become one of history's biggest bonanzas, the ordeal had taken an enormous emotional toll on the studio and no one at Fox wanted to relive it in any shape or form. The mantra at the studio for summer '98 was clear: No risky, $100 million movies; no temperamental filmmakers.

Hence in spring '98 when Jan De Bont, the Dutch-born former cinematographer responsible for directing *Twister*, *Speed*, and, regrettably, *Speed 2*, turned in his script and budget for a sci-fi western called *Ghost Riders in the Sky*, the reaction of the studio was prompt. Good project, said the studio, but we won't go near it. De Bont's budget hovered above the $100 million mark.

The reason *Titanic* had traumatized the studio surpassed issues of mere cost. Every studio feels a sense of panic when a project goes over budget, but *Titanic* represented a new experience for Hollywood. Its costs had spun wildly out of control and the whole town had followed it obsessively. *Daily Variety* even developed a logo depicting a sinking ship for its almost daily *"Titanic* Watch" stories, covering each new tribulation.

To this day, no one will confirm the film's ultimate cost, partly due to normal studio obfuscation and partly due to legitimate differences over accounting. An enormous ten-thousand-gallon water tank was constructed in Ensenada, Mexico, for the movie, for example. The facility was later used for other productions, so it was open for debate whether all of its cost should be charged to *Titanic*. Perhaps partly as a response to James Cameron's extraordinarily contentious personality, the two studios backing the film tended to charge everything against it out of sheer petulance. According to educated estimates, the final cost of the movie, including prints and advertising, was in the range of $300 million—the most expensive film ever made by any standard.

The movie became a sort of cinematic virus that sucked the life out of Fox. Conversations between Fox and its financial partner, Paramount, became so ugly during production that executives routinely hung up on each other. Bill Mechanic, Fox's chairman of filmed entertainment, normally a good-natured, unpretentious man, was transformed into a snapping, irritable studio functionary.

Certainly the personality of writer-director Cameron was a principal cause of the virus. Like most filmmakers, Cameron could be glibly ingratiating in social situations—a very thin disguise to conceal his nastiness and incivility. "I've never known anyone who can be smiling one second and turn absolutely vile for no reason," observed one Fox executive who worked with him. When *Titanic* started spinning out of control, Cameron's response to worried Fox executives was one of utter contempt. Mechanic himself turned up on the set in Mexico one day, and Cameron simply retired to his trailer with the message that he would resume shooting only after his visitor was on his way back to Los Angeles.

"Making a movie with Cameron is like contracting a disease," says one Fox executive. "Even after the movie is released, it still takes a long while to shake off the symptoms."

Though Rupert Murdoch, chairman of News Corps., never commented publicly about the *Titanic* ordeal, his reaction was vividly reflected in terms of his policy decisions. The billionaire had never exhibited much enthusiasm for the movie business to begin with. His ideal business model was to control the global distribution pipelines but let someone else bear the risks of financing movies. "Rupert's mentality is that of the archtypical satellite or cable guy," declared the CEO of a rival entertainment company. "He wants to make one sale, then lay his cable or launch his satellite and collect the money. The idea of having to sell each new movie, customer by customer, drives him crazy. It's like the water torture."

Consistent with these instincts, Murdoch had, from time to time, conducted furtive negotiations with various financing partners, with the hope of laying off the cost of his film production, but so far without success. Instead, Murdoch, like other entertainment patriarchs, had retreated from the studio's previous policy, under which Fox had to own world rights to all its productions. The company now sought financial partners on all of its films, to the point of making overall deals with entities like New Regency, which cofinanced movies on an ongoing basis.

Given this conservative approach to moviemaking and the bitter memory of James Cameron, Fox's plans for summer '98 were severely circumscribed. The basic strategy was to make a series of modestly budgeted movies targeted at specific demographics, with the hope that one or two might break out and become a mainstream hit.

The biggest gamble was a $70 million comedy called *Dr. Dolittle*. Fox had made a previous *Dr. Dolittle* thirty years before and it had been an unmitigated flop. That project, however, was a glossy, old-fashioned musical starring Rex Harrison. The new *Dolittle*, by contrast, would have attitude: It would star Eddie Murphy as the physician with an unlikely, long-repressed ability to talk to animals. But the real stars would be the animals themselves, all of which would be able to talk back to Murphy thanks to the miracle of special effects. Not a new idea to be sure; just ask Mr. Ed and Babe. Some at the studio were openly worried that the novelty had worn off, but they were overruled in studio meetings. *Dr. Dolittle* was put on the fast track.

A second project also had its skeptics. While "The X-Files" had built a loyal, almost cultish following during its five-year run on television, there was a serious question whether or not this audience of 20 million would pay seven dollars to see it on the wide screen, and whether or not a still larger audience could be attracted. There had been very, very few precedents for this exercise, whereby an ongoing TV show would be expanded into a movie. Certainly the success of the Star Trek movies was a positive sign.

But there were a few built-in problems with *The X-Files*. One was the creator of the show, Chris Carter, a brash and abrasive man who one Fox executive describes as "an ego in search of a human being." Crass and fast-talking, Carter believed his TV series represented not just good storytelling—it was art. He made it very clear in his initial meetings that his objective was not to transform "The X-Files" into a movie, but rather to put "The X-Files" on the big screen as is. Sure, a few wide-canvas scenes might be added along with a big-screen special-effects climax, but Carter intended to write the script and have one of his key TV directors shoot the movie. The editing, scoring, and other facets of the movie would also be done by the show's existing TV staff. The Fox folks bit their lips and kept quiet. After all, Carter represented an important franchise to Fox TV. "I'm confident that the 'X-Files' TV audience will turn out for the film in its first week," observed Mechanic. "Whether the movie will be able to build from there depends on how good the movie is."

Three other releases, all of them modestly budgeted, also carried Fox's hopes for summer '98. A light, female-skewed item called *Hope Floats* starring Sandra Bullock and Harry Connick Jr., showed promise as a possible sleeper. So did a Rabelaisian comedy called *There's Something About Mary* from the Farrelly brothers, Peter and Bobby, who had been responsible for Jim Carrey's vehicle *Dumb and Dumber*.

And then there was the ultimate stealth missile—*Bulworth*. Since the film had been made amid the utmost secrecy, no one at Fox knew what to expect from the mercurial Warren Beatty. He had been given free rein on the movie: Once the initial concept had been approved, the studio exercised no further controls, providing Beatty deliver it on his $32 million budget. A skilled producer, Beatty almost hit his target. The studio advanced him an additional $4 million without demanding final cut or otherwise limiting his controls. Indeed, no one within Fox was even sure who had green-lighted the movie, or under what conditions. All that was certain was that it was a holdover from a previous regime—indeed, two previous regimes—and that, as such, the wisest course was to put it into the marketplace and suffer the consequences.

With the approach of summer '98, therefore, the mood at Fox was in sharp contrast to that of other studios. While rivals braced for combat, Fox seemed almost relaxed; its movies did not pose big risks. Where other studios were gambling the store on big disaster movies, Fox had survived its disasters as well as its disaster movie. The *Titanic* may have gone down, but Fox was still upright—miraculously.

Sony

For the new executive team at Sony Pictures, summer '98 represented a moment of truth. Studio chief John Calley and his troops had freely admitted their good fortune in inheriting a string of hits from a discredited regime. Their luck was virtually unprecedented in the annals of Hollywood. When the leadership of a studio implodes, as did the administration of Peter Guber and Mark Canton, it inevitably leaves behind a string of disastrous movies. This time, however, the leavings turned out to be lucrative surprises: *Air Force One, Men in Black,* and *My Best Friend's Wedding.* So when John Calley kept repeating his signature line to the press—"I make it a point to choose my predecessors very carefully"—he was kidding on the square.

At the time of their ousting, Guber, Canton, and their colleagues had been blasted by the press, by their Japanese overseers at Sony, and even by the government for their costly flops and for the company's creative accounting.

Indeed, in 1998 the Securities and Exchange Commission had taken the extraordinary step of fining Sony $1 million, charging that the Japanese company had obfuscated the magnitude of its earlier losses from shareholders—the highest fine ever leveled against a company in a case that did not involve fraud. According to the SEC, Sony had kept boasting about its few hits, like *Sleepless in Seattle,* while deferring the cost of its losers until it took its massive $3.2 billion write-off in November 1994—a write-off that came as a shock to Wall Street.

All this notwithstanding, the fact remained that Guber and Canton had left in their wake an imposing array of hits that John Calley would be hard-pressed to replicate. Indeed, to Calley's frustration, most of his releases in summer '98 would also turn out to be leftovers. *Godzilla* and *The Mask of Zorro,* though green-lighted by Calley, had been acquired and nurtured by the previous regime. Both projects had been bobbing and weaving in development hell for several years at Columbia or TriStar, Sony's two filmmaking divisions. One of Calley's first actions before officially taking office at Sony was to put *Godzilla* on the fast track and to nudge *Zorro* into production.

At the age of sixty-eight, John Calley was not anxious to waste any time in establishing his presence. Having effectively retired from the business for a decade, he was not disposed to replicate this period of idleness. Coming out of the advertising business, Calley had built a successful producing career in the sixties and seventies in partnership with the rotund, freewheeling Martin Ransohoff. The team had been responsible for a formidable array of films, ranging from *The Loved One* to *The Cincinnati Kid,* from *Catch-22* to *The Americanization of*

Emily. Calley had left producing to become production chief at Warner Bros. under Ted Ashley, where he fostered movies like *Deliver-
ance, Dirty Harry,* and Stanley Kubrick's *A Clockwork Orange.*

After Steve Ross bought Warner Bros., however, Calley walked
away from the business. He had simply had enough. For a decade he
lived in the East and dabbled in the stock market and real estate. In
1996, Frank Mancuso, president of MGA/UA, hired Calley to take
over the UA division of his newly re-formed company and Calley,
despite his long hiatus, hit the ground running. Under his stewardship
the company released *GoldenEye,* the most successful James Bond
opus in many years, *The Birdcage,* the Mike Nichols movie, as well
as a few turkeys such as *Wild Bill.*

Though Calley was relishing his return to the fray, he also came
to understand one harsh limitation facing his new company. MGM/UA
simply did not have the financial strength to mobilize a substantial
program of movies. It was going to have to subsist on modestly budgeted projects backed by limited marketing efforts. To Calley, this
represented a potentially disastrous scenario. In order to succeed, he
reasoned, a company would have to put forward a mix of inexpensive
projects and a few big-ticket, "tentpole" movies, and would have to
support them with huge TV advertising budgets to wedge into the
crowded marketplace. At the same time, Calley told friends that he
was convinced Mancuso was going to pull the rug out from under him.
In Calley's view, the MGM chief had lost faith in the movie business.
Mancuso, he felt, wished he didn't have to make any movies at all and
could fire his production staff.

So when Sony sent some trial job offers his way, Calley did not
hesitate. Despite the $3.2 billion write-off in 1994, Sony was deter-
mined to resurrect its Hollywood entertainment empire and transform
it into a profitable operation. And John Calley seemed like the sort of
sober, experienced hand who could make it happen.

In taking office, Calley was determined to make his life easy in at
least one respect. He had witnessed the severe personality clashes at
the top of other studios—indeed, the Guber group at Sony had been

fiercely politicized—and was eager to create a team of kindred spirits. For this end, Calley seemed to have all the right instincts. His inner circle of executives consisted of Gareth Wigan, sixty-eight, an insightful, straight-shooting Brit who had managed to survive under Mark Canton's stewardship; Lucy Fisher, a coolly intelligent executive who had served for ten years at Warner Bros.; and sharp, sophisticated Amy Pascal, who also had worked her way up the studio ladder. "This group was amazingly distinctive in at least one way," Lucy Fisher later observed. "We actually liked each other."

Some producers, agents, and others pitching material to the studio felt that perhaps the new team liked each other too much. New projects were assessed so thoroughly, and discussed so relentlessly, it was charged, that few new movies were actually entering the pipeline. Exacerbating this problem was the tinge of snobbishness that seemed to permeate the studio. "Everybody seemed just too well read, too hip, too sophisticated to get behind anything," complained one director, who managed to extract his project from Sony and set it up elsewhere.

One of John Calley's closest friends was director Mike Nichols, and "when the two of them are together, it's like a fight to see who can be more elitist," said one Sony producer. "Calley had such an I've-seen-it-all mentality that it was almost impossible to get him excited about a project." Part of the problem, too, was that many key players in Hollywood couldn't figure out Calley's style. While Warner Bros.' Bob Daly was the prototypical Brooklyn Irishman, Calley was a sort of Man from Nowhere. He grew up in New Jersey, but barely knew his father. Though he never attended college, his accent seemed Ivy League Mid-Atlantic; his reading habits bordered on the cerebral and his conversational style was witty and urbane. He did not fit into an easy stereotype, and Calley was not above using that as a device to keep lawyers and agents off balance.

His management style was perplexing to his own colleagues as well. In his initial months at Sony, Calley, who never wore a suit or tie, presented himself as a maverick who would resist the encroachment of a corporate culture. As time wore on, however, Calley increasingly dropped references to "zero-basing" and "value chain." No longer was he railing against bureaucracy; rather, he was talking about "re-engineering" his echelons of executives to render them more effective. To save costs and avoid duplication, Calley folded TriStar Pictures into Columbia, thus creating one big organization instead of two smaller, more responsive ones.

Since Calley was very savvy in placing his bets, his willingness to gamble the store on *Godzilla* surprised many. Producers Roland Emmerich and Dean Devlin, in presenting that project, had made no representation that they were eager to emulate Mike Nichols or Francis Ford Coppola. They had come out of B movies like *Universal Soldier* and *Stargate*; they professed an addiction to "popcorn pictures," as they liked to describe them. Yet, throughout the spring, it was clear that Calley was giving them full control of their project and had no intention to second-guess them on script or budget.

The power dynamics on *The Mask of Zorro* were vastly different, of course. No studio executive tried to second-guess Steven Spielberg, who was producing the film. You either made his movie, or you passed. Calley took the first option.

Calley's other entries for summer '98 represented a mixed bag. There were a couple of films aimed at the teenage market: *Dance with Me* and *Can't Hardly Wait*. *Madeline* was a small film from producer Stanley Jaffe slanted at young girls. A Jean-Claude Van Damme movie, *Knock Off*, was clearly aimed at the late-summer action crowd.

Calley was not happy with the thinness of this slate. When I spoke with him in late spring he acknowledged that he would have liked another solid adult movie on the level of the 1997 Jack Nicholson picture *As Good As It Gets*, which had surprisingly grossed $148 million in the U.S. and another $148 million overseas. He had also hoped to marshal sequels to such megahits as *Men in Black* and *Jumanji*, but had found it more difficult than he had thought to line up either the rights or the talent. A possible *Men in Black* sequel, for example, would have to involve Spielberg's production company, Amblin, and probably DreamWorks, of which he was a partner, as well. And

Barry Sonnenfeld, the director of *Men in Black*, now had a rich deal at Disney—that studio might also have to be involved. Plus it was a rule of thumb in Hollywood that all the participants in a sequel expected to get their just rewards in the form of exponentially higher pay and contingent compensation. As a result, while *Speed* cost $37 million to produce, by contrast its sequel cost $140 million. The upshot: The profitability of the sequels business had been sharply diminished.

This having been said, another *Men in Black* seemed predestined to be a global blockbuster, and Calley was determined to get one underway, irrespective of how many partners he would have to invite to the party. Though his summer '98 lineup was undernourished, he felt confident that his company was positioned to release between twenty and twenty-four movies during the following twelve months, and that this total would be bolstered with acquisitions and pickups. He hoped to start a new division specializing in movies in the $4 million to $12 million budget range that would embrace art movies as well as genre films. He also was stepping up Sony's coproductions overseas, working with local companies in Britain, Germany, Hong Kong, and Brazil, where the product would be mainly geared toward the local market.

In attempting all this, Calley was turning over more and more responsibility to Amy Pascal, who held the title of president of Columbia Pictures. Calley had dismissed Robert Cooper as president of TriStar (Cooper subsequently took over a similar title at Dream-Works), and Pascal's star obviously was rising on the Sony lot.

With the approach of summer '98, however, Calley's prime focus was on marketing and distributing his two tentpole movies, *Godzilla* and *Zorro*. If these two films could be propelled into hits, then the extraordinary momentum of the studio could be sustained. If not, Calley worried that the Sony renaissance might falter, a prospect that would not please the long-suffering Sony hierarchs in Tokyo. The Japanese felt they had waited long enough for the big turnaround. They wanted their euphoria to continue.

Disney

Tough-minded and resolute, Joe Roth, chairman of the Disney Studios, was in an ugly mood at the start of summer '98. For one thing,
Disney's stock, long the darling of Wall Street, had been sinking
steadily, dropping from $128 a share to near $100 in only two months.
Skepticism about the Disney-owned ABC network and its plunging
ratings was one reason why analysts were downgrading their earnings
forecasts, but they also were pointing to weaker results on the film
side, and this angered Roth. He had been explaining for months that
the Disney year was back-loaded insofar as the program of movies was
concerned, but the analysts apparently weren't listening. Movies come
together in different ways and at different times, he'd lectured, and in
1998 they would cluster during summer and winter.

Certainly, Roth could cite summer '97 as an example of the sort
of results he was used to delivering. The studio had scored not only
with such $100 million–grossing Disney-produced hits as *Con Air* and
George of the Jungle, but, thanks to some shrewd negotiating, the company ended up with foreign distribution rights to *Air Force One* and
Starship Troopers, two films released domestically by Sony, as well as
an international split-rights deal on Paramount's hit, *Face/Off.* Disney
also did solid if unspectacular business with its animated features
such as *Hercules,* which grossed roughly $99 million in the U.S. alone.

With the onset of winter, however, the combination of good movies
and good luck suddenly came to an end. A succession of projects
fizzled at the box office. Indeed, even their titles seemed to suggest
failure—*Krippendorf's Tribe, Meet the Deedles, Kundun,* and *Deep
Rising.*

None of this took Roth by surprise. The Disney chairman had
been masterminding production schedules for more than a decade,
first at Morgan Creek, a self-financed independent, then at Twentieth
Century Fox, and finally at Disney, and he knew that the fortunes of
studios seemed to follow their own rhythm. Starting with summer re-

leases like *Armageddon* and *Mulan,* Roth felt he could unleash a very promising array of movies for the second half of 1998. There would be comedies like Jim Abrahams's *Jane Austen's Mafia* and *The Water Boy* starring Adam Sandler; there would be dramas like *Beloved,* directed by Jonathan Demme, *Enemy of the State,* directed by Tony Scott, and *A Civil Action* starring John Travolta. Finally, Roth planned to unveil a major animation feature, *A Bug's Life,* about which there had been favorable buzz, in winter '98, right around the time that rival DreamWorks was releasing its much-heralded *Prince of Egypt.* Roth had inadvertently heightened the year's back-loading by shifting the release of *Mighty Joe Young,* a remake of the old RKO picture, from summer to Christmas. Roth liked the movie and didn't want it to get lost amid the clutter of summer.

Thus, despite the studio's weak start, Roth felt that Disney would rank either in first or second place in market share by year's end—and this despite a significantly curtailed production schedule. Reversing the policies of his predecessor, Jeffrey Katzenberg, Roth had been steadfastly reducing both the size of his executive staff as well as the number of releases. At the start of summer '98, he had shut down the Touchstone label and terminated its chief, Donald De Line. Under his blueprint, Disney would release only sixteen theatrical features during 1999 compared with twenty-three in 1998.

Roth did not consider this a retrenchment, however. In his view, Disney had been scattering its energies and resources among too many projects in an effort to capture market share. He believed there should be more focus—and more money—aimed at an elite group of movies. And by early spring of 1998, Roth left no doubt as to which would be his star summer attractions: *Mulan* and *Armageddon.* They would be supported by massive ad campaigns, fueled by record sums of money, not just from Disney itself, but from its marketing partners like McDonald's. No one could ever accuse Joe Roth of hedging his bets.

Roth had demonstrated a talent for resiliency during his career in Hollywood. He turned his first gig, managing a low-rent improvisational group, into a bonanza by producing an inexpensive TV spoof called *Tunnelvision,* which became a modest hit. Capitalizing on this concept, he then attempted a comedy called *Americathon,* a parody telethon designed to save a supposedly cash-strapped America from its mounting debts. The movie flopped, but this didn't slow Roth down. Joining with a producing partner, Harry Ufland, he cobbled together a modestly successful group of films, even trying his hand at directing a few forgettable offerings: *Streets of Gold, Coupe de Ville,* and a sequel to *Revenge of the Nerds.*

By 1990, Joe Roth, always a realist, had come to the conclusion that his talents as a director were at best modest. Further, he was frustrated by the fact that he was still considered an outsider and not part of Hollywood's A-list of producers and wheeler-dealers. Acting on this, he approached James Robinson, a burly, tough-talking Baltimore automobile wholesaler, about forming a company called Morgan Creek. Financing its own films, the company fostered several successful, modestly budgeted movies such as *Young Guns, Dead Ringers,* and *Enemies: A Love Story.* Their performance was sufficient to impress Rupert Murdoch, who in 1989 appointed Roth chairman of the movie division at Fox. Roth's new boss was Barry Diller, a man who made James Robinson look like a pussycat.

Again, Roth's candor and decisiveness served him well. Though Murdoch had constructed a taut little empire of suits, Roth made no effort to conform. He ambled about in jeans and sports shirts and stuck to his casual manner. He billed himself as a filmmaker, not a corporate yes-man. He made eye contact with his visitors and he followed up on his commitments. He also had some good luck. Just as Roth checked into Fox, Warner foolishly put into turnaround a little movie called *Home Alone* that John Hughes wanted to direct. Roth snapped it up and it went on to gross $188.9 million internationally. Other successes followed: *Sleeping with the Enemy, The Last of the Mohicans,* and *Edward Scissorhands.*

After three and a half years, the pressures of mobilizing product for Rupert Murdoch's assembly line began to wear on Roth, who had never been comfortable in Murdoch's presence. The Australian-born newpaper czar had no passion for movies, in Roth's view. He had to finance them to feed his distribution machine, but he distrusted them—and perhaps Roth as well. To Roth's good fortune, it was at about that time Jeffrey Katzenberg decided to step up production at Disney with what he liked to call "singles" and "doubles." That is to say, instead of focusing on high-priced blockbusters, Katzenberg was to release a steady stream of high-concept middle-budget comedies and action pictures that together would buy a leading market share for Disney. The 1986 release *Down and Out in Beverly Hills* was essentially the blueprint for this genre: With no major stars, it nonetheless had a very respectable U.S. box office gross of $38,618,144. But Katzenberg knew he needed an inner circle of producers who could create this sort of dependable product, and he asked Roth to jump ship to Disney.

Roth found Katzenberg's notion appealing on several counts. He would have the opportunity to get closer to the moviemaking process once again and not simply play the role of the suit. Moreover, he would have a major stake in the films he would produce, and the opportunity to make millions of dollars. It was an offer Roth couldn't refuse.

Within months Roth and his longtime producing partner, Roger Birnbaum, were at Disney churning out seventeen instantly forgettable projects like *Angie, I Love Trouble,* and *Angels in the Outfield,* exactly the sort of product Katzenberg had in mind. Every time Roth started a movie, he became a million dollars richer. He also began to see the flaw in Katzenberg's strategy. The public was simply not interested in Disney's stream of high-concept movies: Either the concepts were not high enough or the marketing campaigns were woefully inadequate. The singles and doubles were turning out to be bunts. Katzenberg was grinding out product, but he wasn't winning market share.

Roth was not the only one in the Disney hierarchy to notice the failing strategy. Katzenberg's boss, Michael Eisner, was increasingly troubled by the fact that his studio's live-action product was losing more and more money, in contrast to the extraordinary results of *The Lion King* and other animated films. In 1994, however, Eisner, a fierce workaholic, was felled by a serious heart attack. For weeks the vast Disney empire was paralyzed as its hands-on boss remained virtually incommunicado.

Then one day, late in 1994, Joe Roth received two urgent communications. One was from Katzenberg, who confided that he was moving up in the Disney hierarchy. With Eisner seriously ill, Katzenberg would be taking over the number two job in the parent company, a post unoccupied since a helicopter crash had killed Frank Wells, the brilliant attorney who had effectively reinvented Disney with Eisner. Given this promotion, Katzenberg wanted to sound out Roth about taking over his former post.

The second communication was from Eisner himself, and it carried quite a different message. Eisner wanted Roth to take over Katzenberg's former job, but the man he would replace was moving out, not up. The Disney chief, it turned out, was furious with Katzenberg for campaigning so aggressively for Wells's job even while Eisner was bedriddden in the hospital. Eisner had previously admired Katzenberg's intensity, but now it struck him as simply nasty.

Roth accepted Eisner's offer, even as an ousted Katzenberg set about establishing DreamWorks with his two new partners, Steven Spielberg and David Geffen. He also filed a $250 million suit against his old employer, charging that he'd been cheated out of important bonuses earned during his Disney tenure.

Roth wasted no time setting a new agenda at Disney, not only making new deals but also reducing overhead and curtailing development. Katzenberg had placed such importance on the role of his development staff that he once challenged each of them to come up with his own concept for a film, hire a writer, and nurture it into script form. The implication of this program was that good movies could spring from the bosom of studio bureaucrats—even those whose only credential was an M.B.A. No one except Katzenberg was surprised when not one of these projects carried enough weight to move beyond a first-draft screenplay.

What Joe Roth wanted to achieve was a lean and mean production staff. Equally important, he wanted to mobilize a ferocious advertising and marketing strategy that would be capable of hitting not singles and doubles but base-clearing home runs. "I was blown away by his thinking," acknowledged one member of the Disney marketing staff who left for protective cover at another studio shortly after Roth's arrival. "I had been raised on the philosophy of spending, say, $15 million to launch a new movie. Here was Joe Roth talking about $50 million launches. I though I was, well, in Disneyland."

Roth's approach to decision-making was equally bold. Not one to equivocate, he responded to projects quickly and decisively. Agents and producers accustomed to bureaucratic infighting were surprised to get prompt calls from Roth stating, "I read the script myself and I want to make it." Or, "I pass." Either way, the answers came fast and the community responded. Disney quickly became the number one place to bring new projects.

While Roth was getting high marks as a studio chief, he nonetheless represented something of an anomaly to the town's players. Hollywood tended to trust executives who repaired to Morton's restaurant at night to schmooze with the boys. Roth resolutely ignored these social rituals, heading home instead to be with his wife and kids. The executive style at the TV networks and movie studios called for a great deal of hugging and back-slapping. Roth's style, by contrast, was distanced and, indeed, rather chilly. As conversations became more intense, his narrow eyes would become mere slits, and his nasal New York cadences would become more abrupt. "As long as I've worked with Joe, I have never seen him embrace anyone or display any sort of affection," said one associate. "I assume he saves all that for his kids."

As summer '98 drew near, however, those close to Roth noticed a sharp rise in intensity. Though his reign at Disney had thus far been a hearty success, Roth had a lot riding on the next three months.

There were corporate pressures, in addition, that had focused unusual attention on the performance of his movies. Not only was Disney stock drifting downward, but there had also been a series of executive defections from the Disney hierarchy, headed by Richard Nanula, the company's brilliant young chief financial officer. Wall Street in particular was perplexed by the absence of any clear line of succession beyond Michael Eisner; hence the departures of several prime candidates for the top spot was all the more troubling. Given this dilemma, Roth's name was increasingly being advanced as a potential Eisner successor, even though Roth himself had expressed ambivalence about taking on added responsibilities.

All this focused even more attention on Joe Roth's gambles for summer '98. The first scheduled summer picture, Robert Redford's *The Horse Whisperer,* was considered a safe bet, despite its $70 million price tag. Redford was a major star with strong appeal to the female audience over twenty-five years of age. He also commanded a solid following overseas.

Armageddon was the biggest gamble of summer. Though the project was always talked up at the studio as a $100 million movie—in itself a milestone because Disney had never before invested that much in a live-action project—those close to the film knew full well that it would surely go over budget. There had even been a debate among senior executives about bringing in a financial partner for *Armageddon.* Even Eisner had pressed for such a link, but Roth was stalwart in his resistance. As Eisner explained to me in late spring, "I had said to Joe, 'Do we really want to be out on a limb with a movie that could end up costing us $150 million?' But Joe believes in this movie. He believes Bruce Willis gives us insurance overseas, especially in Asia. He argues that if we're going to take the gamble, why give away the upside? And I support him on this."

Eisner and Roth did acknowledge one cloud hovering over this project: namely, *Deep Impact.* In talking to the press and to colleagues at Disney, Roth always emphasized that the Paramount-DreamWorks co-venture represented a vastly different story than *Armageddon.*

"They're going for a remake of *On the Beach*," Roth told me in April of 1998. "They're doing a movie about what happens to society when the world is coming to an end. We're doing an action picture about a bunch of guys who go on a space mission to save the world." Though all this was true, the overriding fact was that both films spring from the same premise: An asteroid soaring through space threatens the existence of the earth. And both movies employed special effects to depict scenes of massive destruction.

Joe Roth was utterly exasperated that *Deep Impact* would come out before *Armageddon*, but executives at Paramount and Dream-Works were similarly offended by *Armageddon*, fearing it would shorten the commercial life span of their project. Everyone was aware that a similar face-off had occurred only one year earlier, when two volcano movies had gone head to head. In that case, the second one, Fox's *Volcano*, suffered badly despite the fact that many considered it to be a better movie than the first, *Dante's Peak*.

Two Wyatt Earp movies had suddenly emerged in 1994. Four movies about an adult trapped in a kid's body came out at roughly the same time (*Like Father, Like Son, Eighteen Again, Vice Versa,* and *Big*) and, ironically, it was the last in line, *Big*, starring Tom Hanks, that did the best. In perhaps the weirdest face-off, two studios, Warner Bros. and Fox, had tried in 1995 to make movies about flesh-eating viruses, but only one, Warner's *Outbreak* starring Dustin Hoffman, made it to the starting line (*Crisis in the Hot Zone*, which was to star Jodie Foster and Robert Redford, was canceled even though it shaped up as the more interesting of the two projects).

Various theories had been offered to explain this phenomenon. Clearly a curious form of inbreeding grips middle-management—everyone was basically reading the same scripts, doing lunch at the same restaurants, and even working out with the same trainers. In this sort of hermetically sealed environment, one person's bright idea instantly became everyone's brainstorm.

During spring '98, I questioned the principals of *Deep Impact* and *Armageddon* to see if I could determine a common point of origin, but my inquiry was without success. For some undefinable reason, the notion of asteroids crashing to earth had simply filtered into the atmosphere. Indeed, at one point it looked as if four asteroid movies would go into production. Peter Hyams, a veteran director who had done several sci-fi epics, including an ill-conceived remake of Stanley Kubrick's *2001: A Space Odyssey,* had decided to develop an asteroid movie at Fox. Dean Devlin and Roland Emmerich, having struck gold with *Independence Day,* wanted to do an asteroid movie as their next project (they abandoned it in favor of *Godzilla* when they found out about *Deep Impact*).

While Hollywood wondered if two asteroid movies were still one too many, Joe Roth harbored no such doubts. *Armageddon,* he knew, would win the day. He wasn't being cocky, he explained. He had assembled the right team that knew how to get the job done and he knew they would bring home the prize.

Warner Bros.

For almost two decades the venerable Warner Bros. studio had marched from summer to summer with a confident swagger. The team of Robert Daly and Terry Semel had won the respect of Hollywood with shrewd decision-making as well as consistency. While other studio chiefs would advance lofty theories about the crafting of blockbusters, or the care and feeding of stars, the Warner duo cast themselves as by-the-numbers pragmatists. They stayed with what worked, and what worked for them were expensive, star-driven projects and name directors. Daly and Semel didn't give many speeches and they didn't take many chances. And year after year they kept their studio at or near the top of the market-share charts.

On the surface, Daly and Semel seemed like unlikely partners. Brooklyn Irish to the core, Daly, sixty-one, was a hard-bitten numbers guy, an ex–CBS accountant who had learned to curb his trigger temper and sharp tongue. Semel, six years younger, was wary and soft-spoken, a man who picked his words carefully. Semel, who was Jewish, worked his way up through an equally unglamorous side of the business—distribution—earning a reputation as a cool deal-maker and patient strategist. In 1997, Daly decided to take the extraordinary step of making Semel his partner as co-CEO of Warner. Together they presided over an empire encompassing not only movies but TV, music, video, the Warner retail stores, and other enterprises.

Though they dressed in conservative business suits and avoided the party scene, Daly and Semel relished the accoutrements of wealth and power. They lived in palatial homes in Bel Air, traveled the world in studio-owned jets, and vacationed aboard yachts that Greek shipping tycoons would covet. At the studio, a chef prepared their austere, low-cholesterol lunches served in their private dining room. Since the studio's financial numbers were buried under the giant Time Warner umbrella, there was no formal listing of their salaries and bonuses, but guessing games about their wealth had become a favorite indoor sport at the studio. Most estimates put each executive's annual salary plus bonus well in excess of $10 million, and with Time Warner stock more than doubling from $41 to $92 a share in the two years since the merger with Turner Broadcasting, their options were valued north of $150 million. "Daly and Semel both try and keep it all very low-key, but the fact is they are the princes and this is their fiefdom," said one of their senior associates. "When we are summoned, we come and kiss their rings."

Colleagues noted that both executives, from time to time, went to pains to downplay their regal living style, but, as one associate put it, "When Terry Semel plunks down $12 million for a New York co-op, his vows of poverty seem a little strained."

With the approach of summer '98, however, it had become vividly clear that the swagger was missing at Warner. After their remarkably smooth ride, Daly and Semel suddenly were confronting potholes wherever they looked. At the corporate level, it was an open secret at Time Warner that some board members—especially Ted Turner, now the corporation's biggest single stockholder—had become critical of the partners on several grounds, profligacy being high on the list. To Time Inc.'s senior bureaucrats, Daly and Semel were living too high and spending too big. A bruising fight with Michael Fuchs, the former chief at HBO, also had taken its toll. The brillant but volatile Fuchs had been elevated to the top job at Warner Music but had clashed repeatedly with Daly on a wide range of issues, with Daly at one point barking, "You and I, Michael, are like oil and water." Though Fuchs had now been banished from the Time Warner empire, Daly himself had experienced a troubled time trying to restore momentum and esprit de corps at the music division.

Even the well-oiled movie company had suddenly sputtered. Franchises like *Batman* had run out of steam. Franchise players like Clint Eastwood, who had gone from hit to hit, had bombed with his movie adaptation of the best-seller *Midnight in the Garden of Good and Evil*. Kevin Costner's $100 million postapocalyptic epic, *The Postman*, loomed as one of history's biggest money-losers with a U.S. gross of only $18 million. Daly and Semel had spent hundreds of millions of dollars in an effort to challenge Disney in the animation field, but the studio's early warning system carried dire reports about its first pure animation effort, *The Quest for Camelot*.

A lawsuit over the never-made *Pinocchio* had ended in an $80 million judgment against the studio and further deflated morale. Director Francis Ford Coppola had argued in his plea that he'd set up a deal to develop his script at Warner Bros. Unable to reach an agreement on his salary, however, Coppola had rewritten the script, then taken his project to Columbia, where he was given a green light. Daly and Semel, out of spite according to Coppola, barred him from making his film elsewhere, even though they had declined to make it. Warner Bros., which has appealed the case, came off to the jury as an arrogant band of fat cats, and the jury completely bought Coppola's side of the story.

Nothing seemed to be going right at Warner on the management side. Eager to restore some energy and initiative to the studio, Daly and Semel had embarked upon a curious experiment. In 1997, they decided to replicate their partnership by creating a similar alliance between two young production executives, Billy Gerber and Lorenzo Di Bonaventura. The two would share responsibility for supervising the acquisition, development, and packaging of future movies. To be sure, final responsibility for green-lighting movies would still reside with Daly and Semel. They would review the casts and budgets, scrutinize the qualifications of the directors, and read the screenplays (though staff personnel insisted that it was rare for either Semel or Daly to read the full material, relying instead on synopses). Projects they favored would move ahead into production; others would go back to the drawing board or perhaps be abandoned—that is, put into turnaround for other companies to pick up.

During their lengthy reign, Daly and Semel had positioned a number of men in the role of production chief, always relying up to now on a single individual. Most had been dismissed as lightweights by the community of agents, producers, and others who regularly submitted projects to the studio. Some, like Robert Shapiro and Mark Rosenberg, were former agents who had wanted to graduate into production. Others, like Mark Canton and Bruce Berman, had worked their way up through the Warner hierarchy, a process that required more bureaucratic guile than creative skills. None had experience either as a producer or, on the creative side, as a writer or filmmaker. While other studio chiefs, like Joe Roth and John Calley, had long lists of production credits and a wealth of frontline experience, the Warner executives were essentially studio bureaucrats. Not only were they hampered by this lack of experience, but also by the limits of their authority. Important directors and producers, mindful of the fact that only Semel and Daly could flash the green light, tried to circumvent the Warner functionaries whenever possible.

Canton was perhaps the prototypical Warner executive, both in style and substance. The son of a press agent, Canton made no effort to disguise his fondness for schmoozing with celebrities and exchanging trade talk with producers and agents. During his six years as president of production, he had mastered the technique of marshaling projects for the Semel-Daly gauntlet, focusing on those star-driven, down-the-middle films that his bosses favored. As such, he had to compete with several fiercely aggressive producers who had expensive production deals on the lot as well as longstanding personal relationships with Semel. These included Joel Silver, the bombastic action producer whose credits included the *Lethal Weapon* franchise; Jerry Weintraub, a smooth-talking onetime manager who had briefly headed his own production company; and Jon Peters, the fierce-tempered onetime partner of Peter Guber. Steering a course through this thicket of bureaucratic intrigue proved no easy task, but Canton, for a time, ably demonstrated his manipulative skills.

Some agents and filmmakers, however, faulted Canton on several grounds. His attention span was, to say the least, limited. In the middle of a meeting he might start munching an apple or pacing around the room with a distracted expression on his face. The extent of Canton's intellectual resources were similarly dubious. The gossip among directors and writers was that Canton rarely read their screenplays or, if he read them, showed little comprehension. Nonetheless, Canton was recruited in 1994 by another onetime Warner producer, Peter Guber, to take over the top production job at Sony Pictures, a post he would hold for a stormy four years.

Given the precarious tenure of Warner's top production executives, the appointment of Gerber and Di Bonaventura to replace Canton was greeted with considerable skepticism. As visitors started trooping through their offices for their initial meet-and-greet sessions, the atmosphere of doubt intensified. For one thing, their personalities seemed to clash even more strongly than those of Daly and Semel. The forty-year-old Gerber was chatty and frivolous, the ultimate Hollywood insider. Di Bonaventura, forty-one, was more reserved and cerebral. While Gerber was a fast-talking, fast-moving former manager who had worked with such rock groups as Devo and The Cars, the rather somber, bespectacled Di Bonaventura had received his undergraduate degree in intellectual history at Harvard and his M.B.A at Wharton. His father, Mario, was a symphonic conductor.

From the outset, Gerber and Di Bonaventura had difficulty matching the seamless behavior of their bosses, occasionally arguing with each other in the midst of meetings. While they regarded these spirited disagreements as healthy, their visitors who were nervously pitching their projects found them, at best, distracting. Noticing this reaction, the two then tried dividing up their responsibilities and avoiding joint meetings. "This didn't seem to work either," Gerber later told me. "Agents and producers started playing us off against each other. One guy would call me and say, 'Lorenzo has agreed to pay a million for the script, why are you balking?' Of course, Lorenzo had never agreed to any such thing."

Only weeks after assuming their new responsibilities, Gerber and Di Bonaventura knew that their jobs were in jeopardy. Their bosses had grown impatient over their inability to evolve a smooth partnership. Important agents were taking their best clients and most promising packages to other studios where they felt they could get quicker decisions.

When I had lunch with the two in spring '97, I couldn't help but admire their candor. "Look, I know we're catching it from all sides," Di Bonaventura said with a helpless shrug. "The studio's in trouble. We're in trouble. It's as simple as that."

"The wonderful thing about the movie business is that all it takes is one or two hits and you've got a whole new ball game," Gerber interjected. Where would those hits come from? From the outset, the two had felt that the two brightest prospects were *Superman Lives*, which hopefully would breathe new life into that dormant franchise, and *I Am Legend*, a massive sci-fi epic that would star Arnold Schwarzenegger. Both projects, they said, had blockbuster written all over them.

The *Superman* sequel had been entrusted to the care of the erratic Jon Peters, the onetime hairdresser and former boyfriend of Barbra

Streisand who, in partnership with Peter Guber, had presided over the *Batman* franchise at Warner. Peters's attempt to reinvent himself as a top executive at Sony had failed and he had returned to Warner in a producing role. *Superman* represented an important step in his new Warner career, and the studio had shown its support by signing Tim Burton to direct and Nicolas Cage to star. Kevin Smith, the brilliant young filmmaker responsible for 1997's underground sleeper hit *Chasing Amy*, was signed to write a first draft.

To be sure, all these commitments depended upon Peters's ability to deliver a coherent script, and this was like entrusting an art gallery to a graffiti scrawler. With his temper tantrums and lack of focus, Peters was feared by writers and studio functionaries alike. "Jon kept bitching about the drafts, but I don't think he ever read them," commented one ex-employee of Peters's production company, who made no effort to mask his disdain for his former boss. "Let's just say politely, Jon can't read."

By January 1998, it had become clear that the rebirth of the *Superman* franchise would have to be postponed until the following year, and attention would have to be focused on the Schwarzenegger epic. "This is a movie I'm dying to make," Gerber had told me exuberantly. "We're not only creating a great script, we've got a team of animators and special-effects experts at work creating a whole new race of people."

By early spring, however, these efforts, too, while heroic, kept running into one immutable obstacle: budget. The studio's production staff kept crunching numbers, but could not figure out how to make the movie for less than $120 million, and any special-effects movie starting at that level would surely soar higher. Gerber and Di Bonaventura knew full well that Daly and Semel would not be inclined to green-light a project that pricey after the troubled year that they'd endured. *I Am Legend* was put into turnaround.

With their two would-be blockbusters knocked off the schedule, Gerber and Di Bonaventura realized that their fate rested on the stu-

dio's ability to cobble together a long-shot venture—the fourth iteration of *Lethal Weapon*. Though basically B pictures, the *Lethal*s
collectively had grossed $660 million worldwide. They did not depend
on complex plot, subtleties of script, or special-effects wizardry; all
were directed by Dick Donner, a sixty-eight-year-old veteran who
liked to keep the action straightforward, using real stunts and real
settings.

The big stumbling block, of course, was that there was no way of
making *Lethal Weapon IV* without the man who was arguably the biggest star in the world, Mel Gibson, not to mention his sidekick, Danny
Glover. The entire picture rested on the tension in their relationship,
their improvised banter, and their stunts.

The studio dealmakers promptly swung into action. They managed
to sign Gibson and Glover, then made additional deals for Rene Russo
and Joe Pesci, paying the character actor an unprecedented $1 mil-
lion a week for three weeks. Eager to add new energy to the cast, they
also agreed to pay $2 million for the young comic Chris Rock, and
signed martial arts star Jet Li for another hefty sum. The troops at
Warner were mum about what this package had cost. Producers and
agents close to the studio estimated that the aggregate cost of cast
salaries approached $50 million. In addition, the studio surrendered
40 percent of its gross receipts, much of it going to Gibson. While
vague on the specifics, Semel acknowledged that "everyone gave a
little because they wanted to make this thing work." They knew that
on past *Lethal* films their percentages had brought them big returns,
so they were all willing to take a little less than they normally would.
In point of fact, Mel Gibson's agent, Ed Limato, had demanded that
his client receive a very rich deal—$20 million against 17 percent of
the gross.

What made the project acceptable for the studio were the relatively modest below-the-line numbers, the actual production cost. Because most of the movie was to be shot on the studio lot on a fairly
tight schedule, the overall cost would hopefully be kept to between

$100 million and $125 million. "If this had been another movie dependent on computer graphics, we never could have made it," acknowledged Donner.

With *Lethal IV* in place, Warner's summer agenda was rounded
out with *The Quest for Camelot,* an animated movie set in King Arthur's England; *The Avengers,* an adaptation of the sixties TV spy
series starring Sean Connery, Ralph Fiennes, and Uma Thurman; *Almost Heroes,* the last comedy made by Chris Farley before his death;
The Negotiator, a dark thriller starring Kevin Spacey and Samuel L.
Jackson; *A Perfect Murder,* a mystery styled along the lines of *Dial M
For Murder,* starring Michael Douglas and Gwyneth Paltrow; and finally, *Wrongfully Accused,* a Leslie Nielsen comedy.

No one in the Warner hierarchy, least of all Gerber or Di Bonaventura, held this out as the ultimate summer slate. There was no project
that clearly appealed to the burgeoning teen audience; there was none
keyed to a female demographic; there was no sharp effects movie for
young males. It represented, in fact, a sort of holding action designed
to elicit an acceptable market share for the studio. As one executive
put it, "It wasn't going to send us back to the top, but it also wasn't
going to get anyone fired."

Yet in late April, even before the summer movies were rolled out,
Billy Gerber was led off to the guillotine. "It just wasn't working,"
Semel told me. "Why drag out the agony?" The studio put out an
announcement declaring that Gerber had received the standard exit
visa, a producing deal with overhead covering offices, secretary, and
a couple of development assistants. It was now up to Di Bonaventura
to lead his weary troops through the battles of summer.

In early May when I sat down again with Semel and Di Bonaventura, their mood was subdued. "The lessons of the recent past are
clear," Semel told me in his customary soft-spoken, measured tones.
"We were rushing into projects to meet release dates. We're not going
to do that anymore. We're going to be more careful that the scripts are
ready and the budgets are realistic. To achieve that, we're going to

release fewer pictures—only twenty over the next year compared with twenty-eight the previous one."

Di Bonaventura sat next to Semel for nearly half an hour before he finally had a chance to interject a remark. He then quietly recited a list of younger, more cutting-edge producers and directors who had quietly been signed during the course of the previous six months. He, too, was clearly measuring his words. Warner would be making more movies on modest budgets with younger directors, he related. "Of course, we're not backing away from star vehicles," Semel put in. "Definitely not," Di Bonaventura agreed. But the $100 million movie would be rare indeed, they reiterated. These were times, after all, that called for caution. Even at free-spending, freewheeling Warner Bros.

Universal

When Seagram, the huge Canadian-based liquor empire, bought control of MCA in 1995, Hollywood had high expectations that the venerable motion picture and TV company would be reenergized. Edgar Bronfman, Jr., the forty-one-year-old scion of the Bronfman dynasty, seemed like a sharp and daring young executive, sporting his Van Gogh beard, jeans, and Armani jackets. He wrote song lyrics in his spare time and had even dabbled in film producing. He was more than the son of a rich man; he was the very hip son of a very rich man.

There was no doubt that Bronfman's enthusiasm was badly needed. For five years MCA, or Universal as it was soon to be renamed, had suffered from a sort of benign neglect under the ownership of Matsushita, the Japanese conglomerate. While the company had sustained its position as an important supplier of motion pictures and TV product, it had squelched any proposals for significant expansion or acquisitions. Rival companies were pursuing scenarios of vertical integration to keep pace with Rupert Murdoch or Time Warner, but Universal's aging management of Lew Wasserman and Sidney Sheinberg felt increasingly immobilized by Matsushita's indifference.

But now the Japanese were gone and it was Edgar Jr. who was calling the shots. During his initial forays in Hollywood, he seemed to say all the right things. In a town known for abrasive manners, he was studiously polite, even deferential. "Edgar Jr. understands that the easiest way to flatter someone is to ask him questions," said one associate at Universal. "He doesn't really listen to the answers, but he asks the right questions."

His impeccable manners did not extend to scheduling, however. Occasionally he would be two or three hours late for an appointment, sauntering into the room without a word of explanation. Ron Meyer, the affable CAA talent agent who was to become president of Universal, observed: "If you are born a billionaire, you don't wake up in the morning and say to yourself, 'All of this can be taken away from me at a moment's notice.' You know in your heart that none of it can be taken away."

To be sure, those close to Edgar Jr. understood that one reason he seemed deferential was that he was awed by Hollywood power. Keenly aware of the town's curious brand of meritocracy, he was eager to tap into the power brokers, such as the ubiquitous Michael Ovitz, the high-profile CAA agent who had furtively helped negotiate Seagram's $5.7 billion acquisition of Universal. Indeed, when Lew Wasserman and Sidney Sheinberg learned that Ovitz seemed to be working for Seagram behind their back, they were furious. For some years the two had argued about Ovitz—Wasserman, himself a onetime agent, had always disliked Ovitz, while Sheinberg had defended him. When Sheinberg learned that Ovitz was also negotiating with Edgar Jr. about becoming CEO of Universal, he went ballistic. This was complete betrayal.

The Ovitz negotiations quickly hit a dead end, however. Edgar's allies claimed that he wouldn't meet Ovitz's financial demands, but Ovitz said he'd decided that he just didn't want to work for the Bronfmans. He said he wasn't persuaded that they had a tenable game plan for their company.

The collapse of the Ovitz negotiation scored points for Edgar Jr. with Hollywood's other power players, who had long bridled over Ovitz's supposed bullying tactics. (Ovitz went on to enjoy a brief reign as president of the Walt Disney Co., which yielded him a settlement well in excess of $100 million.)

Among those who applauded Edgar Jr. for holding firm was David Geffen, a music industry player who had emerged as a sort of Hollywood seer. Geffen made no secret of his dislike for Ovitz. Geffen felt Ovitz was arrogant—a label some applied to Geffen as well. With Ovitz now banished from Edgar Jr.'s inner circle, Geffen was more than pleased when the Seagram scion turned increasingly to him for advice. Thus when Edgar Jr. made his first acquisition—a 50 percent interest in the Interscope record label, which had prospered with such controversial gangsta-rap labels as Death Row—it was Geffen who turned up on Universal's behalf to hammer out the terms. With all the legal firepower at Universal, Edgar Jr. had relied on an outsider to make his first important deal.

Geffen, too, was instrumental in urging Edgar Jr. to hire Ovitz's former right-hand man at CAA, Ron Meyer, as president and chief operating officer of Universal. A short, compact man who traditionally wore jeans and sports shirts even to corporate meetings, Meyer had a genial personality and excellent contacts in the creative community, but lacked management experience. Yet Meyer, in turn, orchestrated the hiring of his close friend, Howard Weitzman, a prominent litigator, and Sanford Climan, another former CAA agent, to key administrative positions. In a matter of several months, the seasoned but rigid managers of the old Wasserman-Sheinberg regime had been replaced by a new team that was high on energy and good intentions but low on corporate savvy.

While wrestling with management changes at Universal, Edgar Jr. also had to deal with opposition within his own family. Early in 1995, Edgar Jr. had successfully urged his family to sell Seagram's 24.2 percent stake in DuPont in order to facilitate the MCA acquisition. Powerful figures in his family had opposed the move—especially

Charles Bronfman, Edgar Jr.'s uncle who was cochairman of Seagram. In the ensuing period, while Seagram's shares had remained flat, Du-Pont's price had more than doubled, and relatives were reminding him that, in selling DuPont, the Bronfman family had surrendered roughly $9 billion in potential gains.

Late in 1997, Edgar Jr. decided to launch an initiative that would demonstrate his ability to orchestrate dramatic change within Universal. In plotting this startling deal, he once again ignored the existing hierarchy at Universal. His plan was to spin off most of Universal's cable and domestic-TV assets, including the USA cable network, to HSN, Inc., the parent company of Barry Diller's Shopping Network in a complex stock swap. To Edgar Jr. this was a brilliant stroke: It gave Universal a stake in Diller's enterprise along with the possibility of regaining control of its assets at some time in the distant future. Clearly the most important asset to Edgar Jr. was the fifty-six-year-old Diller himself, whom Wall Street considered a media visionary. Diller was also a longtime ally of Geffen.

Edgar Jr. expected this deal would be applauded by Hollywood. He was wrong. To the Hollywood establishment, the deal was fuzzy-minded. By separating TV from movies, it violated the fundamental laws of synergy. Even the math failed to make sense. Edgar Jr. had to pay $1.7 billion to buy out Viacom's share of the USA network and Sci Fi Channel. Diller, however, managed to acquire all of USA and Sci Fi and most of Universal's TV assets for only $1.2 billion in cash and about $3 billion in HSN paper.

Aside from the numbers, Hollywood also was critical of the manner in which Edgar Jr. had kept his senior managers out of the loop. Neither Ron Meyer nor Frank Biondi, his respected CEO, were aware of the Diller deal until it was a fait accompli. A former president of Viacom, Biondi's expertise lay in cable and TV, so the disposal of Universal's assets in this area seemed to strip him of his constituency.

If morale had plummeted on the corporate side of Universal, the situation seemed equally bleak at Universal Pictures, whose slate of movies had suddenly unraveled. Edgar Jr. had hoped that summer '98 would represent a repeat of the previous year, when the Jim Carrey comedy *Liar, Liar,* combined with Spielberg's sequel to *Jurassic Park,* had delivered nearly $2 billion in box office grosses. In focusing so intently on his corporate deals, however, he had taken his eye off the film side, and he was in for a rude surprise. The centerpiece of summer '98, *Meet Joe Black,* could not possibly be ready in time for its July release date—indeed, not for any summer date. Directed by Martin Brest, who was notoriously slow in editing, *Meet Joe Black* told the story of an otherworldly creature who took human form as none other than Brad Pitt and who, while earthbound, fell in love with a beautiful young woman, played by Claire Forlani.

With *Meet Joe Black* off the schedule, Edgar Jr. realized that Universal's total program for summer '98 consisted of a low-budget comedy called *BASEketball*—directed by David Zucker, who'd created *Airplane*—and a quirky thriller called *Out of Sight,* based on a novel by the prolific Elmore Leonard. Also on the program was a film adaptation of Hunter S. Thompson's *Fear and Loathing in Las Vegas* starring Johnny Depp.

None of these offerings shaped up as another *Liar, Liar,* to put it mildly. Indeed, some in the company had complained to Edgar Jr. that the drug-addled *Fear and Loathing* was a loathsome picture that could prove an embarrassment to the company. Its director was Terry Gilliam, a career contrarian who relished tweaking Hollywood power players and, as such, might even have helped promulgate these rumors.

Early in May 1998, I had lunch with Casey Silver, the chairman of the Universal Pictures Group, and he made no effort to conceal his apprehensions about the approaching summer. "I could have pulled the trigger on Marty Brest," he said. "I could have forced him to put on extra editors and start a round-the-clock schedule. But I'm convinced this would have compromised the movie artistically. It would have been one big mess."

A thoughtful man with saturnine features who looked rather ominous in his dark gray suits and perpetually worried frown, Silver conceded that ideally he should have had one or two backup releases. This is easier said than done, he added, observing obliquely that "the atmosphere" at his company hadn't been conducive to green-lighting expensive pictures. "We've had a lot of consultants running around the place," Silver said, alluding to the expensive "reengineering" program that Edgar Jr. had initiated months earlier. The intent of the program was to improve decision-making, heighten synergy between divisions, and consolidate the use of outside vendors such as law firms and ad agencies. While Edgar Jr. had heralded the achievements of his program, insisting that it would save the company at least $75 million a year long-term, many at Universal felt that the ubiquitous consultants had inhibited dialogue within the company and, in fact, stalled decision-making.

If Casey Silver had indeed been lobbying for more green lights, however, his spring releases had done nothing to inspire Edgar Jr.'s confidence. Universal had invested in a lavish ad campaign to launch *Primary Colors,* the Mike Nichols–Elaine May collaboration, but the movie ended up hitting the wall at under $40 million, far short of the nearly $70 million it had cost to make. Whether the moviegoing public simply wasn't interested in political satire or whether John Travolta's broad impersonation of President Clinton had struck a negative chord was unclear. A more conventional, down-the-middle thriller called *Mercury Rising,* starring Bruce Willis, didn't even do as well as *Primary Colors,* grossing a little over $30 million in the U.S. "It has been a tough spring," conceded Silver.

It was about to get tougher. Edgar Jr. let it be known that he was dissatisfied and that heads would have to roll. The body count already had been mounting in the Black Tower, the town's nickname for the forbidding office building that housed Universal's administrative offices. Howard Weitzman, the litigator and friend of Ron Meyer, was out the door. So was Sandy Climan, the former Meyer colleague at CAA, now returned to that agency—"gratefully," he told associates.

When movies fail to perform, the customary practice in Hollywood was to shoot the messenger—in this case, the advertising and publicity staff whose job it was to sell whatever product was handed them. True to form, Buffy Shutt and Kathy Jones, who had run Universal's marketing efforts as a team and were highly regarded in Hollywood, were blamed for the latest flops and let go. No one at Universal was critical of their work other than to say that Shutt and Jones had focused too much on the company's big movies, neglecting its smaller, needier films. The ax also fell on Mark Platt, a taciturn apparatchik who served as president of production under Silver. Again there was no public criticism of Platt's performance, other than to suggest that his style was out of synch with Silver's.

Clearly the mood in the Black Tower had grown ugly. When Connie Bruck, a writer for *The New Yorker,* interviewed Edgar Jr. in May, she was surprised by his demeanor. Told to expect his usual self-deprecating politesse, the Edgar Jr. she encountered "seemed edgy, defensive and bitter, the veneer of graciousness worn thin."

Rumors were rampant that other heads would roll—possibly Silver's and even Ron Meyer's. Producers and talent agents, fretful about the studio's instability, let it be known that Universal was the last place they would take their new projects. Even if they could elicit a decision from the nervous executives at Universal, they were loath to deal with a management that might shortly be dismissed.

In the midst of this crisis at Universal, I decided to write a column in *Variety* and *Daily Variety* that sought to analyze the adverse competitive effects of this sort of corporate instability. Emphasizing that my column often delivered unsolicited advice to those who neither needed it nor wanted it, I observed: "If you hear a curious whirring in your ears, Edgar, it's the sound of the town turning against you." Hollywood simply did not understand what he was trying to accomplish at Universal, I said, and only he could change that perception.

A day of indignant silence followed publication of the column. Then came a sudden flurry of phone calls, first from Meyer, then from the normally close-mouthed Biondi, and finally from Edgar Jr. himself.

"I just want to assure you I'm not going to be fired," Meyer told me, his tone less affable than usual. "Nor is Casey Silver going to be fired. All that is behind us. If you don't believe me, ask Edgar Jr."

Whereupon Edgar Jr. called me. His voice had an edge to it, but he was surprisingly good-humored. He reiterated the mantra—no more firings, no more Diller annexations. "I have a plan," he said. "I realize it may not seem like I do, but I do." He embarked on another sentence, then cut himself short as though not wanting to reveal secrets.

"Does your plan involve acquiring a music company?" I persisted, fishing for information. "A company like, say, EMI?" *The New Yorker* had just published its profile of Edgar Jr. suggesting the EMI deal was all but sealed.

"Yes on the first question, no on the sec—" Again he stopped himself. "These are publicly owned companies," he said. "I have to be careful. The SEC has all these regulations."

"I know. But I'm glad you haven't lost your appetite for the music business."

"It's got a lot more possibilities than movies," he said, his tone lightening. "Like profit margins. There are actually profit margins in the music business."

He shifted the subject, reminiscing about his younger days when he had tried his hand as a film producer. "I was schlepping around projects no one wanted to make," he said. "I remember bringing some of them to you. At least you were polite in turning me down, which was better than most. That's why I can't get too pissed at you for the column. Look, if the town has turned against me, it will turn again. We've both seen that happen often enough."

"We sure have."

It was only a matter of a few weeks before I understood why Edgar Jr. was reluctant to reveal his hand. His appetite for the music business had indeed been rekindled, but it was not EMI he was going after. Those talks had long since broken down. Now Edgar had a much more intriguing target in his sights: Polygram.

During the last week in May, Edgar Jr. disclosed that for

$10.6 billion, Seagram had acquired the giant music and film company from Philips, the Dutch electronics conglomerate. In a single stroke he had reinvented his family's stolid liquor company into the biggest music company in the world, with annual sales of $6.2 billion. Suddenly the Universal stable included hot pop groups like Hanson, important labels like Mercury and Motown, and the enormous classical repertoire that Polygram had assembled.

In addition to the Dutch company's music arm, Edgar Jr. also found himself in possession of an important film company that owned a library of 1,500 titles as well as controlling movie labels like Interscope, Propaganda, and Working Title. The latter entity, presided over by two bright young Brits named Tim Bevan and Eric Fellner, had produced international hits like *Four Weddings and a Funeral* and *Bean.*

Edgar Jr. could scarcely conceal his jubilance. Finally, he had bought himself a major niche in an industry in which he felt at home. As he told me earlier, the music business offered the prospect of higher profit margins than movies, even though music sales had slowed noticeably over the last couple of years and there seemed to be no hot new wave on the horizon to stimulate a recovery. But business would turn around, Edgar Jr. insisted—he knew he could engineer it. He had proved to Hollywood that he had a plan, after all, and that he could bring it off. So much for the naysayers.

The reactions to the Polygram acquisition from around the world were not so ebullient. Some analysts on Wall Street felt the price had been too steep. Others fretted over the concentration of power. "One fewer player in the music business is not good for artists," warned Jay Cooper, a leading music attorney. "And the restructuring that will take place is making a lot of people very nervous."

Movie executives in Europe were even more disturbed about the ultimate disposition of Polygram's movie labels. Polygram was the one major distributor, after all, that was not controlled by Hollywood—it was truly a European-based company. Yet given Edgar Jr.'s sharply diminishing appetite for the movie business, it was clear he wanted to dispose of the Polygram labels, and Hollywood's buyers would inevitably be the most voracious. Pierre Lescure, the powerful chief of Canal Plus of France, said that "a European solution" to this problem would have to be arrived at.

Even as Edgar Jr. and his executive team were shifting their focus from TV and movies to music, they had to confront a final indignity involving their summer '98 movies. Though Polygram's movie assets were aggressively being shopped, there was one Polygram movie that could be of help to Universal's anemic summer schedule. It was an $85 million sci-fi love story starring Robin Williams called *What Dreams May Come,* and Polygram had engineered a positive buzz about the film. There was one catch, however. Since much of the action in the movie took place in what its producers called "the hereafter," the movie was heavily dependent on elaborate special effects.

In the process of adding up its new assets, Universal quickly learned that its newly discovered Robin Williams vehicle wouldn't be available for summer after all. The special effects weren't even close to finished. It would be a long, lean summer.

Other Studios

Aside from the six major studios, none of the other production and distribution entities were prepared to play more than a marginal role in summer '98. Most of the companies supplying so-called niche product, whether art movies or other genres, tended to avoid the summer frenzy. Even Miramax, which had astonishing success with sleepers like *Pulp Fiction* and *Good Will Hunting,* liked to release films at the end of the year, when they would be lodged firmly in the minds of Oscar voters. Miramax would try limited forays in summer '98 with *Smoke Signals* and *Rounders,* but it was clearly saving its heavy ammunition for winter. The same held true for companies like October, Gramercy, and Live.

Trimark would bravely release in August what it described as its first crossover gay film, *Billy's Hollywood Screen Kiss.* Gramercy would wait until some of the smoke cleared in mid-August before going out with its new project from Neil La Bute called *Your Friends and Neighbors.* But with all the blockbusters fighting for elbow room, none of these companies expected to hit real pay dirt.

New Line, a mini-major that had cooled off considerably over the past few years after an earlier hot streak with *Seven* and *Dumb and Dumber,* would not be a significant player in summer '98, but would offer a cluster of promising movies in the fall. Its biggest summer push would be behind *Blade,* a vampire movie starring Wesley Snipes that was slotted for general release in mid-August.

Among all the niche companies, the virtual absence of MGM/UA in summer '98 ranked as the most surprising. Three years ago maverick investor Kirk Kerkorian had taken over the company for the third time after twice buying and selling it, announcing his intention to sink well over $1 billion into the studio. Not once in the history of Hollywood had an owner returned for a second try, not to mention a third. In a baffling series of transactions, Kerkorian had previously sold the company, or parts of it, to such assorted players as Ted Turner (who ended up in possession of MGM's library of films), Giancarlo Parretti (who ended up in jail), and Christopher Skase (who ended up in exile), but the old Armenian always returned to the scene as though out of habit. The MGM he found himself owning once again in the summer of 1998 was a far cry from the powerhouse studio of the thirties and forties. The company was badly undercapitalized; it operated out of rented offices and controlled no production facilities; unlike its rivals, it was solely dependent on features and TV and did not own synergistic businesses like music, theme parks, and cable TV.

Nor could it look ahead to summer '98 to bail it out. The buzz was not good on its sequel to *Species,* a sci-fi movie that had performed well three years earlier. *Dirty Work,* starring Norm McDonald, and *Disturbing Behavior* didn't offer much hope either. In fact, the only film on MGM's release schedule that looked promising was an action movie called *Ronin* starring Robert De Niro and directed by veteran John Frankenheimer.

Kerkorian had let it be known through his associates that he was growing impatient with MGM's lack of progress since he had returned as boss and owner, but he got little sympathy from the town's players. After all, he had been there, done that. By his third try, it was reasoned, he should have gotten it right.

The Press

By the end of the first week in May of 1998, the nation's leading magazines and newspapers had all published their annual summer forecasts. The ritual of handicapping the summer movies had been growing since the early nineties, with more and more editors acknowledging the summer season as a key barometer of pop culture.

With each passing year the analyses had become more detailed and the forecasting procedures more adventuresome. It was as though the press, having corrupted the moviegoing experience by spotlighting week-to-week box office performance with pervasive "top five" charts appearing on every TV news show and in every local newspaper, was now prepared to take the process a step further. It would tell the public what it was going to like in the future.

Given this mission, a predictable similarity characterized most magazines' summer movie coverage. ASTEROIDS! ALIENS! AVENGERS! AND A REALLY BIG LIZARD! heralded *Entertainment Weekly*. AIEEE! IT'S SUMMER! screamed a *Time* magazine headline. "We know how much the season's first big monster movie will earn—Godzillions! But what about mere mortals like Hanks and Willis, Uma and Mel?" said the subhead. *Business Week* took an only slightly more subdued approach: YIKES! MONSTERS, METEORS AND MANAGEMENT SHAKEUPS.

Newsweek's banner was the most restrained. THE JOYS OF SUMMER, it announced optimistically in its May 11 issue, and its introduction was the most candid. "In last year's summer movie preview we tried to predict how much money *Titanic* would make at the box office. We were off by $410 million—and the movie got postponed till Christmas," the magazine acknowledged. As a result, *Newsweek*'s preview was a more modest endeavor, limiting itself to a mere twenty movies and avoiding the practice of forecasting precise box office returns.

Having said all that, *Newsweek* flatly predicted that *Godzilla* and *Armageddon* "would no doubt be colossal hits"—a forecast that was not supported by any documentation. Ranking the summer movies that *Newsweek* writers said they "most wanted to see," however, *Godzilla* ranked fourth and *Armageddon* eleventh. The top-ranked want-to-see was *The Truman Show*, possibly because it had been the film most available for advance viewing. *Saving Private Ryan* ranked second and, curiously, *Fear and Loathing in Las Vegas* third.

The list contained the predictable commercial entries like *Dr. Dolittle* and *The X-Files*, but also some obscure ones, such as *Your Friends and Neighbors*, directed by Neil La Bute, whose previous picture was *In the Company of Men*, and *Smoke Signals*, the Native American film that had been a succès d'estime at the Sundance Film Festival earlier in the year.

Time was equally circumspect. Richard Corliss, one of the magazine's movie critics, stated merely that *Godzilla* had been so widely hyped that the only debate revolved around "which film would come in second." On that issue, he decided to quote, of all people, two Wall Street analysts: Alan Kassan of Deutsche Morgan Grenfell and PaineWebber's Christopher Dixon. *Saving Private Ryan* was clearly the second choice, Corliss reported. "I'd take points in that," said Kassan.

The magazine decided to duck the most-favored list by dividing the films into categories: "Boy Toys" (*Armageddon*), "Girl Power" (*Madeline*), "Idiots' Delight" (*Jane Austen's Mafia*), "Star Re-Turns" (*Bulworth*), and "Weird TV" (*The X-Files*). Corliss admitted candidly that his "tout sheet" was based on "watching trailers, listening to sages and making stuff up." He continued: "Fact is, no one knows what works. Barry Sonnenfeld, director of last year's gigantic *Men in Black*, says he's in the dark."

Premiere faced no such inhibitions. It not only presented its top ten, but even predicted their precise U.S. box office results. Each film listed contained a plot summary ("The Pitch"), some inside dirt on the film ("Off-Camera"), and a hint as to how the project was going ("News from the Front").

Having arrayed all this incidental intelligence, *Premiere* listed its top ten, appending their domestic box office predictions as follows:

Armageddon	$260 million
Godzilla	$250 million
The Mask of Zorro	$150 million
Saving Private Ryan	$135 million
Small Soldiers	$130 million
The Truman Show	$115 million
Mulan	$105 million
BASEketball	$100 million
Lethal Weapon IV	$95 million
The Horse Whisperer	$85 million

Relegated to the "also rans," and without forecasts, were movies like *The X-Files, Six Days, Seven Nights,* and *Dr. Dolittle,* all of which made most forecasters' top ten lists. *Bulworth* had to settle for yet another subspecies, labeled "Best of the Rest."

In advancing these forecasts, *Premiere* was clearly not deterred by its rather patchy record of the previous summer. In 1997, the magazine had been reasonably on the mark in forecasting that the *Jurassic Park* sequel (*The Lost World*) would hit $250 million (its actual U.S. results hit $229.1 million), but from that point on the crystal ball got cloudy. *Premiere* had guessed *Men in Black* at $170 million; it rolled to $250.1 million. It had been too high on *Batman and Robin* (prediction, $160 million; actual, $107 million). Its biggest summer miscalculation, however, turned out not to be a summer movie at all. *Premiere* had thought that *Titanic* would have a U.S. box office gross of $190 million. The film ended up doing $565.7 million, starting at Christmas.

In forecasting that eight summer movies would surpass the

$100 million plateau but only three would break the $150 million barrier, *Premiere* did not thrill either Hollywood or the Wall Street analysts. On the same week that *Premiere*'s presumptuous predictions appeared, *The Wall Street Journal*'s new weekend edition came out with its own summer scorecard, reminding readers that $100 million in U.S. grosses was no longer the mark of a hit. The *Journal* quoted Jeffrey Logsdon, managing director of Cruttenden Roth, an investment banking firm in Irvine, California, as stating, "We're moving to a day when the benchmark is $150 million to $200 million for a block-buster."

In analzying the cost of the fifteen top summer films, the *Journal* estimated that fourteen of them would have to bring in more than $100 million at the U.S. box office to reach hit status. The *Journal*'s tally was as follows:

Deep Impact–Production cost $80 million, worldwide marketing $60 million. Benchmark for hit status $140 million

The Horse Whisperer–Cost $60 million, worldwide marketing $60 million. Benchmark $120 million.

Bulworth–Cost $35 million, worldwide marketing $40 million. Benchmark $75 million.

Godzilla–Cost $120 million, worldwide marketing $120 million. Benchmark $240 million.

The Truman Show–Cost $60 million, worldwide marketing $50 million. Benchmark $110 million.

Six Days, Seven Nights–Cost $70 million, worldwide marketing $50 million. Benchmark $120 million.

Mulan–Cost $90 million, worldwide marketing $60 million. Benchmark $150 million.

The X-Files–Cost $60 million, worldwide marketing $60 million. Benchmark $120 million.

Dr. Dolittle–Cost $70 million, worldwide marketing $50 million. Benchmark $120 million.

Armageddon–Cost $140 million, worldwide marketing $80 million. Benchmark $220 million.

Small Soldiers–Cost $60 million, worldwide marketing $60 million. Benchmark $120 million.

Lethal Weapon IV–Cost $120 million, worldwide marketing $60 million. Benchmark $180 million.

Saving Private Ryan–Cost $70 million, worldwide marketing $50 million. Benchmark $120 million.

The Mask of Zorro–Cost $70 million, worldwide marketing $60 million. Benchmark $130 million.

The Avengers–Cost $60 million, worldwide marketing $50 million. Benchmark $110 million.

By the end of June, the *Los Angeles Times* was chipping in its own projections. Based on the initial openings, the *Times* projected ultimate box office receipts and profitability, hypothesizing that "U.S. box office usually accounts for only a fifth of a movie's revenue stream." The *Times* broke the releases down into four categories, listing their projected U.S. box office receipts, as follows:

Mega-moneymakers: *The Truman Show* ($130 million); *Deep Impact* ($140 million); *The X-Files* ($90 million) and *Mulan* ($115 million).

Moneymakers: *Hope Floats* ($50 million); *Godzilla* ($145 million); *Can't Hardly Wait* ($25 million).

Toss-ups: *The Horse Whisperer* ($72 million); *A Perfect Murder* ($70 million); *Six Days, Seven Nights* ($70 million).

Money Losers: *Bulworth* ($28 million); *Dirty Work* ($11 million).

The *Times*'s cost estimates varied to a degree from those of the *Journal*. *Deep Impact*, for example, was listed as costing $100 million while the *Journal* estimated $80 million.

The *Times*'s and *Journal*'s numbers were instantly challenged on all sides. Studios habitually go into denial about their high marketing costs, and the press consistently understates the actual production expenditures—the actual negative cost of *Godzilla* was $30 million higher than the *Times* or *Journal* estimated. Then, too, the *Journal*'s formula for profitability, which is also used by some analysts, is nothing if not controversial. Star-driven action movies that may look like flops in the U.S. could soar into profitability as a result of foreign box office returns. Disney's extraordinarily successful video division turns expensive animation movies that are marginal box office performers into moneymakers. On the other hand, few disputed the *Journal*'s basic premise that if a movie does badly in the U.S., all other revenue streams are dragged down. Hence, the *Journal*'s main message resonated with the Hollywood community: "This may be the dawn of the $100 million box office flop."

It was going to be a long, hard summer.

The Blueprints

The Truman Show came into being because an obscure young New Zealander named Andrew Niccol, a man admittedly gripped by paranoid fantasies, desperately wanted a vehicle to launch himself as a film director. *Lethal Weapon IV* was set in motion because Warner Bros. was panicked that it would find itself with no major summer picture on its release schedule. *Bulworth* was launched because Warren Beatty not only had a thesis about American politics he wanted to explore, but also a superbly convoluted business scheme for bringing it to reality. *Armageddon* came to life because a shrewd young screenwriter named Jonathan Hensleigh decided that the first screenplay about an asteroid striking the earth would surely make millions. The "X-Files" TV show became a movie because its creator, Chris Carter, felt confident that the cultish devotion of his twenty million viewers was such that they would be willing to pay seven dollars to see an expanded version of the show.

Screenplays come into existence for a myriad of reasons, ranging from fervent idealism to rampant avarice. Creating a script is akin to entering a lottery; the chances of winning are extraordinarily remote. And even if a writer beats the odds, it is highly unlikely that his or her name or vision will make it to the big screen.

All this notwithstanding, some thirty thousand screenplays are registered annually with the Writers Guild. Walk into the office of any development executive or literary agent and you confront appalling towers of screenplays stacked to the ceiling, each embodying the dreams, or greed, of a wannabe screenwriter.

Most screenplays are written on spec, which means the writer was not paid to write the material. However, each studio has between two hundred and three hundred screenplays in development at any given time. This represents an investment of hundreds of millions of dollars and is a major contributor to the roughly $300 million-a-year over-head that is run up by each major studio. One Hollywood screen-writer, Ron Bass, is guaranteed no less than $10 million a year by Sony Pictures, not only to create his own scripts but also to do what is called body-and-fender work—rewrites—on existing projects, some of which are already shooting.

In order for a spec script to gain the attention of a producer or studio executive, it must, in the argot of Hollywood, have "heat." This often comes about when a top agent gives his or her seal of approval to a script—sometimes it's harder for an outsider to get an agent to read his work than a producer—but even this is not enough. Of the major movies of summer '98, only two, *Six Days, Seven Nights* and *The Truman Show*, started out as true spec scripts. *Six Days, Seven Nights*, written by Michael Browning, an occasional prop man and actor who had previously sold a sci-fi script that was never produced, was optioned by Caravan Pictures in 1995 as a vehicle for Julia Roberts. Ultimately it starred Harrison Ford and Anne Heche.

The writer of the other spec script, Andrew Niccol, was a twenty-nine-year-old commercials director in London in 1993 when he sat down to write *The Truman Show*. "I had planned to move to Holly-wood and I knew no one," Niccol recalls. A friend told him about Lynn Pleshette, an independent literary agent in Los Angeles who, unlike most of her colleagues, actually read unsolicited material that was sent to her. She read Niccol's script, liked it, and sold it.

One other project, the much-ballyhooed *Armageddon*, might tech-nically be called a spec script since no one paid its writer, Jonathan Hensleigh, to sit down and write it. Hensleigh, however, was hardly the obscure screenwriter hammering away in relative isolation. He had worked as a writer on several big-budget Disney movies such as

The Rock and *Con Air*, on which he also had an executive producer credit. His wife, Gale Anne Hurd, had produced some big-league movies on her own, including *Aliens* and *Terminator*s 1 and 2. Hensleigh was close to Michael Bay, who had directed *The Rock*, and to Jerry Bruckheimer, its producer, who also had a lucrative overall deal with the Disney studio. When Bay expressed interest in the first draft of *Armageddon*, Hensleigh promptly took him to see Joe Roth at Disney. Hearing the idea, Roth did not even want to read Hensleigh's first draft. He liked the pitch well enough to say, then and there, "I'll make it."

The *Armageddon* experience notwithstanding, most studios have become leery of the spec script and try to play a more proactive role, supervising the development of in-house projects. In some cases, such as *Dr. Dolittle*, this development process required only twelve months. In others, it took many painful years. *Deep Impact* dates back twenty years; *Small Soldiers* was in development for ten. Even *Godzilla* took almost a decade of writing and rewriting before it could be coaxed into production.

Not a single summer movie of 1998 reached the production stage without undergoing rewrites by squadrons of screenwriters. In some cases, not even the producer and director were entirely certain how many writers had toiled on their project. *Lethal Weapon IV* started shooting before a final script was completed and at one point five writers were working simultaneously, trying to hone it into shape. There were five credited writers on *Armageddon*, and four more listed in press material, all with credits such as "written by," "story by," and "adaptation by."

The result of this writing-by-committee on the big action-adventures is often wobbly characterization and patchy dialogue. But even on more intimate films, directors may turn to familiar writers to spice up a scene or add color to a section that seems to be dragging. Hence Ivan Reitman, a director best known for comedy (*Meatballs, Ghostbusters*) turned to veteran comedy writers Lowell Ganz and Babaloo Mandel to jazz up a stretch of *Six Days, Seven Nights*. Among their contributions was a pirate encounter that struck many viewers as highly derivative.

The overriding reality of the movie business is that while every director and studio executive pays obeisance to writers, and while everyone professes to be looking for that great piece of material, the writer really doesn't matter, especially for the summer movies. What a director wants in a screenplay more than anything else is a role that will attract a major star, and consequently make the studio happy. Though Disney professed great ardor for *Armageddon*, it was not until Joe Roth enticed Bruce Willis to commit that the green lights started flashing.

Studios need packages—the right script, the right star, the right director at the right price. Each of the movies of summer '98 met these criteria as they swung into production. Here's how the principal movies came together.

The Truman Show

In which Jim Carrey derived curious comfort from the fact that his new movie would inspire more paranoia than it would laughter

Venturing from New Zealand to London to study filmmaking, Andrew Niccol counted himself both a success and a failure. He had gotten a foothold in the London advertising scene, which didn't really interest him but gave him a chance to try his hand at directing commercials. This was a road that had previously been traveled by filmmakers like Ridley Scott and Hugh Hudson, among others.

Nearing his thirtieth birthday, Niccol decided it was time to take the next major step—a move to Hollywood. "I knew absolutely no one in Hollywood," Niccol says. "All my time in London that I had spent shooting commercials I had also been scribbling away on screenplays. I was obsessed with writing my stories."

On the face of it, Andrew Niccol's *The Truman Show* was hardly a commercial story. The basic plot line was slow in revealing itself and the naive protagonist, Truman Burbank, did not seem empathetic. It was hard to imagine any star wanting to play Truman since he didn't perform any memorable deeds, nor did he suffer from the sort of physical deformity or mental handicap that in the past had won Oscars for top stars.

In the screenplay, Truman was a thirty-year-old man who unknowingly had grown up from birth on America's TV screens. His entire life constituted an all-day reality show, the ultimate "Real Life" taking place on a mammoth sound stage that looked like an idyllic oceanside village. Hidden cameras were situated throughout the faux town as Truman lived his synthetic made-for-TV life with his wife and best friend, who were, of course, actors. The mastermind of this universe was a genius named Christof, a godlike czar of the media world.

"I've always felt that the people around me were acting, if not overacting," Niccol explains. "I suffer from a semi-paranoid belief that most people are lying to me." As it turned out, Jim Carrey, who ultimately was to star in *The Truman Show*, shared the same obsession; indeed, he had long thought about trying to write something on the subject.

The process of translating this paranoia into a screenplay took Niccol two years. Once he had finished he got in touch with literary agent Lynn Pleshette. An acquaintance had told him about Pleshette, a plumply convivial woman who loved what she did and who, as a result, actually read what are called "cold submissions"—that is, material sent in by authors without the endorsement of a professional in the business. Taking the shot, Niccol dispatched to her an earlier script that he'd written called *The Undressing of Sophie Dean*, a piece that also dealt with paranoia. Its central figure was an attractive young woman whose life had been systematically invaded by a series of faxes, e-mails, and phone calls. As luck would have it, the day it arrived at her office, Pleshette's lunch date had canceled and she had decided to attack her stack of unsolicited material. She liked Niccol's piece and sent it to producer Melinda Jason, who promptly optioned it at MGM. Startled yet encouraged, Niccol decided to send Pleshette *The Truman Show*, which he felt was his strongest—if least accessible—piece. In his heart he knew that, since he'd gotten lucky with his first Hollywood foray, the odds were that his second one would be shot down.

But he was surprised again. Pleshette had taken a plane to visit her daughter at Boston University and took along Niccol's script. "I was transfixed," she recalls. "I was reading along and it was getting to me and when I read about the boat hitting the sky, I literally started shaking with excitement. I felt I was in the presence of something brilliant."

Spurred by this encouragement and armed with notes from Pleshette, Niccol went back to work on his script. "Here I was, working on it in Hollywood, in the belly of the beast," he says. "If you want to write about people lying to you, this is the place to do it." Niccol kept hammering away at his script up until an hour before Pleshette was scheduled to make her submissions to producers. The heralded scene in which the star fell out of the sky was added barely moments before the material went off to be Xeroxed.

To the delight of Niccol and Pleshette, the responses came surprisingly fast. They were not always felicitous. "We pass," growled one producer. "Andrew Niccol is clearly a quite disturbed individual." One of the prime candidates on Pleshette's list was the husband-and-wife production team of Frank Marshall and Kathleen Kennedy. They had spent many years working with Steven Spielberg and were shrewd judges of material. Somehow a script from their office, however, fell into the hands of one of Hollywood's ubiquitous trackers, story spies whose job it is to identify and secure hot new properties, and suddenly Scott Rudin, a volatile and voluble producer, also had a copy. His response was almost instantaneous.

"I got this frantic message in my office saying that Rudin would call me at home at night," Pleshette recalls. "I know how arrogant he is, so I said he couldn't call me until eleven P.M., Los Angeles time. I didn't say why—actually I just wanted to watch 'NYPD Blue,' which is my favorite TV show. Also, I wanted to enjoy my moment of power."

Within a couple of days, Pleshette and Rudin had closed a deal for $750,000, with additional fees if the film got made, and a $200,000 penalty clause if Niccol was not permitted to direct. The money was supplied by Paramount, where Rudin had a producing deal.

Rudin had been building an impressive record not only in Hollywood but also on Broadway. He was responsible for such movies as *In and Out, The First Wives Club*, and *The Rainmaker*, and on Broadway, for plays like the revival of *A Funny Thing Happened on the Way to the Forum* as well as *Skylight*, *The Judas Kiss*, and Ralph Fiennes's *Hamlet*.

"This may sound weird," Rudin said, "but I even liked the name of the script. Titles mean a lot to me. I also loved the metaphor. I think most people believe that the world holds them back, that they were meant to be more than they are. This script dealt with ideas that people don't articulate, but which mean a great deal to them. I wanted to make this picture really badly. I also realized the potential traps. It all rested on the directing. I needed a filmmaker who could figure out how to make the movie seem real and unreal at the same time. The danger was that it would be so overdesigned no one would take it seriously."

One candidate Rudin did not seriously consider was Andrew Niccol, despite the writer's aspirations. Indeed, the screenplay deal called for Niccol to be afforded a test in which he could choose his actors and direct a scene of his choice. Rudin and Paramount would view the scene and then pass judgment. Though new to town, Niccol sensed that this was a standard ploy to get rid of an obnoxious *auteur*, but he decided to go through the motions anyway. At least his agent had built the $200,000 penalty clause into his deal; he was renting a small flat in West Hollywood and had no intention of going Hollywood and spending all of his money. Even though he was batting two for two in terms of screenplays, he still distrusted the town.

Niccol had been well briefed for his initial meeting with Rudin. A beefy, round-faced man with thinning hair, a woolly black beard, and a robust voice, Rudin knew how to play the friend of the artist. He, too, was a renegade who had worked inside the Hollywood system, but had opted instead for the New York theater scene.

"He was very seductive," Niccol recalls. "He would quote whole scenes from the script. He understood the material. This wasn't someone who'd just read studio coverage. On the other hand, there was something eerie about the meeting. Looking at him, knowing how he got the script, I could sense it was Rudin who had a camera on all of us. That's why he related to the material."

There was indeed a darker side to Rudin, as Niccol was to discover. He was a man of mercurial moods, a mythic figure in the odd little world of interns, trackers, and production assistants. He was rumored to have caused a bigger body count of casualties among his personal staff than any other working producer.

"I sensed what I was up against," Niccol says. "This was going to be a long tough road, even though everything had started so brilliantly."

His premonition was correct. For one thing, Rudin was under pressure from several directors who were interested in the material. From the outset Niccol had urged that, were he himself denied the opportunity to direct, Peter Weir be contacted, an idea to which Rudin had responded favorably. Weir was responsible for such remarkable films as *The Dead Poets' Society*, *The Year of Living Dangerously*, and *Witness*, which had been a big hit for Paramount. On the other hand, Weir's last movie, *Fearless*, had been a disheartening flop and he had not worked for four long years.

Rudin knew, too, that Weir was notoriously tough on material, a fact that Weir himself understood all too well. When we met to discuss the movie in December 1997, Weir acknowledged to me that he'd become completely depressed by the material his CAA agents had been sending to him. "I asked my agent, 'Am I on the A-list when it comes to material?' He told me that I was. So I said, 'Fine, take me off it.'" What he meant, Weir explained, was that the A-list material was all "cut and dried." It was calculated commercial fare, material designed to attract a top star and build the groundwork for an expensive Hollywood movie. "I wanted scripts from the bottom drawer," Weir said. "I wanted scripts that were broken."

Knowing all this, Rudin decided to take a shot and dispatched

The Truman Show to Weir in Australia. He assumed it would be a long wait. He also assumed the response would be negative. And meanwhile there were other directors to pursue.

An agent, Martin Bauer, was aggressively pushing his client, Brian De Palma, for the project. Certainly De Palma had had his share of hits, including *The Untouchables* and *Mission Impossible*. But a recurring theme in De Palma's work was voyeurism and this was a hot button for Niccol. Truman Burbank's entire life had been televised, so there was ample opportunity for voyeuristic display, but Niccol had resolutely stayed from that. If anything, the screenplay was overly discreet in dealing with the intimate details of Truman's life.

Rudin felt obliged to meet with De Palma, and the two hammered out a short outline. As they worked, the movie was growing darker and more distasteful. Ultimately De Palma decided it wasn't working, and said he'd like to move to another project. Rudin was relieved.

Even as this was taking place, Paramount's creative team had inevitably come up with its own rewrite ideas. The movie needed more comedy, it was decreed. Who better to lend it laughs than Michael Leeson, a veteran body-and-fender man who was both quick and clever. Part of Leeson's assignment was to develop a subplot involving the network that was broadcasting "The Truman Show." The network would have ratings problems and this would add pressure to the fictional producers of "The Truman Show."

All these brainstorms because instantly irrelevant, however, with the mounting interest of Jim Carrey in playing Truman. Rudin had sent him the original Niccol screenplay and was both thrilled by and apprehensive about Carrey's positive reaction. In Hollywood, the process of landing a superstar was somewhat like deep-sea fishing. The initial bite was encouraging, but far from definitive. It was followed by a lot of meetings and hand-shaking, then by intense negotiations over script, salary, perks, locations, and—most important—director.

In the case of *The Truman Show*, all this was even more dicey than usual for a variety of reasons. While several of the top executives at Paramount, especially Michelle Manning, president of production, were excited about the material, Sherry Lansing was less than exuberant. Though she made no effort to block the project, she was concerned that the original material was too "special" to support a big-budget Hollywood movie. When she heard of Jim Carrey's interest, her skepticism was heightened. This was not the standard Jim Carrey vehicle, she pointed out. There were few, if any, big laughs. If Carrey really wanted to do the movie, Paramount would not be willing to pay him anything close to the $20 million figure he had been demanding on his comedies.

There was also the problem of the script. The draft to which Carrey had responded was set in New York City, and everyone agreed this was a mistake. The story didn't seem believable in New York. As even Niccol had acknowledged, "The whole thing would play better against a prisoner-in-paradise setting."

And now came the Peter Weir problem. He had read *The Truman Show* and had passed. It was, as Weir tactfully put it to Rudin, "a difficult piece." Rudin pointed out that that was exactly why he thought Weir would like it. Besides, wouldn't it be sensible at least to meet with Carrey to trade ideas? Maybe an accommodation could be reached.

Weir had seen *Ace Ventura* and rather liked it. It appealed to that part of Weir that once ran an improvisational comedy group in college. He liked Carrey's willingness to explore, and take risks. Then, too, Weir got to thinking about the Gulf War, which reminded him of *The Truman Show*. The war was, after all, a live event, but one that was rigidly orchestrated and controlled, like a sanitized video game. "I was reminded that the line between reality and unreality had become blurred," Weir reflected.

And so it was that Peter Weir decided to get on a plane, fly to Los Angeles, and talk to Jim Carrey. As they did so, Andrew Niccol sat on the sidelines, feeling helpless. This is the moment in which the writer feels most irrelevant. He had created a canvas and some characters; now a director, an actor, and a producer had laid claim to that canvas and adopted his characters as their own. They alone would decide how those characters will change and develop and what fate they will meet. It was their show now.

Carrey and Weir liked each other immediately. Carrey had seen all of Weir's movies and found them challenging. Weir had seen Carrey's work and had approved. Carrey closely identified with Truman's fishbowl life, and with the paranoia that was incipient in that condition. "It's all very parallel to my life," he confided to Weir. "Everybody gets to a point where they have to separate themselves, and to do that you have to go into unknown territory and run a risk of losing everything."

All that was good news. The bad news was that, like most actors, Carrey's life was essentially out of control. As much as he wanted to do *The Truman Show*, he was first committed to act in *The Cable Guy* at Sony and *Liar, Liar* at Universal. It would be at least a year before he could be available.

Peter Weir took a deep breath. He had already been out of action since 1993. Could he afford to be idle another year? "At first my main motivation had been to be in Australia during my son's senior year in high school," Weir explained. "I had been away too much. I wanted to be home. I wanted to turn off my turbines. But the years had now stretched out. It was time to work."

Yet Weir decided to wait. While Paramount was hammering out details of the deal with Carrey, Weir began rewrites on the script. To begin with, he made it clear that he wanted no part of the material created by De Palma or Michael Leeson. He wanted to go back to work with Andrew Niccol and try to get it right. That in itself startled studio executives: Here was a director who actually wanted to stay with the original writer.

Over the course of several months, Weir and Niccol turned out roughly nine drafts of the screenplay. Their efforts focused on several key issues: When did the audience learn that Truman's entire life was being photographed? How does Truman react to the knowledge that, as Weir puts it, "the people around him were all ambitious actors.

He's been brought up by wolves"? There was also the ending to contend with, realigning the scenes involving Truman's escape. Toward
the end of their effort, Weir and Niccol adjourned to an isolated hotel
in Big Sur where they read the script aloud to each other, hour after
hour, letting each phrase and metaphor resonate.

By this time Weir's wife, Wendy Stites, had read a magazine article about a curious little community called Seaside, on the Gulf Coast
of Florida. It was a quaint, antiseptic planned community of picket
fences and porches that seemed to Weir and Niccol like the perfect
set for their film. Seaside solved the logistical problems presented by
Niccol's original New York location. Why would anyone go to the trouble to build a TV set replicating Manhattan? The script was thus
changed to accommodate Seaside and the new locations on water that
it presented.

Finally came the issue of budget. Paramount liked the Seaside
location, but insisted that the film be shot for $50 million. Weir,
Rudin, and their line producer, a burly veteran named Ed Feldman,
all recoiled, pointing out that the above-the-line costs already had
reached $29 million, including Carrey's $12 million fee. "We told
them their budget was fine, except that we couldn't do it for that,"
Weir said.

The studio caved. A budget of $60 million was agreed upon.
Sherry Lansing still had her concerns about the commercial viability
of the project. Jonathan Dolgen still fretted because there was no financial partner. Several studio production executives were worried
that there weren't enough laughs for Jim Carrey and that his audience
would be disappointed.

To everyone's surprise, however, *The Truman Show* kept rolling
ahead, as though it had a life of its own.

Armageddon

In which the destruction of the world resembled a macho video game replete with splashy effects and nervous editing

Red Adair was a legend in Texas and Oklahoma, a macho figure with a remarkable expertise in extinguishing oil well blazes. Jonathan Hensleigh, a young Hollywood screenwriter, never understood why a new movie hadn't been done about the firefighter. He'd admired *Hell Fighters*, the old John Wayne film about Adair, and in fact, late in 1992, Hensleigh scrawled some notes to himself about just such a movie. An asteroid was threatening the earth and Red Adair would be dispatched into outer space to save the planet. He would land on the asteroid, drill a big hole to house some atom bombs, and then blow it up. Hensleigh even had a name for his Adair character: He would call him Harry Stamper, after Hank Stamper in Ken Kesey's *Sometimes a Great Notion*. In Hensleigh's mind, Hank Stamper would die trying to save civilization. Heroes didn't die in action movies, Hensleigh understood. For one thing, it eliminated opportunities for sequels, but he felt it was about time this rule was broken.

During the six years Hensleigh played with his idea, he became a hot writer at the Disney studio, working first on an action thriller called *The Rock*, directed by Michael Bay and starring Sean Connery and Nicolas Cage. He'd also written *Con Air*, starring Cage, John Cusack, and John Malkovich.

Both films had done well for Disney but had left Hensleigh feeling battle-scarred. He'd written ten drafts of *The Rock* and been paid by the studio to stay with the film through principal photography. Despite his conviction that he'd written every scene in the movie, the Arbitration Committee of the Writers Guild of America decided to give screenplay credit to the author of the original spec screenplay and to another rewrite man. Calling this a travesty, Disney had offered Hensleigh executive producer credit, but this was vetoed by the Guild, which warned sternly that such an action was tantamount to overruling its arbitration process. Disney agreed, instead making Hensleigh an executive producer on *Con Air,* for which he also received a screenplay credit, this time without arbitration.

By summer '96, Hensleigh had decided to turn his attention back to Red Adair. The town seemed to be buzzing with asteroid stories. Even his fiancée, producer Gale Anne Hurd, had been wrestling with a project called *Premonition* about a man who was obsessed with the notion that an asteroid was headed toward earth. Disney development executives had felt it was a good idea, but not a big idea. Hensleigh felt he knew how to give it more size and theatricality.

But time was of the essence. Hensleigh and Hurd had learned that Paramount was reactivating the long-dormant *Deep Impact* for veteran producers Richard Zanuck and David Brown. There was talk of yet another asteroid deal at Fox. When she'd made *Dante's Peak* a year earlier, Gale Anne Hurd had demonstrated the importance of being first. Her volcano movie helped bury *Volcano,* which Fox had released three months later.

By this time Hensleigh felt he had enough of a story to make his assault on the studio. He also knew that his pitch would be more effective if he had a director in tow. Who better than Michael Bay, the thirty-two-year-old with whom he had just worked? After finishing *The Rock,* Bay had been unable to find a project that excited him. To fill time and pick up some money, he had gone back to shooting commercials.

Hensleigh knew Bay to be moody and hot-tempered. Strongly influenced by commercials and videos, Bay's style of moviemaking was fast-paced and edgy, which Hensleigh felt would suit his new project.

According to rumor, Bay was the illegitimate son of another director renowned for fast-paced action movies, John Frankenheimer. Bay had confronted Frankenheimer, it was said, but had been rebuffed by the sixty-eight-year-old filmmaker. There were nonetheless clear physical similarities: Both were lanky, charismatic men, who were passionate about their work. Both sized up visitors with an oddly sardonic gaze and played their cards close to the vest.

Upon hearing Hensleigh's pitch, Bay responded with enthusiasm. He confessed that he had always wanted to make a space movie. At the age of thirteen, he had stolen his mother's Super 8 camera to shoot one in his bedroom and had accidentally set fire to some firecrackers and glue. The fire department had ended that shoot; Bay was eager to try again.

For a couple of weeks, Bay and Hensleigh met to further refine their ideas before meeting with Joe Roth at Disney. They were twenty minutes into their pitch to Roth when he interrupted to say, "This will be the biggest movie of 1998. I'm making it."

Roth even had a title: *Armageddon.* The only problem, Roth conceded, was that Joel Silver, a producer at Warner Bros., had registered the title a few years earlier. "I'll do some horse-trading with Joel," he promised, noting that Warner Bros. coveted two titles owned by Disney—*Conspiracy Theory* and *Father's Day.*

Bay recalls leaving Roth's office feeling exhilarated and a bit intimidated. "I was thinking to myself, How am I going to make this movie? So much of it doesn't even take place on earth. We're going to need a lot of stuff—conceptual designs, computer graphics, and so forth."

Joe Roth remembered the initial meeting as riveting: "It doesn't happen often, but every once in a while you hear an idea and you know, 'That's a home run.' I knew this would be our big picture for the year. I also had a gnawing feeling that this would be the most expensive project of the year."

Because of his apprehensions about budget, Roth decided to bring Jerry Bruckheimer into the equation. The fifty-four-year-old Bruckheimer had come to Disney five years earlier with his then partner, Don Simpson, after a long and successful run at Paramount, where they had produced hits like *Beverly Hills Cop* and *Top Gun*. Increasingly bedeviled by drug addiction, Simpson had died of an overdose in 1997. Bruckheimer, an intense but soft-spoken former ad man from Detroit, had by then split off to pursue his own producing career at Disney, working with Bay on *The Rock*. In Roth's view, Bruckheimer would not only provide a sober influence on budget, but could also lend a hand to script development.

Bruckheimer's arrival on the scene was not greeted warmly by Hensleigh. He wanted Gale Anne Hurd to get sole producer credit and to guide the production, resenting the implication that, because of their relationship, she would not be tough enough on script or budget. Besides, by this time, he and Bay already had finished their first draft.

They'd been meeting virtually every day, although there was some disagreement about who was doing what. As Hensleigh saw it, he was hammering out the key issues of structure and dialogue while his director indulged in what he liked to call "visualizing"—working with sketch artists on the content of the scenes. Bay knew he wanted to storyboard every action scene in the movie and was eager to get a head start on this process. As Bay remembers it, however, his role in working out story and structure was easily as important as was Hensleigh's. As a consequence, writer and director had at least one full-fledged shouting match about credits. Bay took the position that he and Hensleigh should share "story by" credit. The writer was equally vehement that Bay was being a credit hog—he already would be listed as director and coproducer, and *Armageddon* would be "A Michael Bay Film." Surely those were enough mentions, even for someone with Bay's formidable ego. At this point Michael Bay did something uncharacteristic: He relented on the "story by" issue. He subsequently admitted to me that he regretted doing so.

Meanwhile, with Jerry Bruckheimer now regularly sitting in on story and production meetings, Hensleigh and his fiancée, Gale Anne Hurd, debated confronting Joe Roth about her role in the production.

Joe Roth was a fair-minded, reasonable man, they knew. He was not one to fly into Jon Peters–like rages. On the other hand, Disney was, in fact, one of the busiest and most decisive studios in town. Given the fact that Hurd and Hensleigh were about to be married, their desire to work together might appear to Disney executives to be motivated by emotion, not business. Gale Anne Hurd thus decided to step aside quietly; it would be Bruckheimer's ball game now.

Joe Roth, meanwhile, was troubled by more practical issues on his new asteroid megapicture. For one thing, he had learned that Paramount had put *Deep Impact* on the fast track, even though Steven Spielberg had decided to withdraw as its director. Spielberg had been fascinated with the film's basic "setup" of how people would spend their final days when they thought that the world was coming to an end. No one can duck out of a project faster than Spielberg, however, if something goes awry; in this case, when he learned of *Armageddon*. The director had no intention of finding himself in a competitive situation, even if he had a clear head start. By this time, too, his emotions were tied up in *Amistad*.

Though Spielberg would not personally direct *Deep Impact*, he nonetheless wanted his company, DreamWorks, to remain involved as cofinancier and codistributor. And he advanced the name of Mimi Leder to replace him. Leder had won awards for her work as a director of the "ER" television series, which Spielberg's company helped produce, and had directed *The Peacemaker* for DreamWorks. Representatives of Paramount and DreamWorks flipped a coin to decide which company would distribute in the U.S. and which overseas, a process they would repeat for *Saving Private Ryan*.

Even though Joe Roth would not have to go up against a Spielberg-directed project, he nonetheless was worried by his risky project. Even as he examined some of Bay's early sketches, Roth realized he was heading down the pike toward $100 million, and this disturbed him. "I had never wanted to get into this $100 million derby," Roth told me. "At Fox and at Disney, I limited my budgets to the

$80 million level. As *Armageddon* began to take shape, I started get-
ting very nervous."

The introduction of a movie star into the mix had always assuaged
the nerves of studio chiefs, and thus it was fortuitous that Roth received an urgent telephone call from Arnold Rifkin, the president of
the William Morris Agency. Rifkin's star client, Bruce Willis, had
found himself in a bit of a jam. For twenty days Willis had been
shooting a small independent film in North Carolina called *Broadway
Brawler* and the movie was not going well. Summoning Rifkin to the
location, Willis ran the footage with him in a state of high agitation.
The work was terrible, Willis fretted. It wasn't cutting together. The
performances were dreadful. What was the point of finishing this
movie when he could smell disaster?

Though Willis presents himself as a glib, freewheeling man, a
decision like this greatly disturbed him. He had started his career
doing light TV comedy like "Moonlighting," but Willis's claim to stardom derived from action movies like *Die Hard.* While other stars
tended to stay close to their signature roles, Willis, with Rifkin's support, had periodically agreed to play small character roles in independent movies. This meant lowering his salary and risking his star
status, but the strategy had paid off royally; *Pulp Fiction* not only
brought Willis new respect as an actor, but also earned him several
million dollars as a result of his gross participation.* Willis hoped
that someday he would own a mini-library of art films to which he
owned all ancillary rights.

Rifkin had not been surprised, therefore, when his star client informed him that he wanted to take a shot with *Broadway Brawler.* Lee
Grant, a fine character actress, was making her debut as a film direc-

---

*A gross participation means a cut of the distributors' share of the money taken in at
the box office. Unless a deal specifies "first dollar" gross, various deductions are made
including checking box office receipts, residuals, taxes, trade association assessments, and
fees and certain overheads. Net receipts don't kick in until break-even—that is, not until the
distributor has recovered production and marketing costs, overhead, print expenses, interest,
and the moneys paid to gross participants.

tor and Willis had wanted to show his support. Funding for the movie had come from an independent company called Cinergi, run by another Willis friend, Andrew Vajna, a Hungarian-born entrepreneur who himself had coproduced some blockbuster action movies such as the *Terminator* series, *Die Hard with a Vengeance, Total Recall,* and the *Rambo* series.

Though Willis's impulses had been generous, the project was now a nightmare problem for Arnold Rifkin. An attractive, extremely hyper man who, in his youth, had worked briefly for his father, a successful furrier, Rifkin knew that his client, in pulling out of the project, was irrevocably dooming it. There was no way they could continue to shoot without him, and they were too far into the movie to substitute another actor. Not wanting to appear the bad guy, Willis had offered to personally assume the outstanding $14.8 million production tab. Cinergi would then assign the rights to the unfinished film to him.

Rifkin gulped hard. Movie stars, he knew, liked to make the grand gesture. They also were accustomed to having a studio cover their bets. That way they could play the patron of the arts and still not end up in the hole.

With all this in mind, Rifkin and Roth had a very earnest conversation in March 1997. Roth was worried because he had a potential $100 million special-effects movie on his schedule that lacked a movie star. Rifkin was worried because he had a star who needed a gig and who was on the line for $14.8 million. Clearly there was room for an accommodation.

The deal was relatively simple. Willis would become the star of *Armageddon.* As far as Disney was concerned, his name would provide an insurance policy that the movie would perform well in Europe and Asia. Willis was, after all, a recognized international action star. Disney, meanwhile, would clean up the Cinergi mess by taking over the costs of *Broadway Brawler* as an advance against *Armageddon* and two future films Willis would make for the studio.

The one possible catch involved Michael Bay. Willis was a free spirit; he liked a relaxed work environment. There were days when he wouldn't know his lines, but directors had to be understanding. In the words of one of Willis's former producers: "When Bruce gets to work in the morning, you know one of two things is possible. Either he's prepared, or he's so unprepared, he hardly knows where he is."

Given these work habits, Willis had developed an aversion to high-strung directors who yelled at their actors and their crew. He had heard that young Michael Bay was that sort of director. Mindful of this, Roth decided to escort both Bay and Jerry Bruckheimer on a trip to Willis's Idaho home. It turned out to be an easy sell. Sitting between such sober veterans as Roth and Bruckheimer, Michael Bay displayed his "visualizations" of key scenes and said all the right things to assuage the star's concerns. They discussed story and Willis liked the notion that his character would die to save the world. In fact, he insisted that the ending not be changed. Roth and Rifkin knew they had a deal.

Even as this was taking place, Jonathan Hensleigh had been hammering away at the script. Like most writers, he had felt an exhilaration in developing his first draft as characters had taken shape, ideas emerged. The rewrites were proving more laborious. Michael Bay seemed increasingly obsessed with the physical production problems and set design. Working with Bay on the story reminded Hensleigh of a comment by Janet Maslin, the *New York Times* film critic, about directors who had emerged from the video world: "They haven't just undermined film narrative, they've demolished it."

As for his producer, Hensleigh understood the Simpson-Bruckheimer formula for dealing with writers: Work them hard for a few drafts, then bring in hired guns to handle specific scenes and incidents. Never mind if the voices of characters would vary from scene to scene. This was an action movie and, by the time it had been edited, sliced, and diced, not that much dialogue would remain anyway.

To no one's surprise, Hensleigh soon joined Gale Anne Hurd on the sidelines while Bruckheimer's road company of body-and-fender men moved in, one by one. The ubiquitous Bob Towne, who'd been doing this sort of thing since the days of *Bonnie and Clyde* and had worked on Bruckheimer's *Crimson Tide*, was brought in to develop a mutiny scene. Scott Rosenberg, who had worked on *Con Air*, made a cameo appearance to rewrite lines for some of the supporting cast, while Ann Biderman (*Primal Fear*) spruced up Liv Tyler's dialogue. Tony Gilroy (*Extreme Measures*) focused on devising a new beginning for the script because no one bought the original setup in which two kids first saw the satellite, then were quarantined by the police so their story wouldn't leak out. Writer J. J. Abrams contributed an over-all dialogue polish, since Michael Bay liked his snappy phrases. Meanwhile, still other craftsmen like Paul Attanasio and Shane Salerno breezed in and out, as the script budget soared past $2 million.

It was standard studio practice with script revisions to insert different-colored pages with each new version. The *Armageddon* script soon took on the colors of the rainbow. Even the people in the copy room ran out of colors.

The only color that interested Michael Bay and Jerry Bruckheimer, however, was green, as in green light. Though Joe Roth had assured them that they had a green light to start production, there is an old axiom in Hollywood that nothing is certain until the cameras start rolling. The knowledge that *Deep Impact* had already started shooting added to their disquiet. They had heard rumors that phone calls had been made at the highest levels, that Michael Eisner and Joe Roth had been contacted by Richard Zanuck, by Sherry Lansing, even by Steven Spielberg. Why engage in a foolish competition to make two asteroid epics? Remember how *Dante's Peak* had cut the legs off *Volcano* only a year earlier? It was still not too late to cancel *Armageddon* and give *Deep Impact* a clear field.

If such phone calls had indeed been made, they apparently had fallen on deaf ears. Roth had repeated his rationale over and over. Sure, both films stemmed from roughly the same premise, but *Deep Impact* was more a remake of *On the Beach* while *Armageddon* was akin to *The Dirty Dozen* in space. There was room for both. Indeed, one might even enhance the market for the other.

The bottom line was that Roth felt he was making the more commercial movie. That Steven Spielberg had withdrawn early on as a
possible director of *Deep Impact* in a sense underscored this theory.
Without Spielberg at the helm, *Deep Impact* was just one more
movie—albeit a movie about asteroids. In Disney's mind, *Armageddon* would surely win the day.

Bulworth

In which a superstar negotiated a major studio into backing a sixties-style social protest movie without knowing what it was about

A gifted myth-maker, Warren Beatty liked to veil his affairs in mystery. Given this behavior, it was no surprise that the precise origins of his movie *Bulworth* were difficult to pinpoint.

Now past the milestone of sixty, and settled into his role as husband and father of three children, Beatty had grown more reflective and mature but no less manipulative. His face was lined, but unlike other leading men he apparently had not asked surgeons to snip-and-sculpt him back to youthfulness.

Beatty liked to weave stories, and his own backstory on *Bulworth* was straightforward: He had come up with the high-concept premise, successfully pitched it to Twentieth Century Fox, and then expeditiously set up his movie. That's what he related to me over lunch in May 1998, and also what he told *The New York Times* just prior to the movie's opening.

According to Beatty, his idea was simply this: A depressed man pays someone to kill him, then falls in love and frantically tries to call off his own murder. Others told a different version. According to James Toback, a writer, director, and longtime Beatty friend and collaborator, Beatty approached him in 1991 with an outline for a movie. The storyline was based not on the actor's original idea but on a short story by Somerset Maugham called "Tribulations" and involved a man who hired his own killer. Toback agreed to work on the project, and was paid by Beatty on a week-to-week basis.

Roger Birnbaum, who was the thirty-nine-year-old president of production at Twentieth Century Fox at the time, had yet another account, one that was confirmed by Joe Roth, then Birnbaum's boss at Fox. Birnbaum said the yarn was derived from a Jules Verne story entitled "Trials and Tribulations of a Chinaman," which in 1960 was made into a movie starring Jean-Paul Belmondo. Birnbaum said that it was he who told the story to Beatty to begin with. The occasion was a dinner in 1991 attended by Birnbaum, Beatty, and Barry Diller, who was then chairman of Twentieth Century Fox. At the time, the star had been trying to persuade Diller to make an expensive movie based on the Dick Tracy comic book character. Beatty intended to produce, direct, and star in the film, but he was finding Diller to be a hard sell. Diller knew Beatty wanted to make a highly stylized film, and he was worried about the budget.

A man accustomed to getting his way, Beatty claimed that Diller had given him a verbal commitment to make *Dick Tracy*. Diller, almost formidably stubborn, insisted he'd made no such promise. Having reached an impasse, Diller had arranged the dinner in the hope of finding other projects for the star to work on to get his mind off *Dick Tracy*. Birnbaum was invited along because he had his finger on all the material that Fox was developing.

A convivial man with a sharp ability at matching scripts to talent, Birnbaum started rattling off the studio's hot projects. He told Beatty the plot of the French movie about a man who hired his own killer. Beatty immediately sparked to the idea. Indeed his enthusiasm took Diller and Birnbaum by surprise—both knew how excruciatingly selective the star was about his material. Beatty reiterated that the narrative Birnbaum recited could provide a structure for a very interesting movie, and Beatty felt he knew how to make it work.

What the star did not to say was that the movie he had in mind would also involve provocative elements, such as an interracial love

story, a politician who became enamored of rap music, and a surreal
expedition through the inner city.

Beatty declined to tell me how much of this story was in his head
during that dinner. But by the time Toback saw a story outline some
months later, the rap scene and all its trappings were an intrinsic part
of the movie. The studio, however, did not learn of these other important ingredients until they first saw the script in 1997. By that time
Diller, Roth, and Birnbaum were long gone and Beatty had tucked
himself away to make the film as he saw fit.

There was also a degree of mystery as to why he was allowed to
operate with such autonomy. Ask Beatty and you get a very simple
explanation: Since Diller had reneged on his promise to finance *Dick
Tracy,* which ultimately ended up at Disney, he'd agreed to give
Beatty a "put" picture—a movie that would automatically be green-
lighted for production. Beatty would have complete control of the project, including final cut, and could make it outside the scrutiny of the
studio. The only provisos were that the film would come in at a budget
of $32 million and that Joe Roth had to approve the basic story line.

Beatty agreed to conform to the budget. And his meeting with
Roth was perfunctory because Birnbaum had already told his boss the
story that he'd earlier laid out to Beatty. Roth listened to Beatty's
short narrative, devoid of the rap or inner-city elements, and said,
"Go make your movie."

In turning the story over to Beatty, however, Roth and Birnbaum
had forgotten one important detail: The producer who'd originally
brought the piece to Birnbaum was already developing the project.
This was an omission that ultimately would cause a great deal of angst
and threats of lawsuits.

Lauren Shuler Donner, an accomplished producer, and the wife of
director Richard Donner, had become enamored of the Verne idea
when she was working with the French writer-director Francis Veber
on another movie. She'd told the yarn to Birnbaum when he was an
executive at United Artists. When Birnbaum switched to Fox, he took
Shuler Donner and her project with him.

It had taken Shuler Donner almost a year to negotiate the rights from the Jules Verne estate, and it was her intention to develop the project as a vehicle for Tom Cruise. Now suddenly Birnbaum and his boss, Joe Roth, were trying to persuade her to go into business with Beatty. Mindful of Beatty's unpredictable behavior and maverick ways, she was reluctant to join forces with the star, but Fox was adamant.

Throughout 1991, her worst fears were realized. Though she brought forth one writer after another as candidates to write the script, Beatty vetoed them all. Finally, Beatty went to Diller with a new demand. He wanted to cut Shuler Donner out of the project and produce it himself. Beatty insists Shuler Donner had no input at all and didn't deserve credit. To Shuler Donner's disgust, Diller caved in to Beatty's ultimatum.

But by the time Beatty was ready to start shooting his movie, now called *Bulworth*, a new regime at Fox had come to power headed by Peter Chernin and Bill Mechanic. Learning that Lauren Shuler Donner had been cut out of the deal, they decreed that her contract giving her producer credit and a fee would be honored. Beatty said he'd go along provided she not involve herself in the production in any way. Reacting to this prohibition, she opted instead to be listed as executive producer, a credit that implied a more distanced role, but Beatty suddenly protested. "Warren threatened to 'kill me in the press' if I received executive producer credit—that he'd spread the word that I had absolutely nothing to do with the picture," she said.

In the end, Beatty relented. When Shuler Donner saw the finished picture, however, she discovered that her credit was on screen for a fraction of a second. "That move was pure Warren," she said ruefully.

Beatty was also disturbed about having to credit Jules Verne with the original story, so he persuaded the estate that his movie followed an entirely different line. To the surprise of the studio, the estate agreed. Insofar as the official credits were concerned, the origin of the story remained as Beatty wanted it—the epiphany stemmed from Beatty, not from Jules Verne or Somerset Maugham.

Even as *Bulworth* was shooting, however, a degree of confusion persisted over who had actually green-lighted the project. Beatty, of course, insisted that Barry Diller had made the deal. But Diller, who ultimately left Fox to build a vastly different kind of media empire called USA Networks, denied Beatty's claim. "Since I never agreed to make *Dick Tracy* to begin with, why would I have given him a 'put' picture?" he told me early in 1998. "If I supposedly did it out of guilt, all I can say is that I don't believe in guilt."

After hearing this from Diller, I called Bill Mechanic, who, at the time of *Bulworth*'s release, was the top-ranking executive in Fox's movie hierarchy. "All I know is that Warren got a 'put' picture from somewhere," he said. "That was the deal that was presented to me." Joe Roth, who by 1998 was the chairman of the Disney studio, professed to be similarly puzzled.

Beatty insists Peter Chernin ultimately gave the green light to the project, a claim which Chernin denies. He concedes he could have blocked *Bulworth* from getting made, but was reluctant to do so for several reasons. For one thing, he was concerned about the possibility of a Beatty lawsuit tied not only to his up-front salary but also to his potential gross receipts—the legal cobwebs surrounding the project had become that dense. Moreover, Chernin liked the script and part of him looked forward to seeing the movie. Nonetheless, the Fox executive (who is number two only to Murdock) did not give it a green light and says he is not sure who did.

The only fact upon which everyone could agree was that a piece of paper came into existence granting Warren Beatty the right to make *Bulworth* for Fox and granting him complete creative autonomy. Informed of this confusion, Beatty himself registered a sly smile and added nothing in the way of clarification. Irrespective of the project's history, it was Beatty who got the last laugh.

The basic irony of the situation, of course, did not escape Beatty. "*Bulworth* is certainly the most controversial movie I ever made, yet it was the easiest to set up and it was the only one that stayed at the same studio throughout its life," he told me. With each of his other movies, there had been eleventh-hour crises over story, budget, or casting that caused Beatty to maneuver his film from one studio to another. But with *Bulworth,* such clashes were ruled out. Since the studio had waived all its controls, except that of budget, no one could take issue with any of Beatty's decisions.

The murkiness surrounding the origins of *Bulworth* was sustained throughout the writing process. According to Beatty, he wrote a detailed treatment that served as the basis for the screenplay. He then brought in writer Jeremy Pikser, with whom he had worked on *Reds,* and together they wrote the screenplay. Feeling the dialogue needed further work, he went back to James Toback. "I hired him by the hour," says Beatty. "He worked for several hours."

Toback insisted he worked for three weeks on *Bulworth,* and wrote three-quarters of the first draft. "I turned in seventy-seven pages," he said, "but I couldn't come up with an ending. When I saw the final shooting script, there was a lot of my stuff in there. One reason I ran out of steam on the project was that, at that moment in my career, I was finding it increasingly difficult to write material that I wasn't going to direct." Toback has since gone on to write and direct two movies of his own.

Yet another important contributor to *Bulworth* who was never named was Aaron Sorkin, the brilliant young playwright responsible for *A Few Good Men* and *An American President.* Beatty had hired Sorkin to write *Ocean of Storms,* an astronaut movie he had been developing. Sorkin was in the midst of this assignment, for which he was being paid $700,000, when he received an urgent call from the actor. "Come by my office," the message stated. "It's important."

When Sorkin arrived, he was handed a draft of *Bulworth* and told he could not leave the office until he had read it. Sorkin complied; when he finished, he told Beatty that he liked it, but the material clearly had some problems. Beatty's response was immediate: Set aside *Ocean of Storms* and start rewriting *Bulworth.* Sorkin was stunned by this instruction, but he admired Beatty and could tell that he urgently needed help on his other project. Though relatively new to screenwriting, Sorkin also understood that writers did not argue with movie stars.

After many meetings with Beatty and nine weeks of work, however, Sorkin began to feel like Beatty's house writer. He also realized that he was not being paid. Though Sorkin himself tended to dismiss this as an oversight, his wife, a former business affairs executive for Castle Rock Films, felt Beatty was taking advantage. So did Sorkin's attorney, Richard Heller, a scrupulous New York practitioner who contacted Beatty and demanded payment on behalf of his client.

When further warnings were ignored, Heller filed suit in Los Angeles Superior Court in August 1997, against Beatty and Fox, the studio financing *Ocean of Storms*, on grounds of nonpayment. According to the suit, Sorkin had been diligently working on *Ocean of Storms* when Beatty shifted him to *Bulworth*. During the writing of *Bulworth*, Beatty developed "irrational, incomprehensible and unwarranted personal animus and hostile feelings toward Sorkin." As a result, Sorkin found himself fired from *Ocean of Storms* because he had failed to meet his delivery date. Yet the only reason he had failed to meet his date, the suit pointed out, was that he'd been ordered to work on *Bulworth*.

In the end, the suit was settled and Sorkin returned to work on *Ocean of Storms*, for which he was fully compensated. Sources who worked on *Bulworth* say they found many signs of Sorkin's witty, sophisticated dialogue in the final version, for which he received no screen credit. Beatty insists the basic script was nonetheless the product of his work and that of Pikser and the other contributions were relatively insignificant.

None of the various writers involved with *Bulworth* disputed the fact that Beatty was the prime source of the material that dealt with rap music and the inner city. However, there's some skepticism about how much research he put into this aspect of the film. Beatty explained that his fascination with things black went back many years. In *Shampoo*, which he shot in 1975, Beatty wanted his beauty parlor to be located in a black neighborhood, hoping that Richard Pryor would play his partner. The director, Hal Ashby, was less than thrilled by this proposal, and set it aside. Beatty said that as *Bulworth* took shape in his mind, he sought out the likes of Tupac Shakur, Dr. Dre, and other gangsta rappers. "Rap music is the language of social protest," Beatty liked to say. "They are poets and they must be heard." One of these "poets," Suge Knight, former chief executive of Death Row Records, recalled Beatty "hanging out," trying to get into the scene. Knight, who is now serving a nine-year prison sentence for beating up a man in a Las Vegas casino after violating his parole, told reporters that the actor was "just a pest sometimes."

Some of Beatty's friends, however, suggest that his research consisted more of playing videotapes of "Def Comedy Jam," the HBO comedy series, than spending time in the inner city. Beatty insists he logged many days in on-site research. And while the actor clearly mastered some moves and mannerisms that helped him create his character on screen, the final movie distressed some blacks. In an article published in *Newsweek* in May 1998, N'Gai Croal insists that "for all the hype that Beatty is brave and politically incorrect, he simply peddles paper-thin stereotypes. . . . A failure as both political and cultural satire, *Bulworth* is interesting only as a look into the bizarre subconscious of a filmmaker who wanted to say something but couldn't figure out how."

Once Beatty had completed his research for *Bulworth* and had turned in his screenplay, there was a certain stunned silence from the studio. "They hated it," Beatty concluded. Not so, said one top executive at Fox who preferred to remain off the record. "The script was a shock to the system, but it was pure Beatty. In a sense, we were braced for it."

To be sure, this was one case where the studio's opinion didn't matter. Under the terms of the mysterious deal that no one could find, the studio was not allowed to second-guess Beatty. It was up to him to make his movie, and then it was up to Fox to market and distribute it. And that, of course, was the one problem that even someone as shrewd as Warren Beatty could not solve.

Godzilla

In which the monster was so overhyped that his ultimate arrival in
theaters and toy stores became the ho-hum event of the summer

In the beginning, *Godzilla* was as much an allegory as it was a movie.
Its origins can be traced to an incident in March 1954, when the
United States exploded its new hydrogen bomb on Bikini Atoll in the
South Pacific. U.S. spotter planes failed to detect a Japanese fishing
boat called the *Lucky Dragon* that was trawling for tuna. When the
boat returned to Japan two weeks later, several crewmen showed
symptoms of severe radiation sickness. According to the Japanese
press, the fishermen "were dusted by the ashes of death."

Word slowly leaked out about the *Lucky Dragon* incident despite
an official curtail of silence. Public discussion about atom bombs had
been banned in Japan for seven years after World War II, and even
after sovereignty was restored in 1952 the Japanese government sup-
pressed the topic, fearing that treaties between the U.S. and Japan
would be jeopardized. Anger was nonetheless stirred by the *Lucky
Dragon* incident and a Japanese producer, Tomoyuki Tanaka, figured
out a way to vent it. Flying over the Bikini Islands late in 1954, he
invented a creature he called Gojira, a mix of gorilla, presumably a
nod to *King Kong*, and the Japanese word for "whale." His name was
clumsily translated into English as "Godzilla," an underwater beast
that had mutated through radiation to wreak havoc first on Tokyo and
then, in later sequels, on other parts of the world.

Tanaka's movie was not subtle in its hidden meanings. It opened with an explosion in the Pacific that sinks Japanese fishing boats. When the monster surfaced, his route of destruction toward Tokyo was similar to that of U.S. forces during World War II. The special effects were primitive but effective. An actor in a rubber Godzilla suit stomped on miniature sets and vastly amused American audiences. The Japanese moviegoers, however, perceived another layer of meaning. "The film kindled anti-nuclear activism among the previously pliant Japanese," observed Michael Schaller, a professor at the University of Arizona who has written about relations between the U.S. and Japan. "The horror genre gave the filmmakers the cover they needed to skirt the government's policy of silence."

Unlike most allegories, *Godzilla* became big business. For Toho, the Japanese studio, Godzilla reemerged in twenty-two successive installments in which he not only destroyed many parts of the world, but also grappled with other monsters. Usually Godzilla played the virtuous monster who did battle with evil aggressors. The titles of the movies were themselves campy, some of them sounding like TV wrestling matches: *Godzilla vs. the Smog Monster, Godzilla vs. Magalon, Godzilla vs. the Cosmic Monster, Godzilla vs. Mothra, Godzilla vs. Mechagodzilla*, and finally, *Godzilla vs. Space Godzilla*. Ultimately, the monster's cinematic lure was replicated on TV; Godzilla became a Saturday afternoon ritual for teenagers around the world.

Given Hollywood's desperation to find franchise movies, the rebirth of Godzilla may not have been so much a great idea as an inevitable one. The lure was apparent: Rather than having to reinvent the wheel every time, a studio could summon up the same characters and situations and even the same promotional partners and hopefully repeat the grosses of the original movie: Witness the *Batman* movies, *Indiana Jones, Star Trek*, and *Star Wars*. Hollywood's problem was that it was wearing out its established franchises through the eighties. The production cost of each new sequel was climbing exponentially even as the grosses edged downward. Thus it was simply a matter of time before a studio latched on to *Godzilla*. It was pure coincidence that the studio ultimately would turn out to be Sony, itself a Japanese company.

The proprietors of the Godzilla brand at Toho Films had heard assorted pitches from Americans for years. One producer even proposed a Godzilla musical. None of the ideas were intriguing, however, and, more relevant, none were backed by serious money.

Indeed, Sony's initial overture seemed equally unpromising. Cary Woods, an ambitious young man in his late twenties, was working as an assistant to Peter Guber, then president of Sony Pictures Entertainment, when he started agitating about *Godzilla* in 1993. In Guber's eyes, Woods was a bright young man who, like many of his kind in Hollywood, was too hungry for his own good. Woods was so eager to become a producer that Guber gave him a producing deal at the studio, where Woods linked up with another eager wannabe, Rob Fried.

Searching for properties that offered some presold sizzle, Woods and Fried found themselves in discussion with a veteran producer, Hank Sapirstein, who owned the rights to Mister Magoo. The talks weren't going anywhere, when Sapirstein happened to drop an unexpected remark into the conversation. Besides Mister Magoo, he said he also controlled the U.S. merchandising rights to Godzilla. It was not a pitch, just an inadvertent line dropped to enhance his credentials.

The two young producers quickly forgot about Mister Magoo and were transfixed by Godzilla. "Here was one of the great characters of the movie business," Woods said. "A character that was beloved even though he wreaked damage and destruction. Godzilla was the James Dean of monsters. He caused trouble wherever he went, but he was misunderstood."

Carried away by their own enthusiasm, Woods and Fried tried their idea out on several executives at Sony. To their amazement, doors slammed in their faces. "Yesterday's news," said one young production executive. "Audiences regard Godzilla strictly as camp," said another.

"I was lamenting my futility to my wife," Woods recalls, "and she asked, 'Have you pitched Guber?' I explained that I can't pitch Guber—he's the boss, the head of the company. He doesn't want to get involved in production decisions. She just stared at me and said, 'Pitch Guber.'"

Guber, to be sure, presented an elusive target. Though he himself had once functioned as a highly successful producer, fostering projects as diverse as *Rain Man* and the *Batman* franchise, Guber had barricaded himself at Sony behind bureaucratic layers that were all but impenetrable. To associates, Guber seemed to perceive his role as strategist and seer, not as a hands-on administrator. This grand design also reflected his well-honed survival instincts. Executives who put their imprint on production slates were short-lived in Hollywood. Guber aspired to a higher role; he would be responsible for corporate strategy, not for day-to-day output.

Seizing the moment, Woods flew to Florida where, he had learned, Guber was scheduled to give a speech. Cornering his former boss, Woods mustered his courage and delivered his *Godzilla* pitch with fervor. He fully expected to be chastised for his directness and perhaps even lose his production deal.

Woods all but closed his eyes as Guber's familiar rasping voice started to respond. A man whose words tend to spill over onto each other, Guber can be hard to follow when he's excited or irritated, but, as far as Woods could tell, Guber sounded excited. He talked about Godzilla as "an international brand." His voice raised another decibel as he described not just one picture, but a series of tentpole pictures spanning many years. He would call Norio Ohga, the fabled chief of the parent company, to determine precisely how to negotiate at Toho. Sony and Toho had a solid relationship, Guber said, and he knew a deal could be concluded. He would promptly dispatch Ken Lemberger, a senior dealmaker at Sony Entertainment, to Tokyo to commence negotiations.

Cary Woods could hardly believe it. Not only had he not been summarily dismissed, but an incredible door had just swung open. No longer was he just another kid trying to cobble together a deal. Suddenly he had become the American proprietor of a global entertainment franchise. He would be custodian of a new, high-tech Godzilla.

Except it wouldn't turn out that way. Woods's first intimation of what lay ahead came in the guise of a series of phone calls from middle-level Sony executives. As Guber had started his follow-up maneuvers, word leaked out that Woods had jumped over several decision-making levels at the studio to go right to the top. Though his mission had been a success, this was a transgression that could not be tolerated. "Suddenly, I found myself in never-never land," Woods recalls. "Guber had set up *Godzilla* as a TriStar project, but Mike Medavoy, then president of TriStar, phoned me to say, 'I don't want to talk to you. If you feel you can go directly to Guber for decisions, be my guest, but stay off my phone list.'" Though TriStar was a key sister company of Columbia under the Sony banner, it was an open secret that Medavoy was not getting along with his boss, Guber. Clearly the hostility of Medavoy would be contagious to his underlings.

Nonetheless, Guber came through with his end of the bargain. A complex deal with Toho had been negotiated whereby Sony would finance and distribute *Godzilla* around the world. Toho would retain distribution rights in Japan and Sony would receive a generous fee in that territory. When Guber conveyed this news to his former assistant, Woods reiterated his gratitude. "I've done my bit," Guber told him. "Now it's up to you to get this thing rolling. You have to give it momentum."

"Momentum," Woods knew, was one of Guber's favorite words. He believed that a studio project had to be cloaked with charisma in order to survive the ordeal of studio development. And even though Guber was now giving him the challenge of carrying *Godzilla* forward, he sensed that Guber's involvement ultimately would be more than passive. Indeed, when Woods told Guber of Medavoy's admonition, Guber's reply was uncharacteristically candid. "Don't let Medavoy scare you," Guber responded. "He may find himself off the lot before long."

The task of starting a major studio project amid these political uncertainties disturbed Woods greatly, but his options were limited. Guber had come through for him. Now he and Rob Fried had to find some momentum.

The two young producers knew their first task was to hire a writer. This meant listening to pitches, reading writing samples. When a producer buys a novel, he has the luxury of sending out the basic material and asking writers to describe their approach. But *Godzilla* was more complex. What was needed was a totally original story and fresh characters.

After weeks of meetings, they reached a decision that surprised the suits as TriStar. Woods and Fried fixed on the offbeat writing team of Ted Elliott and Terry Rossio. They were hardly the flavor of the month. While many of the hot young writers in town had gone to Ivy League colleges, Elliott and Rossio were two unprepossessing guys from nearby Orange County who had never gone beyond high school. One worked as a part-time tennis pro, the other as a video technician. They had been writing scripts on spec for years without success. Most of their projects were written in a vinyl-upholstered booth at Coco's Restaurant in Santa Ana. Their first sale, a fantasy called *Little Monsters*, was to a video company called Vestron. It flopped and Vestron went under. "It was a great credential," said Elliott. "We could say that our script was the project that bankrupted Vestron." Eventually they landed a job writing animated films for DreamWorks, and it was after working on *Aladdin* that they got a call from Cary Woods.

"Cary said, 'I have one word for you. *Godzilla*,'" recalls Elliott. Neither Elliott nor Rossio found that word especially exciting. Woods persuaded them at least to come in and talk. Since the boys needed the work, they agreed. Before they knew what hit them, they were hired to write a draft.

The script they developed was slick and thoroughly professional. Like the movie that was ultimately made, it started with the shocking discovery that Godzilla was alive and well. Added to that was the even more shocking discovery of another monster, the Gryphon, who not only breathed fire, but also had the advantage of being airborne. By casting Godzilla as a potential good guy who saved the world from the flying bad guy, the Elliott-Rossio version followed the broad guidelines of most of the Japanese Godzilla movies.

In defeating the Gryphon, Godzilla was able to stalk off intact for a possible sequel. In the movie that was finally developed, however, Godzilla became a bad guy who was killed at the end while some of his progeny escaped. Many moviegoers resented the destruction of the original monster, whom they were prepared to regard as a savior.

Upon reading the Elliott-Rossio *Godzilla,* I found it generally to be a more satisfying movie. It had an entertaining tone; its characters, while hardly profound, were nonetheless tenable; and its monster battles seemed in keeping with the genre. On the other hand, I experienced the dissatisfaction felt by many who saw the final *Godzilla,* a dissatisfaction shared by some of the top executives at Sony who had been kept out of the creative mix until the eleventh hour.

With the Elliott-Rossio script in hand, Woods and Fried tried to sustain their momentum by landing an important director. Among the names tossed around at the studio were James Cameron, Tim Burton, Roland Emmerich, and even the Coen brothers. The Coens were Woods's idea; he'd seen *The Hudsucker Proxy* at the Sundance Festival and felt the brothers were "cool." Unfortunately, their movie did little business and Sony turned a cold shoulder to the possibility of making an offer. (The notion of the Coens even agreeing to meet to discuss a *Godzilla* movie was far-fetched, Woods agrees.)

The young producers soon struck pay dirt. Jan De Bont, the Dutch-born ex-cinematographer who had scored a major hit with *Speed,* read the script and said he was willing to sign on as director. De Bont had demonstrated a keen talent for directing action; he was a sober, responsible man and professed to have a vision for *Godzilla.* Woods and Fried were thrilled. Even though the politics at Sony were becoming steadily more Byzantine, they felt that, with the hottest director in town in their pocket, they could get their project fast-tracked.

They soon realized otherwise. The decision-makers at Sony, having backed too many unsuccessful pictures—*The Last Action Hero* being the most criticized—were essentially looking for excuses *not* to make movies. Rumors were swirling that heads would soon roll at the studio and that the Japanese wanted either to shut down their American entertainment operation or to fire everyone and start over again. Everyone was wobbly, from Guber on down.

Woods and Fried were in constant meetings with their most active supporter at Sony, an articulate young Asian-American executive named Chris Lee, who kept warning them that they were headed for trouble. As a kid, the Hawaii-born Lee used to sneak into the local Toho cinema to see the latest sequel in the *Godzilla* series. He had been a lone supporter of *Godzilla* since his days as a lowly story editor in 1993. In his eyes, the monster could easily translate to a U.S. audience. "The creature was not just menacing, he was also mythic," Lee had told them.

Lee had been rising steadily in the hierarchy at TriStar, moving from the story department to the job of executive vice president for production. Yale-educated, Lee was respected by his colleagues, but some humored him for his support of this absurd popcorn movie. Lee was still far removed from the green-lighting process. The best he could do was to help maneuver his favored projects past the studio land mines.

They were soon to encounter a major one. The production department had been poring over the Rossio and Elliott script, trying to come up with a budget. The task was a difficult one, as Jan De Bont had made it abundantly clear that he wanted to create a high-tech Godzilla. There would be no men in rubber monster suits, no Japanese-style miniatures. The movie would embrace the most sophisticated special effects attainable. No dollar should be spared.

The production experts responded. The movie De Bont had in mind, they estimated, would cost somewhere in the neighborhood of $150 million.

The producers and director gasped collectively. This was a "defensive" budget, they charged, the sort of document created at a studio under siege. The production estimators shrugged. There was no way they could responsibly cut the budget—unless the director would be willing to cut out one of the two monsters. Godzilla's antics were expensive enough to create, but the flying Gryphon put things over the top.

Chris Lee knew exactly what would happen when his superiors learned of the budget number. *Godzilla* was not headed for the fast track after all; rather, it would be parked at the side of the road.

Jan De Bont had been prepared for the worst. He had been meeting with Helen Hunt and Bill Paxton about starring in *Godzilla*. With the picture now stalled, he decided to keep his cast intact. Warner Bros. had been pressing him to direct yet another effects movie called *Twister*. Hunt and Paxton would be perfect for that film as well. De Bont bid Sony good-bye in 1995.

Utterly discouraged, Woods and Fried turned their attention to other projects. Chris Lee decided that the best thing to do with *Godzilla* was to let it lie in silence and await a better moment. With movies of this magnitude, he knew, it was all a matter of timing. In 1996, roughly a year after the De Bont debacle, Chris Lee's antennae started twitching once again. The final vestiges of the Guber regime had been swept from power. Rumors were rampant that the Japanese hierarchs would shortly move in an entire new group of executives to run the studio. Having written off $3.2 billion, they simply had too many big chips on the table to beat a graceful retreat. Often the best time to put a major project into play was during an interregnum, as Chris Lee well understood. And he knew the ideal candidates to help realize his dream of a high-tech *Godzilla*.

For several years Lee had been tracking the careers of Roland Emmerich and Dean Devlin. They were an odd pairing, to be sure. Devlin was a cocky, glib actor who, teamed with Emmerich, had initiated a new career as a writer and producer. Just as Devlin was a failed actor, Emmerich had dreamed of becoming a production designer and instead had found himself directing B pictures. They were as mismatched ethnically as they were temperamentally. Devlin's mother was Filipino, his father was a Russian Jew. What was he doing with a German prince, a slender, rather austere son of a wealthy manufacturer? Devlin felt he understood the Hollywood game. Emmerich knew he had to extricate himself from what he regarded as lowbrow action pictures. There had to be more to challenge him than urging Jean-Claude Van Damme to "please try that line one more time."

Emmerich had started visiting with Lee back in the days when Lee worked in a cubicle and had no authority whatsoever. The German did not feel at home in Los Angeles; he found Lee to be an island of literacy and good story advice. During their discussions, Lee had shared with him his enthusiasm for creating a *Godzilla* for the nineties. Emmerich couldn't see it, nor could his partner, Devlin. "We talked about it and all we could see was farce," Devlin recalled. "We could see the joke. We couldn't see the movie."

But now it was 1996 and the Devlin-Emmerich team no longer was scavenging for B pictures. Their movie *Independence Day,* made for Twentieth Century Fox, was the sleeper of the year, a surprise megahit that was approaching $1 billion in worldwide revenues. Not surprisingly, the team instantly was the hottest item in Hollywood, and studios were bombarding them with scripts.

It was then that Chris Lee came knocking at their door. He brought with him the same Rossio and Elliott script they had turned down at least once before. He could not even compete with other studios that were offering them "go" pictures—all Lee could present was a step deal at a studio that had no head of production.

To everyone's amazement, the two decided to sign on. "I can't give you a rational explanation," Devlin acknowledged. "Both of us thought it was a dopey idea the first time we talked. When Chris came back to us, we still thought it was a dopey idea. We were on our promotion tour for *Independence Day* and we'd been talking about some other ideas that didn't pan out. We wanted to do an asteroid movie, but when we learned about *Deep Impact* and *Armageddon,* we backed away. And then one day in Paris I looked over and saw Roland sketching on his pad. They were *Godzilla* sketches. And I know, when Roland starts sketching, that means he's got the fever."

When executives at rival studios learned that Devlin and Emmerich were committing to *Godzilla,* they were stupefied. This was a risky venture, they felt, a very Japanese project. When the terms of the deal became known, the surprise was magnified. Devlin and Emmerich proposed to write a script on spec, then submit it to the studio with the demand that the studio either commit to make it immediately or let it revert to them.

Mark Canton, still barely clinging to his job as head of production at Sony, was thrilled with the low-risk deal. Devlin and Emmerich had been warned that Canton was mercurial, but they weren't fazed. By the time they turned in their script, an entire new regime probably would be in place at Sony, so why waste time worrying about Canton's mood swings?

Their intuition was correct. The two repaired to Puerto Vallarta, Mexico, where Emmerich owned a home and where he and Devlin could write without interruption. By the time they had finished two months later, Mark Canton was history. Instead, they received a phone call from John Calley, then president of MGM/UA. Calley explained that he had to be cautious in what he said. He explained that he was well advanced in extricating himself from his contract at MGM/UA and would shortly announce his new job as president of Sony Entertainment, a position structured roughly similarly to that held by Peter Guber. Calley then added, "I read your script of *Godzilla.* I want to assure you that I will make your movie. Is that clear?"

"Very clear," Devlin replied.

When Chris Lee learned of the phone call, he was elated. At long last *Godzilla* would become a reality, and under the best possible auspices. It would be the centerpiece of a new regime; with the enthusiasm and resources to spend on production and promotion. *Godzilla* would be an appropriate symbol of the new Sony.

The news was received with less enthusiasm by Cary Woods and Rob Fried. They had not been part of the Devlin and Emmerich discussions. They did not even know the filmmakers. "We understood that we would be shoved to the sidelines," said Woods dolefully. "That is the way it seems to work. You start something, you keep pushing, and when it finally becomes a reality, everyone seems to forget your name."

Peter Guber was less distressed. In negotiating his exit deal from Sony two years earlier, he had reached a secret agreement with Mickey Schulhof, the then CEO of all Sony activities in the U.S. Under terms of that deal, Guber could set up a lavishly financed company whose movies would be distributed by Sony. His new company would be named Mandalay, and its first production would be *Godzilla*. Subsequently Schulhof had persuaded Guber not to make the Jan De Bont *Godzilla*, however, advising him that it would be politically incorrect to start with a $150 million project. Guber agreed to back off, despite his initial enthusiasm. In return, Schulhof agreed to designate certain "put" pictures, films that Guber could green-light without approval from anyone at Sony. This was all for the best, as far as Guber was concerned. Reading about the project later in *Daily Variety*, he was bemused to learn that it was now John Calley who considered himself the father of the new *Godzilla*. No mention was made that Guber had orchestrated the acquisition of the basic rights. Like all former company chiefs, he had become instantly invisible. But unlike most, he preferred it that way.

There's Something About Mary

In which the Farrelly brothers proved yet again that gross-out translates into grosses

Like virtually every other script in Hollywood, good or bad, *There's Something About Mary* was destined to sit around for about ten years. "It's the way things seem to work," reflected Peter Farrelly, who, with his brother Bobby, ended up rewriting and codirecting it.

They should know. For years the Farrellys spent their time writing scripts that went nowhere. Then they became directors and started scouring the town for just such neglected scripts. *There's Something About Mary,* written by John Strauss and Ed Decker, had the core of an idea that fascinated the brothers. A man was so haunted by the memory of his high school girlfriend that he hired a private detective to track her down. "At Disney that idea got developed into the ground," Peter Farrelly said. "The script finally reverted to the writers, so we bought it and started anew." Among the elements added by the Farrellys was a backstory. In the finished movie, we see Ben Stiller as a teenager lusting after Cameron Diaz. We also see him clumsily blow his chances as he lends a whole new meaning to the term "self-abuse."

The iconoclastic Farrellys were down-home boys, but "home" for them was Cumberland, Rhode Island, where, to hear them tell it, they spent their youth "playing baseball, chasing girls, and catching frogs."

Despite their redneck pretensions, clearly the brothers also had other things in mind. Peter wrote a novel, *Outside Providence,* then started batting out screenplays, eventually moving to Los Angeles to ply his craft. Bobby stayed behind in Rhode Island for a time, tackling some bizarre business ventures. He decided to market a round beach towel, for example, so that sunbathers wouldn't have to get up and shift their towels to accommodate the changing positions of the sun. "People liked my idea," he said, "but it proved too expensive to manufacture."

Bobby soon joined his brother on the West Coast, where they started writing scripts together. Nothing got made. "People wanted things in a cookie-cutter mold and we kept wanting to break new ground," Bobby recalled. "Surprise. We weren't winning that battle."

Not until *Dumb and Dumber,* that is. The Farrellys concocted a typically absurdist script about two dopey brothers making their way to Aspen. Jim Carrey, who had made a name for himself in *Ace Ventura* as a sort of rubber-faced, latter-day Jerry Lewis, agreed to star and also accepted the Farrelly brothers as directors. This was a reach, given the fact that the brothers had neither previous experience nor an interest in directing. "We simply decided one day that it would be good for their careers to announce them as directors," recalled Richard Lovett, their CAA agent who later became president of that agency.

"What was different about us was that we didn't want to know all the technical stuff," says Peter Farrelly. "We understood how to tell a joke. We also knew how to write. When we're writing, we often stop and ask ourselves, What is the audience thinking now? Then we give them the opposite. We talked to David Zucker [the Zucker brothers did *Airplane,* among other movies] and he told us, 'Don't let the camera take over your life.' He felt the actors and the director alike should be unaware of the camera. I mean, we all respect the Coen brothers [*Fargo*], but we're not the Coens. We're the anti-Coens."

Life as the anti-Coens turned out to be an up-and-down affair for the brothers. *Dumb and Dumber* resembled a student film, yet its utter simplicity and lame-brain humor captured its audience. It ended up grossing approximately $127 million in the U.S. and establishing the Farrellys as players.

Their second movie, *Kingpin*, however, sent them back to square one. Though it was a far more polished work of filmmaking, the bowling project was appallingly mishandled by MGM/UA. "We liked the picture so much more than *Dumb and Dumber* that it was painful as hell when it crashed," recalled Peter Farrelly. "The movie was released in the middle of the Olympics, but there were zero ads. Some guy from the studio told us, 'Don't worry about a thing. It will do $18 million on its first weekend.' So we waited and worried. And then on Monday, a different guy calls and says, 'It did $5 million.' I say, 'That's just for Friday night?' The guy says, 'That's the weekend number,' and hangs up. So much for *Kingpin*."

Peter Farrelly turned back to books, finishing a semiautobiographical work called *The Comedy Writer*. And meanwhile the brothers kept working on *Something About Mary*. When it was done, they turned it in to Twentieth Century Fox and expected the worst. After all, Fox was the studio of the ultra-straight Rupert Murdoch. Bill Mechanic, its production chief, seemed like Joe Normal, as Peter Farrelly described him. How would these people react to the semen jokes? To the zipped-up penis? To the non-PC references to "retards"? To the terrible accidents that keep happening to small dogs?

"Joe Normal" didn't keep them guessing for long. "Go for it," urged Mechanic. "We're thrilled." Tom Rothman, president of the Fox movie division, admitted, "Maybe I should be embarrassed to say this, but I think this is one of the funniest scripts I've ever read."

The Farrellys braced themselves for what they knew would soon be coming: script notes. Mechanic, Rothman, and all the others would now be checking in with their ideas on how to make the movie funnier.

Nothing came. The only mandate from the studio was that they would have to bring in the picture at $23 million. Just keep it moving and keep it funny, Fox said. To the anti-Coens, this seemed like an entirely reasonable proposition.

Lethal Weapon IV

In which a studio was so eager to launch its hundred-million-dollar sequel that it forgot about a script

There were a lot of sound reasons why a fourth *Lethal Weapon* should never have happened. For one thing, the sequels business seemed to be sagging. *Speed 2* had been a disappointment and Warner Bros. was unhappy with its fourth *Batman*. Though *Lethal Weapon*s II and III had been very successful, the central characters had lost their edge. Riggs, played by Mel Gibson, had been set up originally as a borderline psychotic prone to such endearing acts as putting his gun in his mouth. He'd made *Lethal I* nihilistic and darkly comical, but these qualities had been softened in subsequent versions. Then, too, six years had passed since the last *Lethal,* compared with an average three-year span between sequels. Had the audience forgotten the characters?

Last, there was the issue of economics. In the time since *Lethal Weapon III,* Mel Gibson had become an even bigger star. His *Braveheart* had won an Oscar. Even if Warner Bros. mustered the courage to try for *Lethal IV,* how could they persuade Gibson to do it and, equally important, how could they afford him? The *Lethal* franchise was not like James Bond; when one of the Bonds grew too old or too expensive, the producers simply shopped around for a replacement. Mel Gibson, however, was the focus of the show. He was irreplaceable.

And the relationship between studio and star was not exactly cozy.

When Gibson was trying to cobble together the backing for *Brave-heart,* he approached Terry Semel about cofinancing the movie in return for Warner's ownership of overseas rights. It was an expensive deal, however, since Paramount, which owned the basic material, would advance only $20 million in return for distributing the movie in the U.S. This meant that Warner would have to pony up $60 million in up-front money. Given this imbalance, Semel decided to extract his pound of flesh. "Semel outsmarted himself," observed one of Gibson's associates. "He said he'd make the deal, provided Gibson commit to another *Lethal.* Mel was offended. He felt *Braveheart* was a worthy project that should stand on its own and he didn't want to strike that sort of a bargain."

The chill continued for a year until Joel Silver, the producer of the *Lethal* series, came up with an idea. A bulky, rough-hewn man whose small head protruded from a large, billowing body, Silver had interested Gibson in doing a remake of an old John Boorman noir thriller, *Point Blank.* Gibson agreed, saying he would star in the remake, which was called *Payback,* but he wanted to do the film for Paramount, to whom he had a commitment.

Silver saw his opportunity. *Point Blank* had been an MGM film, but the rights had switched first to Ted Turner when he acquired MGM's movie library, then to Warner Bros. when Time Warner acquired the Turner empire. Hence, Warner Bros. might squirm back into the star's good graces by simply telling him that, though they owned the underlying rights, they wouldn't stand in his way. Indeed, Warner Bros. would even put up half the money in return for foreign rights. In return, perhaps Gibson would consider making *Lethal IV*.

The proposal seemed to satisfy everyone. Gibson and Silver would get *Payback* made and the star would rid himself of his Paramount obligation. But the question remained: Would he actually do the sequel?

Several considerations worked in Warner's favor. Gibson felt comfortable playing the loopy character of Riggs. More important, he enjoyed working with Dick Donner, for whom he had done six movies. A rumpled man with the gruff, booming voice of a longshoreman, Donner had been directing films for over twenty-five years and was a master at the care and feeding of movie stars. Under Donner's tutelage, Gibson felt relaxed as an actor and was encouraged to improvise lines when he felt he could improve upon the script. "In *Conspiracy Theory*, there were moments where I just had diarrhea of the mouth—the words just burst out of me, and the scenes seemed to take on more intensity," Gibson told me. That movie had been a disappointment, but it served to strengthen the bond between Donner and Gibson.

Then, too, Gibson and his savvy agent, Ed Limato, had always liked to keep a balance between the star's commercial and arty endeavors. Gibson was intent on directing an old François Truffaut sci-fi picture, *Fahrenheit 451*, based on the Ray Bradbury novel. The idea of balancing that with a down-the-middle piece of commerce like *Lethal Weapon IV* seemed pragmatically sound to Gibson. To Limato, the *Lethal* series seemed like old hat. He urged his prize client to reject Warner Bros.' pleas. He lost.

With Gibson receptive to the sequel, the next key to the puzzle would be Donner. The blunt-spoken director had gained a reputation for being the ultimate show-business survivor. He'd been an actor in the old days of radio drama, moving on to television and then film, where his career had been on something of a rollercoaster ride. After an early success in 1976 with *The Omen*, he had tried to avoid getting typecast by tackling some more ambitious films. His sensitive movie about the handicapped, *Inside Moves*, ended up being dumped out by its distributor during Christmas and his Richard Pryor film, *The Toy*, also flopped. Two vastly more conventional movies, *Superman* and then *Lethal Weapon*, not only resurrected his career but helped make him a wealthy man.

He married Lauren Shuler, herself a successful producer, and together they owned an island off Vancouver to which they repaired as often as possible. Donner's exact age remained something of a mystery, with the dates of birth shifting from bio to bio, but friends testified he was between sixty-eight and seventy-four, depending on whom you asked.

Though his directing fee had mushroomed from $5 million on *Maverick* to $10.5 million on *Conspiracy Theory*, Donner had been growing increasingly impatient with his home studio, Warner Bros. He felt the studio was rigidly committed to very expensive, star-driven movies and, even though he was a beneficiary of this profligacy, he still wanted to foster more interesting films in the $10 million range. Indeed, he and Silver had developed several low-budget scripts as well as a small stable of promising young filmmakers whom they wanted to mentor.

Another *Lethal* would help underwrite this agenda. It also would wipe away some of the residual disappointment stemming from Donner's two most recent films—*Assassins*, which grossed approximately $30 million, and *Conspiracy Theory*, which topped out at just short of $80 million in the U.S. Both had been pricey star-driven vehicles— Stallone in the first, Gibson in the second—which had been optimistically tabbed as possibly grossing $100 million.

To give a new *Lethal* more appeal, Donner and Gibson agreed that some fresh faces would have to be added to the cast. This would exacerbate the biggest remaining problem—money.

The cost of director, star, and producer was intimidating enough in terms of up-front money plus contingent compensation, but then there was Danny Glover to consider, not to mention Joe Pesci and the possible newcomers. The gross participations alone already added up to 40 percent. Would there be enough left for the studio?

Initial meetings with Terry Semel, however, assured everyone involved that the studio remained stalwart. It wasn't merely a question of wanting it; Warner Bros. needed it. Of the major projects slated for summer, one after another had fallen out and the remaining slate was painfully thin. A weak summer would only heighten the studio's agony over its long list of recent flops, which included *The Postman* and *Midnight in the Garden of Good and Evil*. Semel and Bob Daly were also nervous about such upcoming releases as *The Avengers*, not to mention their dicey animation feature, *Quest for Camelot*. They needed a sure thing, even if it would cost them dearly. But as the deliberations dragged on, time was running out. There was more than a little concern that by the time all the principals had worked out their deals and other perks, there would be no time to write a screenplay.

On November 12, 1997, when I first visited Donner in his cluttered, cavernous office, he was firmly on board as the director and a start date of January 8 had been selected. With only seven weeks left, however, Mel Gibson had yet to give his commitment to the project, since that was based on script approval and there was no script to approve. Donner attempted to make light of this dilemma. "I'm confident I will have a finished script by the end of principal photography," he declared with a wry grin. "Besides, our actors are very good at improvising."

To be sure, the situation was not as dire as it might have seemed. Joel Silver had been quietly planning for this eventuality. A resourceful producer, Silver had his name on some thirty movies over a period of fifteen years, and liked to boast that their combined gross amounted to over $2.5 billion. Many of his most successful films were of the action genre, starring the likes of Schwarzenegger, Willis, and Eddie Murphy. "I make action movies—that's what I do," Silver said unapologetically. Held up to ridicule from time to time because of his specialty, Silver was irritated by the perceived lack of respect accorded him in the industry. As rude as he could seem, Silver was an exceedingly intelligent man who collected art as well as Frank Lloyd Wright homes, and who could be extremely gracious when the occasion demanded it.

Anticipating the inevitability of *Lethal Weapon IV*, Silver had started fishing for a good premise four years ago. Jonathan Lemkin, who had written *Demolition Man* for him, was hired to try a *Lethal* draft built around a ring that smuggled Chinese immigrants to the U.S.

Though Silver liked Lemkin's basic story, he felt the script was thin. He hired Jeffrey Boam, one of the town's highest-paid body-and-fender men, to write yet another script focusing on neo-Nazi survivalists. Silver felt Boam was progressing, but not fast enough. In July 1997, sensing that Warner Bros. interest was peaking, Silver and Dick Donner started looking for yet other writers. They decided on Channing Gibson (no relation to Mel), an amiable, forty-four-year-old veteran of the TV wars. Gibson had spent twenty years working on shows like "St. Elsewhere" and "NYPD Blue" and he felt ready for a shift to film. Silver had tried him out on one of his other Warner Bros. projects, a thriller entitled *Sandblast*, and he'd performed ably. Now the producer was about to bestow upon him the ultimate honor: Channing Gibson was to write the shooting script for *Lethal IV*. And write it fast.

But not alone. While hiring Gibson, Silver and Donner applied to the Writers Guild for permission to hire several other writers simultaneously, a practice banned by the Guild unless prior permission is obtained. Channing Gibson, as it turned out, was not terribly concerned about it. "The only side of it that took me by surprise was that all of the writers who were hired, including me, were instructed to pursue the same story line—the Chinese immigrants," Gibson reflected. "I figured the director and producer would at least continue to try out different plots, but we were all put on the same track."

Channing Gibson, nonetheless, worked assiduously through the fall, finishing a first draft toward the end of October 1997. Another writing team, Alfred Gough and Miles Millar, turned in their script shortly ahead of him, but it was Gibson's that most impressed the producer and director. He was put on salary and told to keep writing until the movie started shooting and beyond. For Channing Gibson, *Lethal IV* would soon become a whole new career.

"One reason I shifted to film was that I didn't want always to worry about next week's episode," Channing Gibson explained. Yet as he got deeper into *Lethal IV*, his mission became TV-like in its relentless pressure. Donner kept adding new cast members, and hence new characters. While the basic story still revolved around Mel Gibson and his partner, Danny Glover, Chris Rock, the brilliant young comic, was suddenly aboard as another detective. Gibson learned about this addition as he was three-quarters through a new draft, so Rock's character appeared in only a few scenes, his role increasing in subsequent drafts. The studio had been unable to close a deal with Joe Pesci, another member of the *Lethal* road company, but at the eleventh hour, he, too, fell into place. Pesci's three-week role at $1 million a week thus had to be written back into the movie. Gibson also was instructed to write in a part for Jet Li, a talented young martial arts aficionado, who would now become the film's primary villain.

All this added up to a situation that surprised even the most grizzled studio veterans. Warner Bros. was about to start a $100 million movie, its most important feature of the summer, with an unpolished script that was only half completed. As the cameras started rolling on January 15—the date had been pushed back one week—actors were being fed new pages day by day from a writer who had never before written a produced feature film and who had never even been on a movie set. Even Channing Gibson, a sturdy, good-natured type, saw the absurdity of the situation. At one point early in the shoot, he found himself standing on the set of the police station, jotting down lines in longhand as Mel Gibson, Glover, Rock, and Donner crowded around him, each throwing out ideas. At the core of the scene was the conceit that the Chris Rock character was gay. As Donner was about to shout "Action," however, it was apparent that none of the actors liked the scene. Mel Gibson felt that the gay element, which was supposed to be facetious, had been planted too blatantly. As Channing Gibson put it, "It all became unseemly rather than amusing." Hence, a group rewrite began as the entire crew stood around, waiting for something to shoot.

Was this any way to make a movie? I put that question to several participants during one visit to the set and was greeted with a series of shrugs and smiles. This was a chaotic, disorganized movie, all agreed, even for old pros like Donner and Silver. But Daly and Semel wanted their sequel, and by god, they were getting it.

Steven's Excellent Adventure

In which the world's richest director assaulted the marketplace with not just one but four pricey pictures

For most filmmakers, summer was a season to be avoided if at all possible. Starting with Memorial Day, the public was bombarded by too many lavish ad campaigns promoting too many expensive movies. In summer if you're not an instant smash, you suffer a quick demise.

By contrast, Steven Spielberg approached summer the same way a general prepares for combat. He arrayed his forces, mapped out his strategy, and hungrily awaited the first encounter.

Starting with *Jaws* in 1975, summer had been good to Steven Spielberg. Year after year, he had uniquely managed to assemble an array of blockbusters. Some thirty of the forty-five movies he'd produced and directed had been released during the summer months, with their combined gross approaching the $5 billion mark, a milestone beyond the imaginings of any other filmmaker. And fifteen of his projects had grossed over $100 million in the U.S. alone:

1982 *E.T.* (Director, Producer)	$399.8 million
1993 *Jurassic Park* (D, P)	357.1
1975 *Jaws* (D)	260.0
1997 *Men in Black* (Executive Producer)	250.1
1981 *Raiders of the Lost Ark* (D)	242.4
1996 *Twister* (EP)	241.7
1997 *The Lost World* (D)	229.1

1985 *Back to the Future* (EP)	208.2
1989 *The Last Crusade* (D)	197.2
1984 *Temple of Doom* (D)	179.9
1988 *Roger Rabbit* (EP)	154.1
1984 *Gremlins* (EP)	148.2
1998 *Deep Impact* (EP)	138.3
1995 *Casper* (EP)	100.3
1998 *Saving Private Ryan*	190 (to date)

Spielberg's most rewarding summer was 1982, when *E.T.* and *Poltergeist* combined to gross $476.4 million in the U.S. His 1997 tally finished close to that, with *Men in Black* and *The Lost World* combining for $472.4 million. In 1984, *Temple of Doom* and *Gremlins* rolled up a U.S. gross of $328 million.

Though mindful of Spielberg's fervid determination to top himself, many expected summer '98 to be a less frenetic year for the filmmaker. He had directed two complex films back to back, *Amistad* and *Saving Private Ryan,* and had stated his determination to focus more on DreamWorks business, stepping up its output of movies. He had even made noises about spending more time with his seven children.

These pledges were soon abandoned. Despite his many responsibilities, Spielberg plunged into an agenda for summer '98 that was far more ambitious than any previous summer. Four projects representing an aggregate cost of well over $250 million were slated for release, and Spielberg was deeply enmeshed in nurturing all of them. Together, he felt, they would appeal to every sector of the filmgoing audience.

Deep Impact represented the ultimate high-tech doomsday movie that also, in Spielberg's mind, had the potential to profoundly move a global audience poised at the edge of the millennium. *The Mask of Zorro,* by contrast, was aimed at those moviegoers who yearned for simpler, more romantic fare. It represented a throwback to the old Douglas Fairbanks–Errol Flynn movies that brimmed with operatic relationships and colorful swordplay. The kids could be counted on to line up for *Small Soldiers*, Spielberg felt, because it had action, fantasy, and video-game effects. And finally, there'd be his pièce de résistance, *Saving Private Ryan*, which Spielberg would personally direct, yet which represented his biggest gamble commercially. Spielberg intended to go for broke with this movie; its glimpse of war would be as brutally realistic as any movie ever made.

That a single filmmaker could advance so formidable and diverse a slate was itself an expression both of daring and arrogance. With the exception of Disney, no single studio would present a more imposing group of summer movies.

To be sure, it wasn't Spielberg's personal money that was on the line, and yet, to a degree, it was. The funding required to develop the projects had come either from Spielberg's personal production company, Amblin, or from DreamWorks, of which Spielberg was a partner. DreamWorks would be putting up half the production money for two of the four films, *Saving Private Ryan* and *Deep Impact*, both in partnership with Paramount.

As the crucial months approached and tensions mounted, even close associates could not help but wonder why the celebrated filmmaker, year after year, would put himself under this sort of pressure. By April and May, Spielberg was ricocheting between the editing room of *Saving Private Ryan* and meetings on his other pictures, not to mention carrying on the customary business of DreamWorks. Though a master at keeping his cool, his staff could tell that it was taking its toll. His meetings were becoming more attenuated, his conversations more abrupt. One writer who'd been working on a Spielberg script for over a year got a call from the director informing him that his new draft had disappointed him. "Are you firing me?" the writer asked. "This is very hurtful." The response from Spielberg was a quick, "I suppose it is," and he was off the line.

In early summer '98, just after *Deep Impact* had opened, I managed to corner Spielberg to ask him the obvious question. "You have so much riding on *Saving Private Ryan*," I said, "why don't you focus on that for the summer? Why do you feel the necessity of bringing out a full slate of movies?" There were elements to that question I decided not to include. I did not ask why a filmmaker with a personal worth of several billion dollars—surely the most money anyone had ever made from the movie business—felt compelled to try and make yet a billion more. Nor did I repeat the criticisms of some associates at Dream-Works and Paramount, who, upon reading the shooting script of *Deep Impact*, openly wondered why Spielberg had allowed the rather clunky screenplay to start shooting. Was he simply spread too thin? they asked.

Spielberg did not seem at all surprised by my line of inquiry. He replied pensively that he had asked himself that very question lately and had formulated what he felt was a tenable response. "It's a question of retaining one's perspective," he explained. "When I focus on one project alone, I tend to obsess on every scene. I shoot something and I fall in love with my own work. On the other hand, when I juggle several projects, that helps me keep a sharp sense of perspective. If I stop what I'm doing to go to a meeting about a script, I find myself wrestling with those problems and then, when I return to my own movie, I see it all in context."

Spielberg had explained it too neatly, even for his own superbly organized mind. "There's also the other possibility," he added after a short pause. "There's the possibility that I'm simply an insecure Jew, that I always was and always will be. It may be as simple as that."

Perhaps, he implied, it was all a question of hedging one's bets. As a young filmmaker he had witnessed that narrow line between success and failure. Spielberg had watched many of his contemporaries self-destruct while still in their prime. They were all bright young filmmakers who had found their place in the sun at roughly the same time—Peter Bogdanovich, Dennis Hopper, and Hal Ashby. Some were defeated by drugs, others by rampant egomania. Spielberg was shocked and scared by this waste of talent.

In fact, while Spielberg's adulatory biographers had described his career as a succession of triumphs, he'd encountered more than a few hurdles in his path. On *Jaws* his shooting schedule had soared from

55 to 159 days and he had gone 300 percent over budget. Spielberg knew that the word was out in Hollywood that "the kid" had lost control of his movie. Indeed, during a one-night stopover at a Boston hotel on his way back from location on Martha's Vineyard, he sustained such an intense anxiety attack that he was physically immobilized. He lay awake all night, feverish, convinced that he would never work again as a director.

Despite the lessons of *Jaws*, he went over budget again on *Close Encounters of the Third Kind* and the studio even fired him early in the shooting schedule. The order was rescinded a day later, but Spielberg ended up paying for some of the special-effects work out of his own pocket.

There had been other debacles in his career that had left their scars. He remembered submitting the script for a war comedy called *1941* to his studio, Universal, only to hear Ned Tanen, its production chief, scream at him that the screenplay was an abomination. In his rage, Tanen tossed the script against the wall so hard it broke from its binding, pages flying around the office. Stubbornly, Spielberg took his project to Columbia, which agreed to make it. Ultimately released jointly by Columbia and Universal, the film was a failure.

His disciplined work on *Raiders of the Lost Ark* and on *E.T.* restored his fiscal credibility, but he ran into big trouble again while shooting *The Twilight Zone*. John Landis was directing on the fateful day when actor Vic Morrow and two children working on the show were killed on the set, but Spielberg had directed an earlier segment and, as coproducer, was listed in subsequent civil suits. Though he clearly was not culpable, Spielberg's friends said the tragedy sent him into a deep depression.

Spielberg was also wounded by repeated snubs by the Academy of Motion Picture Arts and Sciences, winning nominations for *Jaws* and other pictures, but never the ultimate prize. When Richard Attenborough won the Oscar for *Gandhi* in 1982, despite popular sentiment for *E.T.*, Spielberg began to sulk that his work had been unfairly stereotyped.

In the late 1980s, Spielberg's career hit another unexpected cold streak. His wartime drama, *Empire of the Sun*, received a tepid audience response. His remake of *A Guy Named Joe*, called *Always*, was an abject flop. And *Hook*, while a modest moneymaker, seemed ordinary, both in concept and execution. When Spielberg tried to tackle more serious fare, as in *The Color Purple*, some critics attacked his tendency to sentimentalize whatever subject he tackled.

Once again, resiliency seemed a key to Spielberg's success. Starting in the early eighties, his sensitive antennae detected a change in the public mood. The previous decade had been remarkably friendly to daring young *auteurs* who sought to forge a new language of the cinema. Movies like *Taxi Driver*, *The Conversation*, *Raging Bull*, and *The Last Picture Show* had found both an audience as well as studio support for their filmmakers. But by the early eighties, moviegoers seemed to be responding to more commercial fare. The studios, too, had been burned by too many unreleasable films, too many budgetary excesses, and too many drug overdoses. Multinational corporations had started buying heavily into the movie business, and the newly arrived corporate suits were turned off by the style and presentation of the sixties holdovers.

Spielberg was the first of his generation to come to terms with the new economics of the blockbuster. His early movies seemed to awaken that vast sector of the public that had drifted away from moviegoing with the advent of television. And this phenomenon was not limited to the U.S.; audiences around the world were responding to Hollywood's clarion call, and new multiplexes were being constructed to accommodate this surge. Revenues from ancillary markets, especially video, further propelled the incipient gold rush mentality that began to overtake Hollywood. Star salaries were soaring, filmmakers were becoming multimillionaires, and the movie community as a whole began to take on the boomtown hubris of the late thirties and early forties.

Steven Spielberg was to become the crown prince of this reborn kingdom. Year after year, his movies surged to the top of the charts. As each new trend unfolded, Spielberg seemed to be in the vanguard.

His *Raiders of the Lost Ark* and its sequels dramatized for the Rupert Murdochs, Sumner Redstones, Edgar Bronfman Jrs., and other new corporate marauders the importance and accessibility of the franchise movie. *Twister* heralded the advent of the new special-effects cycle where movies were designed to emulate theme-park rides. *Men in Black* demonstrated the clout of yet another genre, the movie—as—comic book.

For almost twenty years Spielberg had managed to foster his extraordinary portfolio of projects through Amblin, which was fast becoming the Microsoft of personal production companies. Amblin functioned with a skeletal staff headed by the bright, personable husband-and-wife team of Kathleen Kennedy and Frank Marshall.

Attractive and highly articulate, Kennedy, born in Weaverville, California, had been working as a camera operator and video editor for a San Diego TV station when she lucked into a job as a production assistant on the ill-fated *1941*. She and Spielberg clicked and she became his associate producer on *Raiders of the Lost Ark*, getting producer's credit on *E.T.* Marshall, a native of Newport Beach, was an assistant to Peter Bogdanovich on movies like *Targets* and *Paper Moon*, later working with Walter Hill and Martin Scorsese before linking up with Spielberg.

In 1991, Kennedy and Marshall informed their boss that they no longer enjoyed their jobs and intended to quit Amblin to go into production for themselves. Both felt that, given the intense pressures, they were growing increasingly distanced from the filmmaking process and that they had become executives rather than filmmakers. All this gave Spielberg pause; indeed, some associates thought he might be motivated to cut back on the scope of his own activities.

They misjudged him. Instead of scaling back, his interests expanded into video games, theme parks, TV animation, and a myriad of other arenas. It seemed impossible for him to resist whatever new opportunity opened up to him. And with the power of the Spielberg name, the horizon of creative and business opportunities seemed limitless.

Given this appetite, the announcement of the formation of Dream-

Works in 1996 seemed inevitable. Together with David Geffen and Jeffrey Katzenberg, Spielberg heralded the formation of what effectively would be the first fully self-sufficient new studio to be established in Hollywood in several generations. The new entity would have an initial capitalization of $3 billion and would, in time, build its own facility to house its production activities.

In announcing the new company, the three partners made it abundantly clear that Steven Spielberg's role would be active, not symbolic. Neither Geffen nor Katzenberg, who had had a checkered record at Disney in live-action films, would be involved in the filmmaking side of DreamWorks. Movies would be Spielberg's sanctum sanctorum and he would now be charged with running the movie division of a major studio, overseeing the activities of Amblin, and continuing his own directing career. While most of the new Spielberg-initiated projects would be siphoned through DreamWorks, Amblin would still hold the incredibly lucrative sequel rights to such hits as *Casper*, *The Flintstones*, *Jurassic Park*, and *Men in Black*. Were Spielberg to take Amblin public, he would probably see a billion-dollar valuation for the company, though he still said that, over time, he intended to phase out Amblin and concentrate on DreamWorks.

To accomplish all this, Spielberg hired yet another husband-and-wife team, Walter Parkes and Laurie McDonald, to head Amblin and also play a key role in DreamWorks. He later supplemented them with Robert Cooper, the former production chief at HBO, whose activities would be limited to DreamWorks.

By the mid-to-late nineties, Spielberg's career and even his personal filmmaking activity seemed to be assuming more and more of a split personality. On the one hand, his serious films, like *Schindler's List* and *Saving Private Ryan*, were becoming increasingly passionate. As an artist and technician, Spielberg seemed to have ascended to new heights of proficiency. On the other hand, those projects that were intended as commerce were becoming filmsy. The very critics who increasingly were taking potshots at Spielberg for *Twister* or *Jurassic Park: The Lost World* were also heralding him as a great filmmaker.

Even his handling of his business affairs reflected this split personality. Talking to actors or members of the crew who worked on movies that Spielberg personally directed, you heard descriptions of a man who was driven yet uncommonly considerate, decisive yet compassionate. Spielberg the director was neither a tyrant nor a yeller and screamer. He emerged as an uncommonly gracious man who, intent on getting the work done, scrupulously avoided trampling on the egos of those around him.

Spielberg the businessman presented a sharply different picture. He was almost paranoid in his dealings with agents for artists he intended to hire. "Steven feels everyone tries to take advantage of him because he's Steven," said one top agent who represents several writers DreamWorks and Amblin has hired. "He says he wants a fair shake, but what he really wants is a better deal than anyone else is getting." On films he directed Spielberg had an unprecedented deal that gave him 50 percent of the gross once a film had reached a certain level of return. Even on films he only produced, like *Men in Black* and *Twister*, his estimated take exceeded $200 million.

Writers and directors working with Spielberg reported they found him soft-spoken but subtly intimidating. "He's like a Mafia boss in that he subtly flaunts his power," said one writer. "You are discussing an issue in the script and he will say, 'We should ask the president that question. He's my house guest next weekend.' " He was referring, of course, to the president of the United States.

While praising the contribution of the screenwriter in his public pronouncements, Spielberg, as a producer, fired writers with a casualness that startled even the most battle-hardened. On movies like *Zorro* and *Small Soldiers*, writers were hired and fired with regularity. Even on those serious films like *Schindler's List* and *Saving Private Ryan*, which seemed to reflect the distinctive voice of the original screenwriter, squads of rewrite men were ushered in to add scenes and polish dialogue.

To be sure, a director is totally within his rights to change writers, though some of the great directors—like Billy Wilder, himself a writer—decry this behavior. But a few of the writers who worked for Spielberg insisted that he could be coldly dismissive. "He might serve you milk and cookies, but that doesn't really disguise the fact that, in his eyes, you are part of his service personnel, like the plumber or the electrician," said one prominent scenarist.

Sometimes even his good manners wore thin. "Steven asked me to pitch ideas on a script," recalled one writer, "and so I came in and we talked and I pitched. It was very nice and he said he liked my ideas very much. Then I got a call the next day from Walter Parkes telling me he didn't like my ideas at all. That's life with Steven."

In his dealings with people in the industry, Spielberg basically behaved like a movie star. He was aware that what was a casual if not irrelevant conversation, as far as he's concerned, might be one of the most memorable exchanges in that other person's career. What to him may be a routine phone call may change the life of the person on the other end of the line. "He is a mythic figure—it's as simple as that," said one of his key associates. "He can reach anyone in the world. Any government will bend over backward to help him. But all that can be a burden, too. It's heavy baggage to carry around."

If Spielberg's celebrity proves a burden, it clearly also energizes him. He is arguably the most important filmmaker of his generation, surely the wealthiest and, improbably, the most driven. It was this drive and persistence that was vividly evident as Spielberg assembled his summer movies for '98.

The Mask of Zorro

**In which the seemingly anachronistic Hispanic Hero made his ump-
teenth comeback**

The moment of conception for *The Mask of Zorro* occurred at an unlikely time and place. Steven Spielberg was shooting *Hook* for TriStar
in 1991 and things were not going as smoothly as expected. Usually
there was a pervasive feeling on Spielberg sets that this was a movie
whose time has come. Scenes were well planned and decisions
quickly made.

But on *Hook* there was a listlessness in and around the set, a sense
that the pieces of this puzzle were somehow not quite fitting together.
Spielberg himself was distracted from time to time. "It was tough
going," Spielberg recalled. "I had fifteen lost boys on my hands.
Sometimes it felt like fifteen too many. It actually made me wonder if
I really wanted to have any more children."

After one take during which Robin Williams performed some awkward swordplay, Spielberg picked up the phone and issued an instruction to an aide. He wanted a search on the rights to *Zorro*. Who owned
the story, when did the option expire, and how much would it cost to
buy it?

No one knows precisely what made Spielberg fixate on Zorro at
that moment. Spielberg himself dismisses it as a form of free association. Watching the swords flashing reminded him of lazy Saturday
afternoons spent as a kid watching old movies. One of the old Zorro
movies had crossed his mind and registered. Perhaps it was time to

revisit that distant world of Errol Flynn and Douglas Fairbanks. Perhaps Spielberg, the man who led the way into the bold new world of special effects, should turn his attention back to a mythic era of moviemaking when the only effect was a trampoline to help actors put more oomph into their leaps.

With that phone call, Steven Spielberg triggered a tortuous seven-year battle to dust off and refurbish the Zorro legend. The project would wend its way through many writers and directors and cause frequent creative clashes. It was to become a subject of extreme consternation at TriStar, whose support of *Zorro* kept wavering over the years. Recalled one senior TriStar executive: "No one at the studio had any real enthusiasm for *Zorro*. We couldn't figure out why Steven wanted to make it. But when we added up the numbers and figured it out, we realized it would actually cost as much as $20 million to abandon the damned project. We figured it would be a lesser gamble to make it than to abandon it." In the end, *The Mask of Zorro* was vivid proof that what Spielberg wants, Spielberg gets.

The Zorro legend had been haunting movies and TV for some eight decades. Douglas Fairbanks starred in *The Mark of Zorro* in 1920, which became one of the classic hits of the silent era. The movie was based on a serialized novel called *The Curse of Capistrano* by Johnston McCulley that related the feats of a romantic hero who fought injustice in the pueblo of Los Angeles.

By the Great Depression of the 1930s, Zorro was popping up all over the place. In 1940 Tyrone Power and Basil Rathbone made their version of *The Mark of Zorro*. The character was also featured in Republic's first color movie, *The Bold Caballero,* and the B-picture studio later turned out a serial called *Zorro Rides Again*. In 1957, Disney introduced Zorro in a TV series starring Guy Williams and by the sixties, Zorro movies were springing up all over Europe. The best-known foreign Zorro was French actor Alain Delon, who played the masked hero in a French-Italian coproduction. There was even an animated Zorro on CBS Saturday mornings in the early eighties and, perhaps inevitably, a camp Zorro, the "Gay Blade," starring none other than George Hamilton. In the 1990s, a plethora of live-action and animated series continued to parade across global TV screens. A stage musical about Zorro opened in London in 1995.

Over the years, Zorro had been scrutinized from virtually every possible point of view and Spielberg, for a time, seemed baffled by all the possibilities. His first attack on the project suggested a smaller, more contained production than was usual for Spielberg. The first director assigned to *Zorro* was Swedish ex-cinematographer Mikael Salomon. He was later replaced by a respected independent filmmaker named Robert Rodriguez, who had made *Desperado,* which Spielberg admired. The initial drafts of the screenplay were written by the ubiquitous team of Ted Elliott and Terry Rossio, who had also tackled the first draft of *Godzilla.*

As one Spielberg associate explained it, "Steven just wasn't focusing on *Zorro.* What he really wanted was a big panoramic *Zorro,* with a wide canvas and huge battles. That's the Spielberg vision. But the *Zorro* he kept developing at TriStar was more like a small independent film."

Since TriStar was a studio of warring camps, production executives there looked on with a mixture of fear and confusion. They realized that, at any given time, Spielberg and his people could walk away from *Zorro* and it would be TriStar that looked stupid. Spielberg was playing with TriStar money and the investment was steadily mounting.

For Lucy Fisher, who had left Warner Bros. in 1995 to become an executive vice chair for Columbia/TriStar, the turning point occurred over Christmas 1997. Another *Zorro* rewrite had come in and clearly missed the mark—discouragingly so. Suddenly her home fax machine came to life and, to her astonishment, in rolled four pages of notes on the draft, all bearing the personal imprint of Spielberg. "I thought to myself, Steven cares enough about this project to send me script notes at Christmastime. And they were terrific ideas—it was starting to come together for him," recalls Fisher.

"Steven's vision of *Zorro* was operatic," said Walter Parkes, who with his wife, Laurie, served as Spielberg's chief lieutenant. "He saw touches of *Sweeney Todd* and of *Indiana Jones*, equal parts action and opera."

But Spielberg made one thing clear: He was in no rush. He wanted a new attack on the script as well as a director to help supervise it.

"The good news was that we could afford to wait, and to try to get it right," said Parkes. "It wasn't like anyone else was lining up to make *Zorro*. It was a bit like our situation on *Men in Black*, which also was a unique project where you didn't have to worry about the competition."

Meanwhile, Spielberg and his group were zeroing in on Martin Campbell, a New Zealander who had just directed the stylish James Bond sequel, *GoldenEye*. Campbell had moved to London in 1966, where he began his career as a TV cameraman, making his directing debut on a British police action version of "Starsky and Hutch" called "The Professionals." His telefilm, *Reilly: Ace of Spies*, also got him attention as a possible feature director, but the Bond epic was his big break. Indeed, within a week of its opening, Campbell returned home to his house in Provence, France, to find three big cartons of scripts awaiting him, all sent by his Hollywood agent, Martha Luttrell of ICM.

Campbell had been tinkering with producer David Foster on a western at TriStar called *Hell and High Water* when he got the call. Spielberg described *Zorro* passionately, then dispatched the Rossio and Elliott script. Within days Campbell signed on, taking producer Foster with him.

Work on the script now took on a new urgency. A new writer, John Eskow, had been brought aboard but, reading his version, Campbell and the Spielberg troops alike felt the movie had become too contemporary. The decision was made to recruit one of the town's more expensive and experienced writers, David Ward, to do what would hopefully be a final polish. "I was thrilled to get the call," said Ward, who had won an Oscar in 1973 for writing *The Sting*, but whose efforts to launch a career as a director had been troubled. "Coincidentally, Zorro had been one of my boyhood heroes. When I read the earlier drafts, I found they were great fun. This was a picture with epic values. I got it. And I think I knew what it needed."

Ward's marching orders were to work on the relationships between the principal characters, especially that of Zorro and his mentor, played by Anthony Hopkins. "I had never met Martin Campbell before this assignment," Ward said, "but I liked him and I liked what he said. He didn't want this just to be an action piece. He wanted the characters to come alive."

Ward did not have much time to accomplish his mission. Only three weeks remained before principal photography was to commence in Mexico. Antonio Banderas, who would play Zorro, had been signed, as had Hopkins. The picture had received a green light from the studio, not once but twice. Mark Canton had given his okay before he was fired. Then John Calley had again approved the project. "What else could he do?" asked one associate. "You don't start a new job and veto a project produced by Steven Spielberg and directed by Martin Campbell, who had just had a big hit with *GoldenEye*."

Yet the fear at Sony was that *Zorro* was too retro. This was unabashedly an old-fashioned movie, one that seemed to revel in its old ideas. It would be Douglas Fairbanks revisited. Equally troubling was the absence of a major star. Banderas was a flashy actor, but definitely not an established star. Nor was Anthony Hopkins, whose role encompassed a good deal of physical shtick rather than high drama.

Even as he turned in his draft at the end of three weeks, David Ward knew what to expect. Within days he got the phone call asking if he would stay on the picture for a few more weeks and keep writing during principal photography. There would be no way to judge the interplay of character until the cameras started rolling and the scenes unfolded.

Ward understood full well how tough it would be, especially on an expensive action picture, to rewrite scenes as the movie was actually shooting. Actors would have to be fed lines at the last minute, and that in itself could be disruptive.

Still, Martin Campbell was a calm and decisive man who gave the impression that he knew what he wanted, and so was Ward. "It's easier for me to do this sort of work because of my directing experience," Ward observed. "I'm flexible. I'm fast on my feet. And Campbell is great. He's very specific about the work that needed to be done."

David Ward ended up spending two months on location in Mexico. By the time he was done, he was grateful to return home. Mexico was hot and dusty and, as usual, many on the cast and crew became ill. But even as he stepped on the plane, he told himself that this *Zorro* was going to work. It was going to be worth all the years of false starts and frustration.

Small Soldiers

In which the killer toys seemed to pack more excitement for the adults than for the kids for whom they were intended

From the outset, *Small Soldiers* seemed like the guest no one was prepared to invite to dinner. The project had been floating around Amblin for almost a decade—a concept in search of a story. On paper the basic premise would seem irresistible to kids: What if your toys came to life? What if they were elite commando toys, implanted with microchips from the Pentagon, that would wage war against their enemies?

Clearly if such a concept could be translated into a tenable movie, the potential was formidable, not only in terms of box office, but also merchandising tie-ins. This seemed like a perfect project for Dream-Works: a savvy bit of commerce that was all about toys—Spielberg loved toys, Jeffrey Katzenberg loved tie-ins. In addition it had a violent edginess that seemed more and more to appeal to Spielberg, whose movies increasingly have been criticized for pushing the envelope in terms of violence.

In short, *Small Soldiers* could either be a hit or an embarrassment. Was it worth the risk? There were those around Spielberg who argued it was not. If *Small Soldiers* were really a movie, they argued, some semblance of a narrative would have fallen into place after almost a decade and eight writers. Besides, they said, it was Universal's development money that went into the project. A write-off would be easy to arrange.

But *Small Soldiers* seemed to have a life of its own. Spielberg had always had a soft spot for the idea. At his urging, Universal had paid $400,000 for a spec script by Gavin Scott, a British writer whose work he'd admired on "The Young Indiana Jones Chronicles." And Spielberg didn't let things die easily.

Early in 1997, the filmmaker had an idea on how to resurrect the project. What *Small Soldiers* needed was teams, he said—the good guys versus the bad guys. The Commando Elite soldiers led by super-macho Chip Hazard would battle their enemies, the evil Gorgonites. Maybe a battalion of warlike Barbie dolls could also be brought into the mix.

His colleagues at Amblin rolled their eyes. Spielberg's teams were a staple of his movies. This formula had worked in *Jurassic Park* and again in *Twister*. There were always bad guys who turned up at convenient moments to propel the action, even though, from time to time, they seemed to have been inserted arbitrarily.

Suddenly, after years of sporadic activity, *Small Soldiers* shifted into high gear. New writers were brought in to reshape the script. Joe Dante, the director of *Gremlins,* was signed to pull together the diverse elements. Stan Winston, the special-effects wizard who had performed so expertly on *Jurassic Park,* was enlisted to work on animatronic puppet toys that could be intercut with computer-animated material developed by George Lucas's Industrial Light and Magic elves. The project was now being characterized by its publicists as *"Toy Story* with an edge." And the merchandising tie-ins began to take off. Burger King was prepared to launch a major promotion to give out *Small Soldiers* toys. (The company later was startled when the violence in the movie triggered a PG-13 rating that militated against the kiddie theme of its campaign.) Discussions with Universal heated up over incorporating the toys into a theme-park ride—"an exclusive experience of high-tech movie magic," a release exclaimed. Hasbro was grinding out *Small Soldiers* toys and a deal was even consummated to paint the *Soldiers* logo and characters on professional race cars.

Under terms of the distribution deal, DreamWorks would handle the film in the U.S. and Universal overseas. Both companies let it be known to the press that they considered *Small Soldiers* the possible sleeper hit of the summer.

Because of the complexity of the special effects, the movie was not available to be seen by marketing and distribution executives until late in the spring of 1998. But from the bits and pieces of the film that were screened, some serious concerns began to arise among those executives. What was the prime audience for *Small Soldiers*? Would it prove too violent and even too nasty for kids or perhaps not quite credible enough for teens?

Small Soldiers had found itself miraculously on the fast track. But was it the fast track to nowhere?

Deep Impact

In which a studio dusted off a fifty-year-old property and prepared to move heaven and earth to deliver summer's first asteroid

David Brown had been around long enough to have mastered the fine art of creative recycling. Still razor-sharp and articulate at age eighty-one, Brown could compete with the most tenacious young producers or book-trackers in ferreting out hot new literary properties. He also understood how an outstanding piece of material may get passed over because the wrong studio executive happened to read it or because a movie on a roughly similar subject had flopped. For years, Brown had been looking for the right time and place to revive certain of his favorites like John O'Hara's *Appointment in Samarra* or John Dos Passos's *USA*.

In 1951, Brown was working as managing editor of *Cosmpolitan* magazine in New York when Darryl F. Zanuck, the brilliant—if erratic—president of Twentieth Century Fox decided that he needed a smart young story mind—someone who understood the East Coast as well as the West, and who could find material for the more than fifty producers and directors he had under contract. Brown was conscripted for the job, and went on to form a partnership with Darryl's son, Richard. Along the way they fostered a remarkable array of movies, including *Jaws*, *The Sting*, and *Cocoon*.

Zanuck, feisty and bantam-sized, tended to focus on deal-making and physical production, while Brown lined up future projects. On the side, Brown would still write the cover lines for his old magazine,

Cosmopolitan, which had been edited for many years by his wife, Helen Gurley Brown. Between takes on a movie, one could find Brown, looking like a dapper academic in his suit and tie, scribbling lines like "The Road to Better Orgasms" or "The G-Spot: An Owner's Manual."

It was in the late 1970s that Brown approached Barry Diller, then chief of Paramount, about the prospect of remaking *When Worlds Collide,* the classic sci-fi novel by Philip Wylie and Edwin Balmer. Paramount had made the movie in 1951, directed by George Pal, but Brown sensed the time was ripe to attempt an updated and more technically sophisticated version. Diller agreed, and Anthony Burgess, the novelist, was retained to write the script. His work proved to be brilliant but unbearably academic, Brown recalls, and Paramount recruited Sterling Silliphant, a far more commercial writer, to rescue the movie. He, too, failed and the project languished.

Two decades later, Brown encountered Steven Spielberg at one of those summer parties in the Hamptons on Long Island where everyone is at once convivial and competitive. Not one to squander an opportunity, Brown told him of his long-abandoned project. To his delight, the filmmaker seemed taken by the idea and the two began discussions about reviving it. Spielberg was not interested merely in producing the film, but directing it as well. They reminded each other that their last collaboration twenty-five years earlier had turned out rather well. It was a movie called *Jaws.*

While Paramount still owned the rights, the studio was always eager to take on partners, especially if a filmmaker of Spielberg's stature would be involved. The new version of *When Worlds Collide,* now called *Deep Impact,* would be cofinanced by Paramount and DreamWorks with worldwide revenues going into a pot to be shared fifty-fifty.

In the initial talks between Spielberg and the studio in 1993, a basic point of view about the movie began to emerge. None of the principals wanted to make another soulless effects movie. The compelling idea about *Deep Impact* related not to the pyrotechnics of the collision between earth and asteroid, but to the doomsday scenario that would envelop the world. How would society react to the knowledge that the end was at hand? Would institutions break down or would a new spirituality emerge?

No one can quite recall who advanced the idea, but an old Stanley Kramer movie, *On the Beach,* based on the novel by Nevil Shute, emerged as the model for *Deep Impact.* That story dealt with a nuclear apocalypse, not an asteroid, but the analogies were clear. Sherry Lansing, for one, was an advocate of character-driven movies, and the notion of developing *Deep Impact* along these lines appealed to her. Spielberg, too, was more than sympathetic. He had scored a big success with *Twister* but had also taken heat from critics who accused him of trying to model his movies after theme-park rides. Clearly, he did not want *Deep Impact* to be another *Twister.*

As executives and agents around town learned of this revisionist thinking, a certain understandable skepticism greeted the idea. Other asteroid projects were beginning to take shape at other studios. To the casual observer, they all seemed like high-concept action movies. Irrespective of everyone's higher aspirations, *Deep Impact* seemed destined to be another special-effects blockbuster.

One such skeptic was Bruce Joel Rubin, a veteran writer best known for the sleeper of 1990, *Ghost.* Rubin was respected as a skilled writer with innovative ideas, but now, at age fifty-five, he had professed his desire to avoid studio assignments. He told his agents he wanted to be left alone to develop his own movies. So when Rubin was contacted by Spielberg about *Deep Impact,* he was astonished. "You get a call from this man who is a godlike figure in your industry and you're blown away," Rubin recalls. "He says he wants to direct this film and he wants you to write it and his enthusiasm is contagious. Beyond contagious."

Despite all this, Rubin mustered the strength to issue a polite no. As persuasively as Spielberg had described *Deep Impact,* to Rubin it still seemed like another popcorn movie. "It sounded exciting, but it was still another writing assignment, albeit a Spielberg writing assignment," Rubin said.

In the end, Spielberg got his man. One reason Rubin gave in, as he later acknowledged, was the delicious opportunity for research into exotic subjects. Spielberg was urging him to visit NASA, the White House, the Pentagon, various Air Force bases, and other such locations. "He hit my weakness," Rubin recalls. "I love doing research. And Steven can open all the doors. His office makes a call and says you're working for Spielberg and suddenly you're in."

It was Rubin's intention to write not just a movie but an epic saga. To that end, in the subsequent months he created a big, indeed a positively enormous, script of 176 pages. Packed with big scenes and grandiose images, his script at one point calls for: "EXT. THE HEAVENS. The image we see can only be described as biblical in its power. . . ."

Rubin felt he had the mandate to write a three-hour movie. During the writing, Spielberg himself suggested some broad-canvas scenes that he later decided not to shoot. For example, at the moment when New Yorkers felt they were imminently doomed, Spielberg conceived that the entire population would simultaneously trek toward the ocean. With the tidal wave approaching, they would stand at the shore, legions of them, holding hands and sublimely awaiting their fate.

To Rubin, this was the kind of scene that *Deep Impact* needed—big, epochal scenes that would inscribe themselves in the audience's mind. At some point in the process, however, Spielberg seemed to change his mind as to just how big he wanted the movie to be. After two drafts, he fired Rubin and brought in Michael Tolkin, a bright but idiosyncratic writer who had made a name in Hollywood with his novel *The Player*. Though Spielberg told Tolkin that he intended to work closely with him, he also confided some other surprising information—he would no longer be directing *Deep Impact*. Disney was preparing its own asteroid movie called *Armageddon*, he explained, and he had no intention of getting into a race. He had even selected his replacement, with Paramount's approval. The new director would be Mimi Leder, who had just finished another film, *The Peacemaker*, for DreamWorks. A matronly woman with a round, benign face and a focused, intelligent gaze, Leder had made her reputation in television, directing several of the most memorable "ER" episodes. On that series she had proved not only her dexterity with the camera, but her keen eye for character development.

In her initial meeting with Tolkin, Leder explained emphatically that her interest was in the people, not the asteroid. "I was drawn to this story because of the human element," she told me over lunch. "This was the ultimate end-of-the-world story, about how people respond when they're facing the end."

One advantage to directing a Spielberg-produced movie, she acknowledged, was that the magic of his name eliminated the pressure to cast movie stars. The biggest names in *Deep Impact*, Tea Leoni and Morgan Freeman, could hardly support an anticipated $80 million outlay at most studios. This, however, was a character picture, not a star vehicle, as Spielberg kept explaining to a nervous Paramount.

Tolkin had never done a studio rewrite before, and he would find the process both fascinating and frustrating with its pressures and false starts. At one point, he recalled, Spielberg had the notion that all the astronaut dialogue would be so steeped in technical terms and mathematical equations that the audience could not hope to follow what they were saying. It was a noble attempt at realism that didn't work. Tolkin tossed out the scenes and went back to the drawing board. He also found the thicket of subplots difficult to cut through. "You have to face the fact that, whatever your contribution, it's still basically not your script," he concluded. "I took Rubin's script and tried to improve it, to isolate and develop its basic themes. But the fact remains, it's someone else's project. It was discouraging. Yet I would often read Spielberg's script notes and say to myself, 'No wonder they pay him millions of dollars to work on a movie.' "

Tolkin was succeeded by the estimable John Wells, who was one of the top writers and producers on "ER," as well as its major guiding force with Michael Crichton. Wells and Leder had worked together countless times on "ER" episodes and were comfortable together. "Wells was amazing," said one Paramount executive. "He'd take a three-page scene and reduce it to less than a page, and it was a more compelling page." But Wells had only a limited period of time to give the project. After a couple of weeks he was gone and it was Mimi Leder's show now. She was on her own. And *Armageddon,* she learned, was prepping to start production in early July of 1997, not far behind *Deep Impact.* She was a pro. She had learned that in television, time was everything, and the same applies to movies. There was no way the top executives at DreamWorks and Paramount would allow *Deep Impact* to start production behind *Armageddon.*

It was going to be a tough race, Leder knew. But she was accustomed to winning races.

Saving Private Ryan

In which Steven Spielberg reinvented the genre of the war movie, and how it should be designed, cast, and photographed

Though great movie ideas are supposed to spring full-blown from a director's sensibility, or perhaps from the ruminations of a distinguished screen writer, the genesis of *Saving Private Ryan* can be traced directly to one studio executive's obsession. Don Granger, an executive vice president of production at Paramount, was a man on a mission, and that mission was to add a movie about World War II to his studio's slate. "Let's be honest about it," he explained. "One reason guys like me get into these jobs is that we were strongly influenced when we were growing up by a few special movies. And whether we realize it or not, we all are driven to remake these movies. In fact, we have this private conceit that we can make them better."

An attractive, well-tailored man in his thirties who would look more at home in an advertising agency, Granger admired movies like *The Guns of Navarone* and *Destination: Tokyo*. And while his studio had virtually every type of film in preparation, not a single war movie was among them. The reason was simple: Everyone believed that movies about WWII had gone out of style.

Granger started spreading the word that he would be glad to take pitches from writers and producers who thought they had a good war movie. His task turned out to be exhausting. He waded through piles of proposals, but they tended to follow a familiar path. The stories usually focused on a top-secret mission to assassinate Hitler's chief nuclear scientist or some other minion. The hero was always a retro John Wayne who came home a hero.

Granger was getting discouraged until he received a call from a producer at Twentieth Century Fox, Mark Gordon, whom Granger knew to be a smart young guy. Gordon wanted to come in with writer Robert Rodat to pitch a war story. The premise was very simple: There were four Ryan brothers in combat during World War II; three had been killed and the army had decided to send a mission to bring home the last remaining brother.

Granger immediately sensed that this was a fresh idea. But he was less than thrilled that Rodat had no reputation as a creator of strong, forceful stories. A little-known writer, he was associated with softer fare like *Tall Tale*, which he'd written for Disney, and *Fly Away Home*, a lightweight family comedy.

Despite this, the tall, erudite thirty-six-year-old writer who walked into his office on June 14, 1995, commanded his attention. Rodat had studied history at Colgate, then earned his M.B.A. at Harvard Business School before veering off to attend film school at the University of Southern California.

The inspiration for his idea, Rodat explained, came from an unprepossessing granite obelisk that stood in a small town near Keene, New Hampshire, where he lived during the summer months. It was a monument that listed the town's war dead. Rodat would walk his child past that monument and, pausing to read the names, he was struck by the fact that one family had lost five sons in the Civil War. Coincidentally, his wife had recently given him the book *D-Day: The Climactic Battle of World War II* by historian Stephen Ambrose. What would happen, Rodat wondered, if the War Department had decreed that an entire family could not simply be wiped out? What would be the implications if several men were dispatched to save one lone survivor?

Gordon and Rodat had pitched the story before to Tom Jacobson, who was at the time head of production at Fox, but he hadn't been interested. Don Granger, however, was not only interested, he was riveted. "As I listened to Rodat, I said to myself, 'My God, this is it! This is exactly what I've been searching for.' " Over dinner that night with his wife, Lisa McCree, the cohost of ABC's "Good Morning America," Granger found himself prattling on nonstop about *Saving Private Ryan.*

Granger saw several levels to the story. The mission, though heroic, had a fascinating moral ambiguity. There were no superheroes. Rather, a small group of ordinary soldiers had been sent to accomplish something they didn't completely believe in. And Private Ryan turned out to be a man who did not want to be rescued.

Many facets to the story would have to be resolved, Granger realized. Would Captain Miller, the man leading the mission, be the conventional career military officer mindlessly doing his duty, or would he understand the built-in irony of possibly sacrificing his men to achieve the symbolic goal of saving one? Would Ryan himself turn out to be someone worth rescuing? These issues, he knew, would doubtless be debated throughout the script stage and well into production.

But first, Granger was determined to get the deal done. To accomplish this, he needed the approval of John Goldwyn, a tall, angular, rather distant man who held the title of president of motion pictures at Paramount. Granger knew that Goldwyn, a son of Samuel Goldwyn Jr., and grandson of the legendary producer, was not given to impulsive judgments. With considerable apprehension Granger gave Goldwyn a two- or three-sentence description of *Saving Private Ryan* along with his request for about $300,000 to buy a first draft of the screenplay and two sets of revisions. He acknowledged it was a high price tag for an original story in a genre that many considered to be extinct. To Granger's surprise, Goldwyn's response was immediate—make the deal.

It was not until he sat in a screening room at DreamWorks three years later watching the finished film that Granger would understand the extraordinary irony of what he had done. He had commissioned a

writer of airy romantic comedies to create what would ultimately become one of the most searing, brutally realistic depictions of war that
Hollywood would ever make.

While Paramount regarded *Saving Private Ryan* as a high-risk
undertaking, Robert Rodat had no such apprehensions. He was determined not to be typecast as a soft writer and, while he had two young
children himself, he had no desire to make a career of family pictures.
With this in mind, he had written a rather somber script about Jack
the Ripper, which had come to the attention of Mark Gordon. Gordon
had tried unsuccessfully to set it up as a feature, but had failed and
ultimately it was produced as an original movie for cable. Rodat and
Gordon had liked each other and decided to continue their association. The writer and producer had sifted through dozens of ideas before focusing on *Private Ryan.*

It took six months for Rodat to deliver his first draft to Paramount.
During this period he conferred frequently with Mark Gordon. Both
knew a lot was riding on the draft and that it was important to make
the right choices. They decided, for example, to keep Private Ryan
essentially unformed as a character. He would not be depicted as
heroic, or as a nasty, ungrateful kid. Rather, as a result of his rescue,
Private Ryan would be reshaped by this extraordinary experience and
by the circumstances that surrounded it. Indeed, Captain Miller would
also emerge as a vastly changed man who felt a little farther from
home every time he kills a man.

As they worked on the first draft, Rodat and Gordon received some
alarming news from Granger. From out of the blue, two other screenplays set in World War II had surfaced at Paramount, and, even more
daunting, major stars were attached to both. A script called *Combat*
had attracted the interest of Bruce Willis, who agreed to do it provided
an acceptable director could be recruited. Yet another war thriller,
With Wings of Eagles, had also been acquired, this one for Arnold
Schwarzenegger. *Eagles* had been written by Randy Wallace, who'd
been responsible for *Braveheart.* While the studio liked the script,
there were two obstacles to overcome. First, Schwarzenegger would

have to accept Wallace as the director. Second, the Austrian-born actor would have to be comfortable wearing a Nazi uniform, something he had never before agreed to do.

What had once been a clear field was now a crowded one. Sherry Lansing had sent out word that all three were worthy projects and that the first to come together would get the green light. "Finish the damn script," Granger instructed Rodat and Gordon. "Let's get it out there."

Stung by the news, Gordon and Rodat hammered together the final scenes and sent the script off to Granger to read and circulate among his colleagues. "My attitude had instantly changed from excitement to resignation," Rodat acknowledged. "I believed in this script. I knew in my heart that it would get made. But now I realized it could take a few years. I resigned myself for a long, hard wait."

His intuition was wrong. Granger read the script the night he received it and said it was great. His one admonition was that Captain Miller not die in the end. The following day, Rodat changed the ending; the captain would live.

As the script circulated among the Paramount executives, it took on a certain sense of déjà vu. Like *Deep Impact*, this was a story that lacked both a star and a name director. Mark Gordon knew at this juncture that the ball was in his court. He knew that the executives who had read it at Paramount had liked the script, and that he could count on Granger's advocacy. But he needed important names to attach to what would be a very expensive project. The studio said it would come up with lists of suggested "elements," such as stars and directors, but studio bureaucracies moved slowly, Gordon knew. Pictures came together because producers hustled and did not wait for studios to make lists.

Gordon's first step was to dispatch the script to CAA, the agency that represented many key stars and directors. Projects could get lost just as easily at CAA as at a studio, Gordon knew, perhaps even more so, since every producer in town sent scripts to the agency in the vain hope that a key agent would take an interest in it.

But Gordon had an association with a ten-year veteran there

named Caryn Sage, who he knew did her homework. When Gordon had made *Speed* at Fox, Sage had represented the writer, Graham Yost, and she and Gordon had maintained a telephone relationship.

Having made the customary CAA move, Gordon next launched a more direct attack. He sent the script to Bob Zemeckis, who'd directed *Forrest Gump* at Paramount. He knew the studio was desperate to do another project with him. Zemeckis read the script promptly and sent word back that he was not interested.

Next on Gordon's list was a director named Rob Cohen, and this submission proved more productive. Paramount had liked a film about Bruce Lee that Cohen had directed and he was in postproduction there on *Dragonheart*. Early in his career, Cohen had twice headed independent, self-financed production entities and was respected as a responsible filmmaker. Sensing that he was about to land his prey, Gordon placed an urgent phone call to Sherry Lansing. "Rob is close to committing," he told Lansing. "If you would take the time to have a meal with him, I think we could get him."

Lansing had promised to maintain her neutrality in the battle of the war movies, but she had also promised to help in any way she could, and she was true to her word. That week she arranged to have breakfast with Rob Cohen.

What neither Lansing nor Gordon knew, however, was that the wheels were turning at CAA. Caryn Sage had read *Saving Private Ryan* and, in the argot of talent agencies, had flipped for it. She told her boss, Richard Lovett, the president of CAA, that it would make a perfect vehicle for Tom Hanks. Sure it was a war movie and Hanks had professed his disinterest in playing characters who carried a gun, but this wasn't some cop movie, this was a truly memorable role.

Sage also had another proposal. Steven Spielberg was making his annual pilgrimage to the CAA office the next day and Sage said she'd like to pitch the script to him. Lovett was taken aback by Sage's enthusiasm, but he knew her to be a savvy, cool-headed judge of material. He shrugged his approval.

When Spielberg seated himself in CAA's aggressively contemporary conference room the next day, he was surrounded by the usual cadre of fifteen agents, all of whom were given a chance to pitch their projects. Since Spielberg had never based any of his films on material submitted by his agents, choosing instead to discover or develop his own projects, they knew this was, at best, a long shot, but they doggedly went through the motions. Caryn Sage did not go through the motions, however. When her turn came, she pitched *Saving Private Ryan* with passion. Spielberg nodded with a trace of a smile and promised to read the material.

Two days later Mark Gordon received the telephone call that was to change the course of *Saving Private Ryan*. It was from CAA's Lovett, a very businesslike young man who conveys both good and bad news in the same matter-of-fact tone. Tom Hanks, he reported, had read the script and wanted to have lunch to discuss it with Gordon and the writer. "Make him feel comfortable with the project," Lovett cautioned. "And don't tell anyone that he's interested."

Thrilled by the news, Gordon felt uncomfortable about the secrecy. Ever since the days of Michael Ovitz, CAA seemed to prefer to keep its operations clandestine, as though it were emulating the Central Intelligence Agency. On the other hand, Gordon understood the foibles of superstars. Tom Hanks did not want to get calls from the studio to pressure him into the role, or read about himself in the trades. He wanted to be left alone to make his decision, mindful of the fact that, by accepting a role, a multimillion-dollar business would spring into action—crews hired, locations selected, and other actors recruited—all triggered by his saying "yes."

Gordon's discomfort was heightened by a phone call from Sherry Lansing. She had just returned from her meal with Rob Cohen and she was encouraged. "I think you have your man," she reported in her customary cheery, high-pitched voice.

She was surprised by the silence at the other end of the line. "I really appreciate your doing what you've done," Gordon replied, his voice tense, "but I think we should all lay low. We should do nothing for a while."

"Do nothing!" Sherry Lansing repeated. This was not the sort of message she expected to receive. A producer in this situation usually is pressing the studio to close the deal. Something was awry, and she couldn't figure out what it was.

Gordon, meanwhile, found himself fielding another nervous-making call from John Goldwyn. "I heard Rob Cohen wants to do *Ryan*," Goldwyn said. "We should start the negotiation." Again, Gordon was forced to backpedal. "We can't do anything," he advised. "Let's put a hold on things for a while." Even as Goldwyn agreed, Gordon knew that the studio must be thinking he was double-dealing. Perhaps he had a star attached but was intent on taking his project elsewhere.

The lunch with Hanks went superbly. A keenly intelligent man, Hanks dissected the character of Captain Miller, analyzing how he would be affected by the events of the mission, how he'd inevitably feel a certain bitterness toward Private Ryan. After all, the captain had survived the devastation of D-Day. Now he had to put his life on the line for an ungrateful kid. Though the script's setup was fascinating, Hanks said, Miller was drawn as too standard a war hero for his taste, with his Medal of Honor, his cigar, and his tendency to say things like, "Come on, you sons of bitches." If Hanks were to play the role, it would have to be redrawn and softened, and Miller would have to be reborn through his experience of rescuing Private Ryan.

"I was intimidated by Hanks at first," Gordon recalled. "Then I realized he had made me feel entirely comfortable. Here was this intelligent, decent guy talking about a movie and changing my life as he talked."

It was an utterly casual remark by Hanks that brought the conversation to a halt, however. "What would you think about Spielberg doing this piece?" he asked. He said it matter-of-factly, as though inquiring about dessert. Gordon was speechless. Before he could recover, the subject shifted once again.

It was a day later, late on a Friday afternoon, that Sherry Lansing got a call on her car phone from Richard Lovett. She was heading up Benedict Canyon toward her home. It was nearly seven P.M. and she was tired, and became impatient that Lovett's voice kept going in and out as the static increased.

Lovett got right to the point. "Steven Spielberg and Tom Hanks want to do *Saving Private Ryan*," he reported with his customary colorless delivery, as though he were disclosing weekend grosses. "What was your feeling about that?"

Lansing does not remember precisely what she replied, but her first thought was that this was a hoax. This is simply not the way things worked in the movie business. *Saving Private Ryan* had not even been submitted to CAA, as far as she knew, no less to Hanks or Spielberg. "To get a Tom Hanks or a Steven Spielberg, you have to do a dance for months," she explained. "You have to beg and implore. You wine and dine. You don't just get a Friday night phone call."

Lovett got an equally skeptical response from Jonathan Dolgen, the tough, hard-bargaining Viacom Entertainment chairman. When informed that Spielberg and Hanks would commit to *Saving Private Ryan*, Dolgen's response was curt. "What's *Saving Private Ryan*?" he demanded.

What motivated these two to make their commitment to *Saving Private Ryan*? Actors and directors are cautious about explaining themselves or their decisions. Clearly, Hanks, like Rodat, remembered the powerful war movies of his youth. *The Dirty Dozen* and *The Great Escape* were two he mentioned. Like most boys, Hanks had acted out his own fantasy versions of his favorite war movies. Captain Miller, to Hanks, could become the perfect Everyman figure with whom he seemed to identify.

Hanks had met Spielberg early in his career when the actor made *The Money Pit* for Spielberg's company. They found that they shared a lot of friends, and had children the same age. Later, they became next-door neighbors in the Pacific Palisades area of Los Angeles. Though Hanks admitted that "Steven made me pee in my pants" when they talked about film, the actor's own self-esteem rose with hits like *Philadelphia* and *Forrest Gump.* Hanks had become one of the top five stars in the world.

The prospect of working with Hanks had worried Spielberg; he feared it might ruin their friendship. But as they talked about *Saving Private Ryan*, they found that they were responding to the same elements. "It was the perfect morality play, except on some levels you have to call it an immorality play," the director said. "I read it and I seemed to just see it."

Spielberg, of course, had long been intrigued by World War II. His father had manned a radio aboard a B-25 bomber in Burma. Spielberg had first dealt with the war in his ill-fated comedy *1941.* He tried again in *Empire of the Sun* with marginal success, and yet again with *Schindler's List*, which he regarded as his best movie. To Spielberg, World War II marked an epic struggle to save Western civilization. The subtext of the Holocaust also resonated with him as arguably the century's seminal tragedy.

Spielberg and Hanks both felt that *Saving Private Ryan* would have to break new ground as a war movie. It would be shot like an independent film, with hand-held cameras and documentary-style footage. It would be cast like an independent film, devoid of the one-dimensional characters that tend to inhabit Hollywood's war movies. It would, in short, be a war movie to end all war movies.

As far as Paramount was concerned, all this was manna from heaven. Don Granger could hardly believe that what had started as a pitch had instantly become the hottest package in town. Colleagues stopped him in the corridors to congratulate him.

Paramount's negotiators, however, were less exuberant. To make this project happen, they realized, the dealmaking would have to be as creative as the screenplay. Spielberg's partners at DreamWorks had decreed that, though the script had been developed at Paramount, DreamWorks would nonetheless split the proceeds worldwide on a fifty-fifty basis. To that end, the company would put up half the financing. A coin would be flipped to decide which entity would hold distribution rights in the U.S. and which abroad (DreamWorks ended up with the U.S., just as Paramount won the right to distribute *Deep Impact* in the U.S.). Spielberg felt he could make the film in sixty days on a budget of roughly $65 million. Both star and director offered to take minimal up-front salaries. On the other hand, each would receive 20 percent of the gross receipts. That meant that almost 40 percent of the gross would be surrendered by the two financing entities. For DreamWorks this seemed less of a blow; after all, Spielberg was a full partner in that company. At Paramount, however, the deal was a hard sell. Executives at both the studio and its parent company, Viacom, bemoaned the fact that Paramount, having risked its development money, would end up with a share of only half the revenues. Even if the movie were a big hit, its upside was anemic.

The dissenters were quickly silenced, however. *Saving Private Ryan*, supporters pointed out, would be the single most prestigious movie of the year with the potential for winning many Oscars. As such, its benefit to the studio would be incalculable. This was not just a movie, it was the centerpiece of a program of movies.

As the deal became a reality, Spielberg and his coterie buckled down to shape the screenplay along the grand design envisioned by the director and his star. A series of meetings were convened with the key players to argue out the story points. Rodat would be given the initial shot at the rewrite, but everyone understood full well that Spielberg's modus operandi was to utilize not one but several screenwriters and that, as the start date drew near, the director would surely revert to form, no matter how well Rodat performed.

At initial story sessions, Spielberg remained at his home in East Hampton, Long Island, communicating with L.A. via teleconferencing. The group in Los Angeles consisted of Rodat, Hanks, Gordon, and Walter Parkes, who, with his wife, Laurie, served as production chief at DreamWorks. The initial focus was on character development—Captain Miller would have to be redrawn to fit Hanks's requirements, and Private Ryan rethought as well. Should Private Ryan be wounded in battle? Should he be likable or brashly annoying, a savant or a fool? The participants went through the same exercise with the other principal characters. Time and again, Spielberg zeroed in on those elements of the script that he described as "movie" moments. The aim was to make the script as honest as possible, and as realistic. Spielberg not only wanted characters altered, but also new characters added, such as the Jewish soldier, Melish, and the tough Italian kid, Caparzo. Soon faxes elaborating on story points started pouring in from Spielberg, along with technical advisories dealing with weaponry and types of vehicles from Captain Dale Dye, the hard-bitten military adviser.

"Steven was making his choices," Rodat recalls. "It was his choice to be very lean on backstory. My preference was to add more backstory regarding secondary characters. To Steven, however, the backstories seemed unnecessary. Here were these kids hitting the beaches—what difference did it make what they did for a living or where they came from? That was Steven's point of view."

Rodat turned in his draft. He waited. Then he was told the inevitable. Spielberg wanted to try a few things, and had decided to bring in another writer, Frank Durabont, who had written *The Shawshank Redemption*. His contribution would be limited to sketching out the combat scenes. Rodat knew he was in good hands, but it was nonetheless frustrating to be shunted aside.

By the time Scott Frank joined the party, things were becoming more urgent. Frank was a brilliant young writer whose credits included *Get Shorty*, *Out of Sight*, *Malice*, and *Little Man Tate*. In three weeks, *Saving Private Ryan* would start shooting, and there were still elements Spielberg wanted to explore. "When I heard how Steven intended to shoot the first twenty minutes," Frank remarked, "my first reaction was, hell, the story is irrelevant. If he could deliver those twenty minutes, you could run a Buick commercial for the rest of the movie."

Spielberg was intent on adding a scene in which Captain Miller's men attempted a mutiny and he asked Frank to write it. He also wanted richer dialogue among the soldiers during a scene in a bombed-out church. Since the captain had been a teacher before the war, the director felt there should be glints of a higher sensibility—a quote from Emerson was added.

Then, too, Spielberg was greatly concerned about the final words Miller would utter in the movie as he lay dying. The script called for Miller to say only two words: "Earn this." Would another phrase be more appropriate? Spielberg fretted. Was a longer speech required to make the point? "More and more," Frank reflected, "I felt Steven moving toward the idea that this movie was really about saving Captain Miller."

In the filmmaker's mind, Captain Miller felt he was losing more and more of himself as he traversed the brutal encounters of war. "Spielberg is at his best when his movies are depicting chaotic situations, when it is perfectly clear who is good and who is bad," explained one writer who has worked with him. "When he is dealing with complex characters, he tends to lose it. He will say, 'Let's try this,' but then he will back away from it."

When the company left for Ireland to start production, Spielberg asked Scott Frank to join them and keep working. Still later in the shoot, Rodat was asked back for some further work. But as Scott Frank and Robert Rodat saw dailies—a screening of film shot the previous day—they realized that, inevitably, there were other forces at work on the script, namely, the actors themselves. Tom Hanks, for example, decided he did not want to give a lengthy speech in which for the first time he revealed his background and beliefs to his soldiers. "It was a monologue that I suppose any actor would kill to have," recalled Hanks, "but I didn't think it was real. It seemed to compromise the integrity of my character for him suddenly to explain himself." The speech was dropped.

Similarly, when Private Ryan, played by Matt Damon, sat on the steps of the burnt-out French town and chatted with Captain Miller just before the German attack, he was trying to recall details about his brothers only to find his mind go blank. The captain suggested he try to think of a context, and suddenly Private Ryan was giving an absurd speech about discovering one of his brothers in a barn trying to make out with an ugly girl. The speech was in none of the versions of the script. When Spielberg yelled "cut," Damon looked a bit defensive, as though he wanted to remind everyone that he, too, was a writer.

Watching the scene in dailies that night, a couple of Spielberg's people said they didn't care for Damon's addition, but Spielberg clearly found it strangely compelling. The ad-libbed speech was neither profound nor insightful, the director acknowledged, but perhaps that's exactly why it worked. It somehow seemed true to this oddly unformed kid who was fated to be at the center of this mission. Damon's speech stayed in.

With shooting underway and one writer after another taking a stab at rewrites, no one except possibly Spielberg knew who was supposed to be doing what. One writer was assigned the task of finding a way to introduce the expression *fubar*, enlisted-man slang for "fucked up beyond all recognition," into the movie. Meanwhile, messages from military advisers kept pouring in and adjustments had to be made in numerous scenes. And Spielberg continued to toy with ideas for the ending.

Throughout the turmoil, Spielberg astonished those around him by appearing relaxed. His action scenes, despite their logistical complexity, had not been storyboarded, but apparently had arrayed themselves in an orderly fashion in his head. *Amistad* was there to be edited at lunch breaks, but this, too, seemed to have taken on a structure, at least in its director's mind. When Robert Rodat came to Ireland to put some final touches on the script, he was alarmed because there were fragments of the screenplay that hadn't been worked out. The ad-libbed scenes that Spielberg had ordered up impulsively did not flow into the rest of the script, at least not in the mind of the original writer, but Spielberg seemed unconcerned. The movie had taken on a rhythm of its own; he saw it and was comfortable with it. Perhaps his was a somewhat disjointed version, but it was a version nonetheless. The writers were now irrelevant. It was his show.

Six Days, Seven Nights

In which a filmmaker set out to tell a story about mismatched lovers without realizing quite how mismatched they were

Along Hollywood's corridors of power, producer and director Ivan Reitman was known as a shrewdly manipulative player who knew what he wanted and stood ready to pay the price. Transferring his hub of operations from Toronto to Los Angeles in the late 1970s, Reitman pioneered a dubious new genre, the gross-out comedy, with films such as *Animal House, Meatballs*, and *Stripes*.

In the 1980s he rode the crest of high-concept comedies with his *Ghostbusters* and *Twins*. He quickly learned how to harness the power of the big talent agencies, becoming a prize client of CAA and a close friend of Michael Ovitz. Some of the prototypical CAA packages of that period made Reitman rich, while others, like *Legal Eagles*, embarrassed him.

From the outset, Reitman displayed an instinctual understanding of how to make and market summer movies. "My career was built on summer," he told me late last spring as he was preparing yet another summer assault. Movies like *Animal House* were created for the summer crowd. Reitman had made it a point to understand the demographics of summer week by week. He knew which weeks belonged to teen boys, fresh out of school and eager for gross-out, and which weeks, later in summer, provided an opportunity for romantic movies keyed to young women.

Reitman exemplified the type of eighties filmmaker for whom movies represented more of an entrepreneurial opportunity than an art form. A thick-set man with bright, feral eyes, he ran a small company that had been involved in producing some twenty-eight projects over a span of twenty-five years. The son of an Auschwitz survivor, Reitman had become immensely wealthy, with homes in Los Angeles and Santa Barbara. Skilled at the Hollywood game, he consistently made money from movies no one even knew he helped foster, like *Private Parts*, starring Howard Stern, or *Space Jam*, the combined animated and live-action movie starring Michael Jordan.

But success hadn't insulated him from the occasional debacle. As the producer and director of *Father's Day* in 1997, Reitman was confident that with Robin Williams and Billy Crystal costarring, he had a major winner on his hands. "Even as we got deep into the shooting schedule, I began to sense something was wrong," he recalled. "Something wasn't happening, but I couldn't figure it out. Then everything started going wrong. The tracking studies were discouraging. The ads didn't create a want-to-see. We came out with the movie too early in summer, fighting for attention against the big special-effects action pictures. We should have waited till the end of June."

The fizzle of *Father's Day* depressed Reitman, who hadn't been praised for his directing since *Dave* in 1993. He admitted that when things went wrong he was not the easiest person to work with. At least two well-known producers involved in previous Reitman movies have vowed they would never work with him again. "There are many directors who won't listen," said one of them, "but Ivan Reitman might as well carry a sign that says, 'You can talk, but I don't hear.' "

In 1996, eager to try something different, Reitman honed in on a spec script called *Six Days, Seven Nights*. It seemed like a safe bet. It was a romantic story with comedic overtones.

He had no way of knowing at the time that it would become one of the most gossiped-about movies within memory. The buzz was triggered by Reitman's decision to cast Anne Heche, an avowed lesbian, as Harrison Ford's love interest. It was a daring move, one that brought the project much unwanted notoriety.

The author of *Six Days, Seven Nights*, Michael Browning, had struggled through years of obscure jobs as prop man, art director, and occasional actor in commercials before deciding to try his hand at screenwriting. He and his wife had moved out of Los Angeles to the Lake Arrowhead area to keep costs down while he labored on his scripts. Though the big money in spec scripts derived from the action genre, Browning decided to try light romance. To his delight, he struck the right chord. Caravan Pictures, a production company run by Joe Roth and Roger Birnbaum, paid $150,000 in 1995 to option *Six Days, Seven Nights* and persuaded Julia Roberts to star. Browning could hardly believe his luck. A script sale with a big star attached meant he had a career.

He soon found out that nothing happens quite that easily. Julia Roberts found something she liked better and left the project. Joe Roth announced he was leaving Caravan for Disney.

For *Six Days, Seven Nights*, it was time to start over. Roger Birnbaum, who remained at Caravan, decided to try casting the male lead first. His submission to Harrison Ford hit pay dirt. Ford had just signed on to do the action thriller *Air Force One*, and he wanted to follow that with a change of pace. *Six Days, Seven Nights* filled the bill, provided the producer was willing to wait a year.

There was another issue as well. Ford wanted the security of working with an experienced director. Like every star, Ford had his list of acceptable directors, and Birnbaum managed to interest one of them, Ivan Reitman. The director liked the script, though he wanted to make some changes. He also didn't mind waiting a year, since he had to finish producing *Space Jam*.

Birnbaum took the package to his old partner, Joe Roth, who was more than willing to make room on next year's schedule for a Ford-Reitman movie. Suddenly the project was back on course. Except— now Ford and Reitman had to find a female lead, and they knew this would not be an easy job. When Ford starred in his *Indiana Jones* movies, he always managed to fit in perfectly with the oddball cast of heavies and good guys. When he tried more personal movies, how-

ever, the results were decidedly mixed. While Ford and Kelly McGil-
lis seemed to mesh smoothly in *Witness*, there was little chemistry
with his leading ladies in *Sabrina* and *Regarding Henry*. By nature a
very reserved, even austere man, Ford came across as downright pa-
ternal with these women, making any suggestion of sexual attraction
seem ludicrous.

With this in mind, Reitman and Ford started to get the script out
to different stars with the understanding that an audition would be
mandatory. Some felt they were above reading for a part, others were
edgy about playing opposite Ford. Anne Heche, however, was enthusiastic. Heche, who was coming off strong performances in *Wag the Dog*
and *Donnie Brasco*, said she liked the script and would be delighted
to tape a scene opposite Ford.

When Reitman viewed the tape of the audition, he was startled.
The two actors seemed to click. He showed it to Ford, who agreed. To
confirm their judgment, they decided to test other actresses, a few of
whom came up with excellent readings, but in the end, they returned
to Anne Heche. "She seemed the most natural," Reitman said. "She
seemed very real. In a funny way, she got under your skin. And she
had that rare quality—an unspoken sexuality."

The precise nature of that sexuality was elusive, Reitman acknowledged. Heche had not as yet gone public with her relationship
with Ellen DeGeneres. "I had heard rumors that Anne was involved
in a lesbian relationship," Reitman acknowledges, but he tended to
dismiss it as a temporary fling and something that would certainly not
become a public issue. After all, no aspiring star—and Heche was
clearly ambitious—would broadcast a homosexual relationship.

Nonetheless, Reitman felt obliged to tell Joe Roth about Heche.
The new Disney boss, according to Reitman, was wary. The Disney
name was sacrosanct, Roth argued, and he had a responsibility to
protect the brand. He asked if there were any other strong contenders
for the role. Reitman replied that Heche was the clear leader. Roth
delivered the verdict: If she's the best for the part, then go with her.

Others close to Reitman and Ford were not so supportive. One of

Ford's key advisers told him bluntly, "You've got to be crazy. You don't make a high-profile love story with a lesbian." A very principled man, Ford resisted these warnings. He liked Anne Heche, and the idea of rejecting someone because of sexual preference deeply offended him. Besides, her private life was her own business.

The presumption of discretion was to prove illusory, however. Heche and DeGeneres soon decided that their relationship was everyone's business. Wherever they went—to premieres, charity events, restaurants—they made it a point to be seen, arms around each other, reiterating their romantic link. They even snuggled in front of President Clinton at the White House correspondents dinner. By the time *Six Days, Seven Nights* was released, theirs was the most ardently self-publicized lesbian relationship in the history of Hollywood. And privately, no one associated with the movie was happy about it.

While dealing with his controversial casting decisions, Reitman also was making some important changes in the script. Browning's screenplay was too one-note, the director felt. It needed to be spiced up with some comedy sequences and, to this end, he turned to Babaloo Mandel and Lowell Ganz, the oddly named writers who had served him well many times before. "Ivan is very specific," Ganz said. "Some directors will tell you something general, like, 'Give me a new third act.' Ivan will tell you exactly what he wants and where it should go."

Among the comic turns that emerged from the rewrite was a scene in which a water snake finds its way into Heche's pants and a series of scenes in which her presumed boyfriend, played by David Schwimmer, becomes romantically involved with a woman who works at the resort at which he and Heche had been staying. Still another addition was a rather long, intrusive section involving some marauding pirates who chase Ford and Heche across their deserted island.

The pirate section in particular aroused the concerns of some executives at the studio and especially Roger Birnbaum, the producer. In an effort to lighten up his movie, Reitman, they feared, was destroying any vestige of credibility. It's one thing for a movie to be funny; it's another to be silly. In Birnbaum's view, *Six Days, Seven Nights* was becoming just that. Reitman's script had lost some of the subtle story points of the original draft, such as a scene in which Ford and Heche discover a long-lost Japanese plane containing a letter from the pilot to his wife.

But Ivan Reitman was the man in charge, and his star, Ford, was going along with his decisions. The studio seemed more worried about Anne Heche than about script changes. These concerns were amplified as Heche began to give press interviews about the movie. To *Time* magazine, she said, "I'd be a fool not to recognize the fear and hesitation around this movie. Obviously it's super-exciting to play opposite Harrison Ford." She paused, lit a cigarette, then added: "But frankly, it wasn't as exciting as finding the love of my life."

The RECKONING

May—June

WEEK ONE Monday, May 11

It didn't feel like summer, the days still foggy and brisk, but by Hollywood's calendar, summer was at hand. The days of reckoning were approaching.

Hollywood was shrewd at concealing its high anxiety. A visitor could traverse studio corridors without detecting traces of panic. Executives proceeded calmly with their negotiations and pitch meetings. Assistants and other wannabes fetched coffee and exchanged gossip, then disappeared behind closed doors.

One happened upon the pockets of tension almost by accident. When I managed to penetrate the building in which *Godzilla*'s special effects were being mobilized in early May, it was akin to entering a homeless shelter. Bodies were passed out in sleeping bags on the concrete floor while others kept plugging away in what had become a desperate night-and-day exercise. Meanwhile, across town at the *Armageddon* editing rooms, the crews were red-eyed and bleary, looking more like hostages than artisans as they struggled to meet their dates and, at the same time, compress the overlong movie into a tenable running time.

All the while, on one project after another, the almost identical dialogue was taking place between the filmmakers and the studio suits. "We need to see the film," the suits pleaded relentlessly.

"We'd be glad to show you something, but the effects aren't ready," the director or producer responded.

"We have to show it to our distribution people, our marketing people, our publicity people."

"What can I tell you? It's a complicated process. . . ."

"The exhibitors think we're hiding it from them. So do the long-range critics. We promised them. . . ."

"We can show them the film without the effects. . . ."

"Bullshit. That's like walking them around a theme park and not letting them on the rides."

"We're working around the clock."

Sometimes the colloquy would end with a plea, sometimes with a veiled threat. Always it would end in frustration. There was simply nothing left to say.

John Calley, among others, was putting on a brave face. *Godzilla* would be wonderful, he kept assuring his troops at Sony. The movie was dragging so far behind schedule, he knew, that exhibitors wouldn't be able to see it until the eleventh hour, which technically meant that deals could not be closed until one day before the actual opening. Roughly 60 percent of the states had laws intended to prevent "block booking," which effectively forbids theater owners from booking movies until they had actually seen them.

Behind closed doors, however, associates reported that the normally good-natured Calley was seething. Having started as a hands-on producer, Calley was talented at suggesting cuts to improve the flow of a film, or reshuffling scenes to speed along the story. Despite his unstinting support for his *Godzilla* filmmakers, Dean Devlin and Roland Emmerich, Calley knew they could lapse into a B-picture sensibility. *Godzilla* would benefit from his input only if he could see it in time, and that was driving him crazy.

"John is brilliant at maintaining a facade," said one close associate, "but I could tell it was white-knuckle time."

For the first movies of summer, however, the moment of truth was already at hand. The town's best screening rooms were booked solid in preparation for the initial onslaught. Caterers were turning away business because of the crush of postpremiere parties.

Caught squarely in the spotlight on week one was *Deep Impact*. Both Paramount and DreamWorks, which had cofinanced the film, had wanted to grab the auspicious presummer weekend that had worked so brilliantly for *Twister* only two years earlier. *Deep Impact* could boast that it was the summer's first and, hopefully, definitive asteroid movie, while Disney's *Armageddon* was a mere blip on the horizon. Both studios could proudly tee off their summers with a Steven Spielberg production—a brand that in summers past had been a guarantee of box office prowess.

In reality, however, everything about *Deep Impact* had proven to be a lot tougher than anticipated, and now the downside of going first loomed large. While everyone on the project was grateful to Mimi Leder for stepping in after Spielberg's withdrawal as director, her presence nonetheless inspired a round of second-guessing. Her first effort for DreamWorks, *The Peacemaker*, released in September of 1997, had been accorded a respectable but undistinguished reception. It had grossed some $42 million in the U.S.

In taking over *Deep Impact*, Leder had little time to solve the problems of a convoluted script that no one felt was fully realized. Her cast, too, lacked a star presence, especially given its $80 million cost. Morgan Freeman was a respected character actor, but much of the movie rode on the unproven Tea Leoni. Inevitably, the questions were asked: Would Spielberg have agreed to direct this film without the security of a major star? Would he have insisted on one last round of rewrites to simplify the multistory format?

Working under intense pressure, Leder exuded a quiet self-confidence that helped mollify the doubters. She was, after all, a ten-year veteran of TV. Moreover, she was a second-generation filmmaker. Her father, Paul Leder, had specialized in B-picture fare—movies like *I Dismember Mama* and a 3-D ripoff of *King Kong* made in South Korea. He had died of lung cancer while *Deep Impact* was in preproduction.

Not long thereafter, Leder suffered another loss. Her director of photography on *Deep Impact* was Dietrick Lohmann, who had cut his teeth on several Rainer Werner Fassbinder films and had shot *The*

Peacemaker for her. On *Deep Impact,* however, he seemed to have trouble keeping up with the pace. His work was curiously inconsistent, and it was Leder who was catching the heat for it. What no one knew was that Lohmann, at fifty-four, was fighting leukemia. Toward the end of the shoot he was often absent from the set, with his camera operator filling in. Three weeks after the movie wrapped, Lohmann was dead. The movie carried a dedication to him in its closing credits.

Even without these side dramas, the ninety-day shoot had been arduous. While Leder understood how to use her camera and was decisive in her choices, she was accustomed to a contained set and to actors who understood their roles. This was hardly the case on *Deep Impact.* Moreover, shooting in and around the huge set that housed the comet had proved especially exasperating to her. What she could not have known was that the set was astonishingly similar to Michael Bay's asteroid that resided in a sound stage half an hour away in Burbank. Both sets were too big for the sound stages that housed them. Both exuded headache-inducing gases. Bay had confided to anyone who would listen to him that DreamWorks was sending spies to his set to copy its design as well as lines of dialogue. Leder and her producers, Richard Zanuck and David Brown, denied any such espionage. Nonetheless, the specter of *Armageddon* loomed over them all. Were they making essentially the same movie? If *Deep Impact* began to slip, would there be any chance that Disney could move up the dates on *Armageddon* and beat them?

All this was especially nettling to Leder. When she agreed to direct *Deep Impact,* she had not been briefed fully about the status of the rival movie. Spielberg's departure from the picture had been explained in terms of other factors—there was the sequel to *Jurassic Park* to contend with, not to mention *Amistad.* It was not until she was deeply enmeshed in her project that she realized that for Paramount and DreamWorks, Disney's *Armageddon* was not only a rival, it was an obsession. "The whole thing made me all the more determined to focus on the human element, not the comet," she reiterated to me at lunch as she was completing her postproduction work. "They would play with their *Dirty Dozen* in space. We had more serious spiritual and emotional issues to deal with."

Even as she was laboring in the editing room, Paramount's ad men were trying to develop a marketing strategy that reflected these loftier objectives without sacrificing the movie's action. It was, as one studio executive conceded, "a tough challenge." Translated, that means "a fucking nightmare." The movie's campaign had to look "Spielbergian." At the same time, the studio didn't want to seem like it was selling *Armageddon*.

Paramount's ad team faced another reality as well: They would never have the massive advertising dollars of their rivals at Disney. Sumner Redstone, the seventy-five-year-old head of Viacom, Paramount's parent company, understood the realities of the marketplace, but he also did not subscribe to what he regarded as Disney's profligate spending. "We knew Joe Roth would spend between $40 million and $50 million to open *Armageddon*," said a top Paramount executive. "This was simply beyond our range. Way beyond our range."

At the same time, Paramount could ill afford to be cautious. With *Godzilla* scheduled to open May 19, only eleven days after *Deep Impact*, an alarmingly narrow corridor of time was available in which to establish the movie in the public psyche. "The nightmare algebra of movies is that you have to grab half your gross in your first two weeks," said Arthur Cohen, Paramount's ad chief. "That's a pathetically small window."

Given these realities, the studio couldn't afford subtlety. Its TV ads and trailers showed the impact of the comet, showed the massive waves overwhelming cities and countryside. This was not a campaign for a thoughtful movie inspired by *On the Beach*. This was a good old-fashioned hard sell of a summer blockbuster. There was even an expensive campaign built around NBA basketball games with an asteroid shooting across the bottom of the TV screen.

"There were some of us who felt the campaign cheapened the movie," said one key member of *Deep Impact*'s creative team. But these pockets of resistance lost their bargaining power as an increas-

ingly negative buzz surrounded the movie. According to the buzzmak-
ers, that ubiquitous cluster of agents, managers, press mavens, and
wannabes who professed to see everything and go everywhere, *Deep
Impact* was too long and too confusing. That was the "inside word"
that was passed around town. And while studio officials tried their
best to combat these rumors, their efforts were severely undermined
by the results of their first test screening. A demographically representative audience had been invited to the Paramount studio theater
to see an initial cut of the film and they didn't like what they saw.

There was loud laughter during some of the movie's dramatic
scenes. People seemed fidgety and impatient for the movie to end. By
the time the filmmakers and studio suits filed out of the theater, they
knew they were in trouble.

The practice of holding test screenings on the lot was supremely
irritating to old pros like Zanuck and Brown. In their era a studio
would take the first cut of a film to a distant city and show it to a
"real" audience under conditions of secrecy. But studio regimes had
been persuaded by their research gurus that on-the-lot screenings
were more accurate, controllable, and considerably less expensive.
The downside was that the results instantly became grist for public
gossip, with precise analyses of the screenings appearing on the Internet the next morning.

Such was the case with *Deep Impact*. The bad buzz was all over
town. Immediately after the first screening, Sherry Lansing led a grim
parade back to her office. No one talked during the ten-minute walk.
"It was like the Bataan March," said one DreamWorks functionary.
In her office, Lansing led the critique and was both specific and candid. The movie had played well except when the teen lovers occupied
center stage. The kids had been miscast. The audience wasn't intrigued by their story. Their scenes would have to be cut back sharply.
Further, a stronger, more upbeat ending would have to be shot—
perhaps Morgan Freeman as the president could deliver an inspirational speech from his wrecked White House.

An intense discussion followed. The assessment of the kids was unanimously accepted. Some were surprised that the scenes between Tea Leoni and her father played as well as they did. The movie needed to be warmed up—more shots of women clasping their babies, farewells to loved ones, that sort of thing.

It fell to Walter Parkes from DreamWorks, working with Mimi Leder, to write and orchestrate the necessary cuts and reshoots. It would be an exacting chore; the time pressures were extreme. Parkes, lanky and laconic, had been through this sort of thing before. He felt the movie was eminently fixable.

It also fell to him to make the necessary call to Spielberg. The filmmaker never attended test screenings. He didn't really believe in them and, besides, they made him nervous. But he wanted to hear the facts and he also wanted to know the proposed solutions. "You don't give Steven a problem without suggesting a response," said one long-time aide. Parkes made the call. Spielberg took it matter-of-factly. He suggested some additional cuts and fixes. Parkes hung up and went to work.

It was three weeks before a second test screening was scheduled. The movie shown to this audience on the Paramount lot was twenty minutes shorter and contained the new ending. The response of the audience was vastly more encouraging. "The movie played well," said a DreamWorks executive. "Not great, mind you, but well."

With the release date now upon them, the studio was cautious about making any box office predictions. An opening weekend in the range of $25 million to $30 million was in the cards, they ventured. No one would proclaim it an instant blockbuster, but it had the potential to build from there.

Their wariness increased after the first screening for the media. Not surprisingly, the studio theater was packed. There was no derisive laughter during the movie; indeed, the audience seemed rapt. Once the screening was over, scores of critics and reporters gathered around the theater to argue about the film—an extraordinary occurrence for the blasé media crowd, which customarily marched off toward the parking lot without a moment's banter. The reaction was sharply divided between the naysayers (weak story, plastic characters, lame effects) and the admirers (great concept, solid character-driven narrative, vivid visuals). It was a good half hour before the debates started to wind down.

Even the most experienced of studio veterans were unsure how to read this reaction. The movie had stimulated public discussion—that was encouraging. On the other hand, a substantial number of media people seemed downright indignant that the movie didn't deliver. This did not augur well in terms of the critics, and the filmmakers had been counting on solid critical support.

By Monday, May 11, however, *Deep Impact*'s naysayers were in full retreat as the numbers rolled in. The movie registered an opening salvo of $41.9 million for its first three days, a number that surpassed the previous record for a May opening set by another high-profile disaster movie, *Twister*. *Deep Impact* totally buried its competition: *City of Angels*, its nearest competitor, took in a meager $4.7 million. And no one was more surprised by these results than the Paramount PR machine. Reacting to the general aura of skepticism, the studio's estimates of between $25 million and $30 million now seemed downright tame.

Exit polls offered even further encouragement, indicating an even mix between men and women. Older moviegoers outnumbered the young, but by a narrow margin. What all this portended was that *Deep Impact* might develop "legs"—that its audience would not melt away after the initial advertising fusillade had subsided.

And if this came true, *Deep Impact* potentially could even cast a cloud over that second asteroid epic, *Armageddon*, scheduled to open only eight weeks later. If the Spielberg picture proved to be a self-fulfilling prophecy—if it had truly made a "deep impact" on the public—that in itself might inhibit the appetite for another movie of the same genre.

The naysayers were quick to point out, however, that while *Twister* had found a relatively clear field last May, *Deep Impact* could cruise for little more than a week before it faced its own potential armageddon—the May 19 unveiling of *Godzilla*. Hence, while *Twister* ultimately grossed $241.7 million domestically and $251.9 million abroad, no one expected *Deep Impact* to approach the magic $500 million circle. The reasoning related not only to competition, but also to the fact that the movie presented itself as a serious picture, not as popcorn fare.

Serious or not, audiences were finding *Deep Impact* to be immensely entertaining, which seemed all the more important given *Godzilla*'s looming presence. To be sure, no one in the media, nor even exhibitors for that matter, had seen the Sony movie because the special effects still were not completed—at least that was the studio's story. Another theory was that *Godzilla*'s producers, having so assiduously concealed the monster's look (the lizard toys were still not in the stores), had opted to build suspense until the last possible moment, even at the studio.

The strategy seemed to be working. Surveys indicated a remarkable 95 percent "awareness" of *Godzilla*, and it ranked as first choice in the want-to-see category among that pivotal young male audience. By contrast, Robert Redford's movie, *The Horse Whisperer*, ranked as first choice among older women and low among the kids. *Bulworth*, starring Warren Beatty, registered abysmal numbers in its tracking studies. Despite the near-frenzy of personal appearances and adulatory magazine articles, Beatty's movie remained off the radar.

While *Deep Impact* clearly was stealing the spotlight, it nonetheless evoked sharply divided responses from critics. Toughest on the movie was Mike Clark of *USA Today*, who wrote: "The dull and ironically titled *Deep Impact* won't have much of one after its opening weekend." Clark, of course, was wrong in his forecast. "*Impact*'s many meaningless story threads leave you praying the Eastern seaboard will finally get smeared," he concluded.

Other critics, while impatient with the conventions of the disaster genre, were appreciative of the film's humanistic aspirations. "Hey guys, how's this for a twist? Let's take the end of the world seriously. Geez, how square can you get?" wrote Richard Schickel in *Time* magazine, but he went on to acknowledge: "There's something curiously refreshing in the soberly inspirational way *Deep Impact* embraces the conventions of the old-fashioned disaster movie."

Kenneth Turan of the *Los Angeles Times* tended to agree: "The latest in Hollywood's almost Biblical procession of disaster films, *Deep Impact*, tries with moderate success to be more than just the sum of its special effects."

Janet Maslin of *The New York Times* also felt that Mimi Leder directed the film "with a distinctly womanly touch. . . . It's rare to find attention paid to rescuing art, antiques, elephants, and flamingos or to see the day care center at the television station." While not delivering a rave, Maslin's mood was one of resignation: "We will survive to be hit by another comet picture in July."

Like so much else connected with the movie business, the reporting of grosses was intensely ritualistic. It was Sunday evening when radio and TV news shows started reporting the rankings of newly released films. Studio executives by late Friday night, however, already had a pretty good sense of the winners and losers. By the time multiplexes on the East Coast had sold their tickets to the Friday late show, the studio crunchers already were sending forth their projections. And distribution executives, even as they sipped their coffee Saturday morning, were dialing up their studio chiefs, producers, stars, agents, and others to deliver the good or bad news.

That information was immediately acted upon. If the initial news is upbeat, studios may step up their TV spots. "The best way to make money is to make a big hit bigger," said Jeff Blake of Sony. If the news was bad, however, the ad budget may instantly be cut and multiplexes will reduce the number of screens on which the film is playing. Since roughly 70 percent of ad dollars were spent in and around opening week, studios were quick to open or close the throttle.

In making their projections, distribution chiefs do not rely on data alone. Exit polls also weighed heavily. The opening numbers weren't outstanding on *Armageddon*, but exit polls indicated that audiences liked the movie and were recommending it to friends. The bullish forecasts turned out to be valid.

It's a delicate art, however. Movies appealing to the young male demographic tended to perform well on Friday night, but adult films do better on Saturday and family pictures may have strong Saturday and Sunday matinees. Some films appealing to blacks, like *Soul Food,* experience a strong Sunday night upswing. Word-of-mouth also figured in. Not that many people saw *There's Something About Mary* on its opening Friday, but they apparently told enough of their friends that, by the following weekend, business already was picking up.

"We can be fooled some of the time, but in 80 percent of the cases, we can predict a movie's ultimate gross within a $5 million margin based on the initial Friday night results," observed Fox's Tom Sherak.

Most filmmakers were hungry for these results. When his first film opened, Brett Ratner, a young director, called New Line distribution executives every fifteen minutes and also dialed theaters in New York and Miami to inquire directly about ticket sales. The movie was appropriately titled *Money Talks*.

Steven Spielberg, by contrast, specifically instructed associates not to inform him about box office results until Monday morning. When producer David Permut had a new movie opening, he habitually checked into the Canyon Ranch in Tucson, Arizona, on a Friday afternoon and took long walks so no one could reach him.

By Sunday morning the distribution chiefs, having filled in their colleagues, start calling key members of the press to spread the word. Often the process of achieving the number one position becomes a test of gamesmanship. A distribution chief, for example, may call *Variety*'s box officer reporter, Andrew Hindes, and inquire what his rivals at other studios have reported. If his film is running neck-and-neck with a competitor, he will offer a higher number. Not until Tuesday morning were the official numbers announced by a company called Entertainment Data, Inc., which based its estimates on hundreds of phone calls made by its employees directly to theaters. By that time the ads would already be in the newspapers claiming that the film in question is "the number one movie in America." Given the herd instincts of the moviegoing public, this information helps build momentum, even if the basic data itself may be exaggerated. The machinery of hit-making had been set in motion.

WEEK TWO Monday, May 18

This was a weekend of dire portents, nasty rumors, and delicious ironies—exactly the sort of weekend Hollywood coveted. It was the weekend when those splendidly narcissistic old rivals, Warren Beatty and Robert Redford, went head to head with their new movies; when the two blockbusters that supposedly would "own" the summer, *Armageddon* and *Godzilla*, both received hostile receptions at their initial public screenings; when Warner Bros. tanked with its expensive new animated movie that had been designed to break Disney's generation-long lock on the animation business.

By Monday, even the most battle-hardened industry hands were doing their best to make sense of their faxes, e-mails, and box office data and regain their equilibrium.

It was the initial reaction to *Godzilla* and *Armageddon* that galvanized attention. Disney had decided to unveil fifty minutes of *Armageddon* before an invited audience at the Cannes Film Festival, but the audience seemed more appalled than awed. Disney spinmeisters dismissed the skeptics, pointing out that Festival audiences, expecially those at Cannes, traditionally were suspicious of Hollywood blockbusters.

Sony's PR brigade was similarly dismissive of the negative buzz following *Godzilla* media screenings in Los Angeles and New York. Since the press had proclaimed *Godzilla* to be the most overhyped movie of the decade, it was inevitable that the media would turn on the movie. The movie would still be the biggest hit of summer.

Despite the spin, however, a good number of marketing and distribution people on Monday were rubbing their eyes wearily and wondering aloud, "Could this be the summer that defies all forecasts?"

Amid all these doubts, there was no arguing with the hard numbers of the weekend. *Deep Impact*, the first surprise hit of summer, pulled in another $23.2 million, bringing its total gross for the first ten days to $74 million. Though the second weekend represented a 43 percent dropoff, the movie nonetheless would clearly join the coveted $100 million club and establish itself as a major international success.

The Horse Whisperer, the Robert Redford vehicle, did not open that impressively, nor was it expected to. The film had a $14 million weekend on 2,039 screens, for a respectable $6,866 average per screen. Optimists at Disney pointed out that these were strong numbers considering its two-hour, forty-four-minute running time and that the national magazine critics, especially *Time* and *Newsweek*, had given it the roughest reviews of any Redford movie in memory. The audiences skewed toward older females according to studio exit polls: A 55 percent–45 percent female-male split was the guess. Disney had decided to spread the movie into many smaller communities rather than saturate the big cities that Fox was targeting for *Bulworth*. The model for this strategy was *The Bridges of Madison County*, the 1995 Warner Bros. movie starring Clint Eastwood, which ended up grossing a satisfactory $71.5 million in North America. *Bridges*, like *Horse Whisperer*, represented an adaptation of a romantic best-seller set in rural America; both also featured older leading men, Redford and Eastwood.

Fox's *Bulworth* battle plan was antithetical to Disney's bucolic strategy in every detail. *Bulworth* opened at only two theaters, one in New York and the other in Los Angeles. And with Warren Beatty all but bludgeoning the media into submission, the movie registered an eminently respectable $135,000. In an era of megascreen openings— *Godzilla* imminently would grab over 7,000 screens for its first weekend—the *Bulworth* approach represented a throwback to the seventies, when studios counted on strong reviews and potent word-of-mouth to build an audience. "This extra lead-in week will help a lot," observed Tom Sherak, chairman of the Fox Film Group and a buoyant cheerleader. "Next weekend will be huge for everyone." By putting its toe into the water, he hoped, *Bulworth* would avoid being obliterated by the onslaught of *Godzilla*.

While *The Horse Whisperer* and *Bulworth* could point to some healthy portents, such could not be said for the Warner Bros. animated entry, *Quest for Camelot*. Grossing a mere $6.4 million on 2,245 screens, the movie's pathetic $2,000 per-screen average hardly justified the studio's massive ad spending of the past two weeks. Throughout this weekend newspapers nationwide ran lavish full-page color ads depicting Arthurian characters posed against a background of warm-and-cuddly creatures. "Exciting and enchanting. Happily-ever-after-entertainment," proclaimed a quote attributed to Gene Shalit on the "Today Show." Shalit was virtually alone in giving the movie a wet kiss. Barry Reardon, the thoughtful if battle-weary Warner distribution chief, said the movie was hurt not only by mediocre reviews but by a premature release date—not enough kids were on their summer vacations yet. "Some animated pictures take a little time to get going," he said hopefully.

Reardon knew his bosses at the studio had been zealous about making a dent in Disney's stranglehold over animation, which remained the single most profitable sector of the film industry. Warner's first effort in this arena, *Space Jam*, a combined animation–and–live-action feature starring Michael Jordan, had grossed a respectable $90 million in the U.S. and also had proven to be a merchandising bonanza. As a result, Warner Bros. had invested between $120 million and $150 million in *Quest for Camelot*—the actual number depended on how the start-up costs of the new animation facility were accounted for. In any case, the potential loss loomed large.

While Hollywood was adding up the winners and losers of Week Two, their colleagues at the Cannes Film Festival were busily trying to create some excitement in the European press for their upcoming releases. Disney, which usually ignored the Festival, decided for a big presence, not only showing the fifty minutes of *Armageddon* but accompanying it with a press conference and party honoring Bruce Willis, Michael Bay, and Jerry Bruckheimer. While some festival veterans thought it was bizarre to show a Hollywood blockbuster to the elitist Cannes audience, Disney's representative claimed that hundreds had to be turned away because of lack of space.

Not surprisingly, many in the audience seemed less than enamored of the high-decibel, effects-laden mayhem, and there were spasms of laughter during scenes that were supposed to hold dramatic tension. These outbursts did not escape the attention of the irascible Willis, who held forth at the postscreening press conference. Willis's behavior had always been erratic at Cannes—one year he hurled epithets at reporters and stalked out of a press conference. He was more restrained this year. "Thank you for watching a fifty-minute commercial for the movie," he told reporters. "And thank you for enjoying the comical aspects of the film. I'm glad you all took the end of the world so well."

When asked why the roles he accepted were so uniformly heroic, Willis responded, "In America my name is in our Yellow Pages under World Saver." Willis and his director could not resist taking a few shots at their rival asteroid epic, *Deep Impact*. "Not to trash their movie, but it's not one I'd want to make," Willis confided. "At least in ours, we have a lot of fun."

One French reporter pointed out, gratefully, that the scenes of mass destruction focused on the U.S., not Europe. "Not so," said Willis. "We're shooting new scenes all around the world, in Paris, India, and Turkey," thus giving away a fact that his studio was hoping to conceal. Following an early test screening, crews had been dispatched at considerable expense to shoot added doomsday material, with the Eiffel Tower predictably among the targets of destruction.

Armageddon's difficulties were minor compared with those of *Godzilla*, whose first media screenings were staged amid great fanfare at New York City's Madison Square Garden and Los Angeles's Dome

Theater. Both venues, not surprisingly, were packed, with long lines forming half an hour before screening time.

Industry interest was such that a substantial number of top executives infiltrated the Los Angeles press screening, strolling in at the side of reporters and trying to look inconspicuous. Many reporters in New York had been puzzled as to why Madison Square Garden had been selected—no one could recall a previous screening at that facility. The explanation became obvious at the point in the movie when *Godzilla* started laying his eggs throughout the Garden and when his raptorlike progeny, looking like escapees from *Jurassic Park*, started breaking out of their shells en masse.

When the critics finally made their escape, they made no effort to conceal their disdain. One Sony publicist, overhearing their remarks, shook his head wearily: "Thank goodness we've just got the second- and third-string critics here. They can do less harm." The top reviewers of the major magazines and newspapers had been sent to Cannes. Nonetheless, a surprising number of those in attendance seemed downright angered by the movie, claiming it was too long, too noisy, and lacking in real tension.

The movie that proclaimed that "size DOES matter" was in fact a seismic disappointment, they declared. The official Sony response was terse—when the movie opens, the numbers will speak for themselves.

By the time I'd entered the movie business in 1967, Warren Beatty and Robert Redford had already become players. Beatty had served a brief apprenticeship in television—his bios never mention his humble supporting role in "The Many Loves of Dobie Gillis"—before hitting instant stardom in *Splendor in the Grass* in 1966. *Bonnie and Clyde* two years later, which he produced and starred in, was to provide him with his credential as filmmaker, a badge which Beatty, always a bit of a snob, deeply coveted. Redford had begun to make a mark doing light comedy in such mid-sixties movies as *Barefoot in the Park* before graduating to the superstar firmament with the 1969 western *Butch Cassidy and the Sundance Kid*.

I knew both in that period; not on a personal level, but in my role as a young studio suit. I served as vice president for production at Paramount, and they were included among my constituencies. We were roughly the same age; the two seemed to respond to the fact that I was not another former agent or attorney trying to shove my way into the business, but that, as a former *New York Times* reporter, I had covered some important stories and was willing, as were they, to haul home my share of screenplays every weekend.

Inevitably, our paths kept intersecting. Beatty and I cooked up a thriller called *The Parallax View*; I worked on such early Redford movies as *Downhill Racer* and *Little Fauss and Big Halsey*. And I had frequent dialogues with both as various hot screenplays were brought to their attention.

Beatty, a master of one-upmanship, would systematically let it be known that he had read and rejected every script to which Redford had committed, including *Butch Cassidy*. "I read that—it was a lousy part," Beatty would relate during his often-rambling phone conversations. Redford, on the other hand, while equally manipulative and self-protective, was more circumspect in his put-downs. Beatty, he would hint, was more interested in negotiating than he was in acting.

The ensuing years would suggest that Redford was indeed the shrewder in selecting his roles. Eight of his twenty-nine movies were certifiable hits compared with only four of Beatty's twenty-one films. Up until summer '98, each had directed only four films—a rather slim filmography—and again Redford seemed the more perspicacious. All of his efforts as *auteur*—*Ordinary People*, *The Milagro Beanfield War*, *A River Runs Through It*, and *Quiz Show*—were memorable in one way or another, though only *Ordinary People* fulfilled box office expectations. By contrast, Beatty's offerings were erratic at best, ranging from the remarkable *Reds* to *Love Affair*, which was a textbook exercise in narcissism. *Heaven Can Wait* and *Dick Tracy* were glossy but eminently forgettable.

As young actors in the sixties, both Beatty and Redford carried themselves with a cocky "I've-got-this-scene-figured-out" air about them. Both could be immensely engaging in conversation when they wanted to be. Unlike other budding stars of that period—Steve McQueen and Marlon Brando, for example—they had the smarts; they not only read scripts, they even read newspapers. At the same time there was a remoteness in their personalities, as though, even then, they knew that they were destined to dwell in that rarefied stratum of celebrityhood that would grant them unique access—social, financial, and sexual. When they wanted to talk about something, they were in your face. When problems arose, you couldn't get them on the phone.

I lived through many problems with both. I talked Redford into doing a Western called *Blue*, which was to be directed by an interesting young Canadian director named Silvio Narizzano, who had just made a hit in London called *Georgy Girl*. Redford met with Narizzano and they liked each other. The deals were put in place and a start date agreed upon. But even as sets were being built and locations selected, Redford had a sudden change of heart. As Redford admitted years later, he simply went for a long drive and decided the movie was a mistake. I never got a call from him; indeed, no one did. His idea of an explanation was a no-show.

On the other hand, as flaky and narcissistic as Beatty could be, when problems arose, his inclination was to roll up his sleeves and get to work. On *The Parallax View*, even as the start of principal photography loomed, the Writers Guild suddenly took the extraordinary measure of calling a strike. Our screenplay was still far from completion—key scenes were being rewritten and Beatty was panicky. "I don't want to start a movie without a script," he complained, withdrawing to his house for several days. Then suddenly a new Beatty emerged: He was coming down to the office to get his picture going, even if it meant doing some of the writing himself. He did, and the movie started on time.

These two incidents focused my understanding of these two curious but immensely talented men. Beatty was the priapic prince who seemed to have memorized the phone numbers of every beautiful woman in America, but there was always a side to him that was accessible and committed. Redford, on the other hand, was distant and nonconfrontational—"the most Presbyterian superstar in the history of Hollywood," one director tabbed him. Significantly, while each chose to live on a mountaintop, Beatty's was atop Mulholland Drive overlooking Hollywood (until it was destroyed in the recent earthquake), while Redford's was in Utah, very far from the madding crowd.

The films Redford chose to direct reflected his view of the world. By and large, they spoke to solid middle-class values and to noble ideals. *Ordinary People*, in particular, was prototypical Redford: mannered, buttoned-up, and a bit forbidding.

In choosing his roles, Redford tended to favor upright characters. His biggest deviation was *Little Fauss and Big Halsey*, a raucous, elliptical film made in 1969 that dealt with the world of motorbike racing. The script was written by Charles Eastman, a brilliant counterculture writer of that period, whose scripts were picaresque and novelistic. Big Halsey was hardly a Redford type of person: He was a charming lowlife who drank and brawled and flirted with every woman he encountered. Coming on the heels of *Butch Cassidy and the Sundance Kid*, it seemed like a risky proposition.

Albert S. Ruddy, who produced the film, recalled that Redford threw himself into his character, but still remained aloof from the free-spirited, down-and-dirty crew. "It was as if he were armored," Ruddy recalls. "If you pressed hard you could get him to relax and have a beer, but by and large, he remained off by himself. There was no dope or booze around him, which in that period set him apart from the rest of the world. He had his wife and kids visit him from time to time. He was Big Halsey on the set, but he was Redford the rest of the time."

While Beatty came out of hiding regularly to participate in political forays on behalf of liberal candidates (he was Bobby Kennedy's confidant, Gary Hart's handler), Redford's major commitment in public life was to his Sundance Festival in Utah, struggling over the years to sustain its dedication to serious filmmaking. As Sundance kept growing, Redford continually battled to limit the incursions of Hollywood at the festival. While sustaining this activity, however, Redford, unlike other stars such as Bruce Willis, focused his personal career on traditional Hollywood vehicles, never straying into Sundance-like independent film.

Given these sharply contrasting styles and attitudes, Hollywood insiders relished the irony that, in summer '98, there would be a serious face-off between these two durable, ego-driven stars. Each had made an extraordinary commitment to his respective project, deciding not only to star, but also to direct (while Beatty had done double duty before, the more conservative Redford had never done so). And the movies they selected could not have differed more dramatically. *The Horse Whisperer* was ennobling and romantic (some called it soapy); Beatty's *Bulworth* was raw and abrasively satiric. Redford presented himself as the rustic hero, Beatty as a neurotic politician whose life was absurdly unraveling. In his film, Redford comes to terms with the forces of nature even as Beatty spins out of control in the inner city. And, typically, while Redford and his project were eagerly courted by Hollywood, Beatty had to scheme and cajole to get his through the back door.

As luck would have it, *The Horse Whisperer* and *Bulworth* opened on the same day, May 15—a fact that annoyed the hell out of Beatty, but didn't bother Redford at all.

It infuriated Beatty that, while *The Horse Whisperer* had owned its weekend for months, it was not until the last minute that Fox had notified him of his release date. This behavior, in Beatty's eyes, suggested game-playing by the studio. It was no secret that *Bulworth* did not represent the present regime, but was inherited from the Barry Diller era eight years earlier. Not until early May did Beatty finally learn *Bulworth* would have a summer release—in itself a controversial time in which to release a political satire.

It was Tom Sherak, a cheerful, high-spirited man who heads distribution for Fox, who notified Beatty. "I have great news for you, Warren," Sherak said, "We're high on *Bulworth*. We want to give it a prime play-date in summer."

Beatty, who even in the best times was given to long conversational pauses, gave this news an especially lengthy time to sink in. He had always feared that Rupert Murdoch, who controlled Fox and who held rather vehement right-wing views, would screen his film and then smother it. But now—summer! "I'm pleased to hear this," Beatty replied in his usual measured cadence. "What's the date?"

"We're going out May 22," Sherak piped. "You'd have only one other film to compete with on that date."

"And what exactly is that one other picture?"

"*Godzilla*," Sherak blurted.

The pause was now especially pregnant. Beatty's gut reaction was the realization that he'd been sandbagged after all. He had his prime date, but what chance did he have against *Godzilla*?

He would think it over, he advised Sherak. But even as he hung up, he grew more disturbed. If he delayed his movie a few weeks, he would run into a firestorm of summer blockbusters—a Spielbergian lineup of $100 million special-effects pictures. On the other hand, he stood a much better shot if he moved it forward by one week to get into the theaters before the summer heated up. The only problem: *The Horse Whisperer* was opening that week and if there was one thing Warren Beatty did not covet, it was running up against his old rival.

In the end, Beatty decided to hedge his bet. He phoned Sherak, telling him the May 22 date would be okay, but he wanted two theaters for the previous weekend. In a way, it was appropriate, he argued. *Bulworth* was a throwback to the personal filmmaking of the sixties and early seventies. He had produced, directed, cowritten, and starred in it. The movie embodied his point of view. Therefore why not do what most companies did a generation earlier—open in select situations and let word of mouth promote the film's prospects?

Remarkably, none of the major newspapers or magazines, in reviewing or writing about the two films, compared their two *auteurs*. Indeed, on the surface the critical reception was almost identical. In *Variety*'s Crix Pix, a weekly canvassing of the national critical response, *Bulworth* was greeted with sixteen "pro" reviews, four "cons" (negative reviews), and four "mixed." *The Horse Whisperer* received fifteen "pros," four "cons," and three "mixed."

The big difference, however, was that the positive *Bulworth* reviews were downright ecstatic, brimming with quotable lines. The Redford reviews, on the other hand, were politely approving, but many commented on the fact that the film, at almost three hours, overstayed its welcome.

Time and *Newsweek* deviated from the national norm, both giving raves to Beatty and pounding Redford fiercely. Even Richard Schickel, *Time*'s veteran critic who had once collaborated with Redford on a documentary, seemed utterly exasperated by Redford's idealizing "the simple, natural life." He wrote: "Doubtless Redford believes in the ideals that animate this movie, as who among us does not. But the very fact that he is so well known and widely applauded for his many good, politically and artistically correct works offscreen helps make this movie seem self-regarding, self-righteous, even smug." Tom Booker, the character Redford designed for himself, is nothing more than "a rustic bore," Schickel protested. "The question is, can we manage nearly three hours in the company of so perfect a male animal, a figure from whom, in fact, everything animalistic, for that matter anything jaggedly human, has been blanched?"

Kenneth Turan, the *Los Angeles Times* film critic, pursued a similar line: "Robert Redford, who for the first time stars in a movie he's also directed, has taken soap opera material and treated it like something inscribed in yak vellum by the Dalai Lama. The lack of identifiable passion is *The Horse Whisperer*'s most vexing problem. Redford directs everything smoothly, but from a distance, with too few natural moments. This kind of story needs to be more vital, to capture audiences by force and make them believe. Redford's careful, respectful style can do a lot, but that is not within its powers."

Newsweek's Jeff Giles was equally brutal, calling Redford "a big bore beneath a big sky." He added, "For a man who has criticized the media's preoccupation with looks, there's an awful lot of sunlight and moonlight and firelight in his hair. It's as if Redford figures he's such an icon he can break hearts just standing still."

By contrast, the important media critics pulled out all stops in heaping praise on Beatty's production and performance. Even the most cynical writers seemed startled that Beatty would take such bold risks—that his performance would be so daring, the targets of his satire so close to home. "Like Bulworth the senator, Beatty the director . . . is throwing caution to the wind, producing a genuinely political movie in an era deeply suspicious of political passion," wrote David Ansen in *Newsweek*. "Savaging Hollywood as well as Washington, Beatty then compounds the risk by sending his discombobulated hero into the inner city for a crash course in socioeconomic consciousness-raising."

Just about every magazine seemed eager to slap Beatty on its cover, even *The New York Times Magazine*, which customarily looked askance at showbiz covers. Lynn Hirschberg, a rather ferocious entertainment writer who had helped trash the careers of several industry figures (her piece on ABC programming executive Jamie Tarses almost cost Tarses her job), wrote a very long, very admiring piece on Beatty, casting him in his favorite role as the embattled underdog.

Though she took the reader through all of the star's seductive tactics—the purring phone voice, the very calculated personal interest he takes in his interviewers, the long conversational pauses of the pained artist—she also succumbed completely to his act. Beatty emerged as a combination of Alexis de Tocqueville and Victor Hugo, desperate to convey his tormented vision to a philistine audience. "When you're making a movie, it's a little like telling a joke underwater in slow motion," she quoted him as saying. "You think, Am I kidding myself? Can you hear me?"

In the days and weeks prior to the May 15 face-off between the Beatty and Redford movies, exhibitors were perplexed by the projects. Redford was late in delivering his finished version of *The Horse Whisperer*, necessitating eleventh-hour screenings for the long-range press and representatives of theater chains. Exhibitors quickly concluded that this was a film aimed at heartland America—a picture that would appeal more to women than to the male audience.

The ever-canny Beatty, meanwhile, decided to take a more aggressive, hands-on approach. He knew that he was surrounded by doubters: Tracking studies had shown that startlingly few regular moviegoers singled out *Bulworth* as their first choice to see. Indeed, despite efforts to publicize his movie, few even knew of its existence.

If there's one thing a star deplores, it's being ignored, and Beatty began to work feverishly to attract attention to his movie. Abjuring the usual press screenings, he took his picture to academics at Harvard; political journalists in Washington; to Julian Bond, board chairman of the NAACP; and to virtually anyone else who could be considered an opinion leader. Deftly obliterating the line between news and entertainment, Beatty even talked his way onto ABC's "This Week," the Washington, D.C., show starring Sam Donaldson and Cokie Roberts, and showed some *Bulworth* clips. An ABC network PR representative conceded that this was the first time an actor had succeeded in hustling his movie on a political talk show.

Not to be outdone, Tim Russert opened a segment of "Meet the Press" with a short taped interview with Beatty. Nor did Beatty limit his attack to the news ghetto. He boldly invaded the daytime women's shows, chatting it up with one gushing hostess after another. He even agreed to a Howard Stern interview, looking like a deer in the headlights as the shock jock peppered him with his predictable questions about women he had bedded. It was Stern who finally blurted in mid-show, "God, you're a lousy interview."

And he was. Beatty never had become comfortable on the interview circuit and, by and large, had absented himself from media blitzes. Part of the reason was his yen for privacy, but another stemmed from a certain intellectual snobbery. He recoiled at dumb questions, usually responding with dumb answers.

It was in the midst of this media frenzy that I had a quick lunch with Beatty at an Italian restaurant near Fox and found him even edgier and more evasive than usual. A column of mine had been published that morning in *Daily Variety,* in which I argued that the economics of the star system had begun to unravel. Pointing to a succession of recent star-driven films that had failed to attract opening-day audiences, I took the position that the $20 million star salary, not to mention the 10 percent to 15 percent cut of the gross receipts, was increasingly untenable in the eyes of top studio executives in town.

Seating himself at my table, Beatty could not wait to do battle. "The column is simply wrong," he said, in his customary urgent tones. "The star system is at the center of Hollywood, and these salaries are at the center of the star system."

"Aren't you uncomfortable taking this position?" I queried. "After all, one of the major points you make in *Bulworth* revolves around the unfair apportionment of income in this country. A tiny minority makes the big bucks and the rest of the nation isn't doing any better than they did one or two generations ago—that's your thesis, right?"

Beatty did not even blink. "Stars are different," he intoned. "We're talking about movie stars." And having made this important distinction, he picked up the menu and started ordering.

Later, relaxed by his heaping portions of risotto, fish, and steamed vegetables (Beatty loves to eat), he confessed his concern about his movie's weak tracking. The problem with focusing the public's attention on a movie like *Bulworth,* he fretted, was that this sort of film depended on word of mouth—that the entire system of marketing movies as it has evolved today militates against this process.

"Today it's all about TV spots," he complained. "You make the big TV ad buy. Maybe a spot during the NBA playoffs. Inevitably, you start tailoring the movies you make to lend themselves to TV spots. Then you spend so many millions of dollars on TV advertising that you have to open the movie everywhere—two thousand screens, four thousand screens, all simultaneously."

What most worried Beatty was whether Fox, his distributor, would continue to support his film if it didn't open to good numbers. Over the years, Beatty had become a master at studio gamesmanship—he knew how to manipulate the studio chiefs and the ad people to play the game his way. I had seen him skillfully playing his role over the years with several studios, cajoling, bullying, flattering, threatening.

In setting up his projects, Beatty had become proficient at playing one studio against another to improve his leverage. Every Beatty project had ricocheted between studios, with Beatty always improving not only the numbers but also the degree of his control.

Even on *Bonnie and Clyde*, his first caper, Beatty had to pull out every stop to hold his project together. Arthur Penn tried to withdraw when he read the final script. Beatty kept him in by hiring Bob Towne to do a quick rewrite, knowing Towne only does slow rewrites. When Jack Warner saw the final cut, the moment the lights went on after the screening, the old man demanded: "What the fuck is this?" Again, it took weeks of cajoling and renegotiation to keep the studio from withdrawing, and even the initial release was more symbolic than real.

"The irony of all this," Beatty told me at lunch, "was that *Bulworth* was my most controversial movie by far, yet it turned out to be the only one that I didn't have to switch from one studio to another." On *Heaven Can Wait*, Beatty, for example, had gotten into an eleventh-hour fight over the deal with Frank Wells, then the top business affairs executive at Warner Bros., and had abruptly pulled his movie over to Paramount. *Dick Tracy*, originally set up at Fox, was yanked over to Disney, a result of yet another power struggle. *Bulworth*, however, with all its potential problems, had remained steadfast at Fox, much to the ultimate chagrin of Rupert Murdoch.

While Beatty was going through his contortions, Redford was having his usual smooth sailing at Disney. Even the process of obtaining the rights to *The Horse Whisperer* had been a well-oiled exercise.

By the time Redford had expressed his interest in the book by neophyte British novelist Nicholas Evans, it already had become a cause célèbre. Even before the book's completion, the first two hundred pages of the manuscript had fallen into the hands of a curious subspecies of the publishing community known as trackers. These are the story scouts who sift through the literary flora and fauna in search of that occasional hot item that could attract the attention of movie studios and foreign publishers.

Thrillers from big-name authors usually provide the grist for the tracker mill, but for some reason the surreptitiously Xeroxed two hundred pages of *The Horse Whisperer* triggered a veritable frenzy. Scott Rudin, the New York–based producer, offered $500,000 in an effort to take the book off the market, but that only served to stimulate still other bids from Peter Guber, Wendy Finerman (who had produced *Forrest Gump*), and Jon Peters, the excitable ex-partner of Guber. The negotiations up to this point had been conducted by a venerable British literary agency called A. P. Watt, the chief of which, Caradoc King, quickly realized that, amid this stratospheric bidding, he was out of his league. He had become acquainted some time earlier with a literary agent at CAA named Bob Bookman, a round-faced bon vivant who thrived on this sort of overheated auction. He had recently consummated enormous deals for a Michael Crichton novel called *Disclosure*, which sold for $3.5 million, as well as $3.75 million for John Grisham's *The Chamber*.

The moment King brought Bookman into *The Horse Whisperer* melee, all the ingredients were set for a splendid bidding war. For one thing, Bookman knew Peters and Guber, onetime partners who now hated each other, would bid furiously against each other.

Bookman also realized that some order had to be brought to the proceedings. He decided to set a price for the book at $1.75 million, and then to arrange a series of conference phone calls during which each of the bidders would explain his point of view to the author. "It was my feeling that if the bidding went beyond that number it would set an ominous precedent," Bookman recalls, thus setting out, in effect, to protect the bidders against themselves.

Bookman explained the ground rules of the telephonic beauty contest. The bidders agreed. "I thought I had a good chance to talk the author into letting me have the rights," said Guber, who is renowned as a fast and facile talker. "Then I found out who was going up against me and my heart sank. I could promise a lot of things, but a Redford can say that he will direct the movie, that he will star in it, that it would be his next picture. He could blow me away."

And that is exactly what Redford did. Like Beatty, Redford understood how to wield the weaponry of stardom and, with his customary spare, taciturn style, persuaded Nicholas Evans that he alone could bring *The Horse Whisperer* to fruition. Redford saw Tom Booker, the protagonist, as "silent, apart, centered—a modern cowboy." In short, Redford identified Booker as himself. What could be more persuasive?

Ask Warren Beatty why he decided to tackle *Bulworth* and you are all but inundated by a blizzard of words relating to the political process, the responsibilities of celebrity, the nature of personal commitment, and so forth. Redford, by contrast, is not given to lengthy explanations. When Todd McCarthy, the chief film critic for *Variety* and someone who, unlike most journalists, has a rather warm relationship with the star, asked him that question, he elicited the following response: "It was basically just a good, solid story with the right amount of complexity. It also utilized East and West, something that I am familiar with, being a Westerner but living in New York. I have a strong love of nature and the West, and the loss of the frontier is interesting to me. I have horses of my own. Having children of my own, even though they are grown up. Being able to draw on areas that you have reference for."

These words, published in an interview in *Premiere* magazine, translated into an expenditure in excess of $70 million for the Disney studio, which included a $20 million salary for Redford. They also resulted in a film that was made with the same scrupulous care and professionalism that the star had lavished on his other directing efforts. The difference here was that Redford set the precedent of actually directing himself, something that the more venturesome Beatty had done twice previously.

Predictably, Redford was not eager to explain why he took the leap this time out. "I didn't think I would ever direct myself because it requires the kind of calculation and an awareness of yourself that I'm not comfortable with," he told McCarthy. "I was never comfortable being too aware of myself as an actor. I was much happier letting myself give in to the moment, and to the director I was working with, and engaging with the story and the other actors." Directing, he found, involved "all aspects of a scene . . . the rhythms, the different levels, the pace and the energy, all in one. . . ." On *The Horse Whisperer*, he confessed, there were times when he would lose himself as an actor and forget to say "cut."

Though Redford professed that he managed to exercise a director's discipline in the editing process, he nonetheless fell in love with his own four-and-a-half-hour cut. He insisted that the movie worked at that length. It was only through a process of agonizing persuasion, aided by his movie star's self-protective instincts, that the cut was brought down to its final two-hour, fifty-minute length.

But running time wasn't the only issue: Less than a month before the movie's release, Redford was still tinkering with the ending, ultimately cleaving away the book's final denouement. In his interview, McCarthy asked Redford to explain why he finally changed the ending, to which Redford replied succinctly: "I'd rather not."

This diffidence continued to manifest itself during the weeks prior to the film's May release date. The Disney publicists were deeply concerned whether they could motivate their star to cooperate with their media blitz and involved Redford's personal publicists, the ubiquitous PMK firm, in their effort. Their final results were a mixed blessing. Reporters who were shuttled to Hollywood on the press junket got a quick hit of time with the star. TV shows like "Access Hollywood" and CNN's "Show Biz Today" were able to scrounge up the usual sound bites showing Redford, reserved and somewhat austere, responding to a chorus of queries. Since Redford had not cooperated with junkets in the past, the Disney soldiers seemed pleased.

They were even more pleased, if not downright astonished, when *The New Yorker* decided to publish a lengthy profile on Redford, entitled "Existential Cowboy," which ran the very week of the film's opening—and, paradoxically, the same week that *The New York Times Magazine* decided to immortalize Warren Beatty. *The New Yorker* in the past had uniformly shunned movie tie-ins of this sort, but Tina Brown, the imperial editor, had lately exhibited a kinder and gentler attitude toward celebrity journalism.

In its publicity material accompanying the issue, *The New Yorker* was careful to emphasize that the Redford profile had been written, not by some ordinary celebrity journalist, but by a Richard Rayner, identified as "an English novelist" and author of four books. The publicity release also emphasized that Redford was "usually inaccessible," and that virtually the first thing the star had said to the writer was "Why do you want to write about me? I don't think I'm very charismatic."

Despite this sly modesty, it was PMK that orchestrated the *New Yorker* piece, and Redford himself who devoted hours to the interviews. And neither Redford nor his publicists were heard protesting the tribute at the end of Rayner's worshipful article that stated: "He has been instrumental in fashioning some of America's most defining images: the investigative reporter, the loner, the defender of the unregulated outdoors, the opponent of mindless corporate culture, the independent filmmaker, the fly fisherman, the athlete. Like the hero of *The Natural*, he's the man with the magic bat, and he's contrived to make us pull for him."

All this was music to the studio's ears, but, while Redford may still have held "the magic bat," he no longer held the magic demos. Exit polls and other research indicated that Redford's potential audience tended to be older and skewed toward women. In short, the young men who lined up to see Tom Cruise or who were now taking a keen interest in Matt Damon would not line up to see a Redford movie unless it held some special appeal for them. From a studio's standpoint, Redford, having passed the age of sixty, had now entered that shadowy zone of heightened economic risk. With a $20 million salary and a $70 million negative cost, *The Horse Whisperer*, to recoup, would have to attract a wider audience than middle-aged women. In short, the movie had to transcend demographics.

As the release date drew near, however, Redford did not respond like Beatty; there was no last-minute flurry of interviews and screenings. While Warren Beatty was determined to give *Bulworth* one frenetic last push, Robert Redford retired to his Utah mountaintop to await his fate.

WEEK THREE Tuesday, May 26

It is hard to pinpoint when the *Godzilla* hype machine started revving up. As early as summer '97, the first *Godzilla* teaser started running in theaters. By fall, *Newsweek* was proclaiming *Godzilla* to be "next summer's surest thing," and a merchandising blitz was ignited that ultimately involved some three thousand products, including Hershey's bars and Duracell batteries.

Over the years Hollywood has unleashed its hype on a succession of blockbusters from *Jaws* to *E.T.* to the *Batmans*, but *Godzilla* was arguably the first such project that seemed to be enshrined as pure commerce. From the outset, its title more appropriately should have been *Godzilla, Inc.*

Sony executives, starting with John Calley, doubtless would take issue with that assertion, insisting that their prime motivation was to create a hit movie—the rest would follow. Nonetheless, in my conversations with the full range of studio executives, their references to *Godzilla* were couched almost exclusively in terms of business opportunity. Sony needed to build a new franchise, they reiterated; tentpole pictures were the key to survival. From Peter Guber through John Calley, I never heard anyone at the studio utter the magic words "I can't wait to see this picture." Significantly, Calley even boasted on more than one occasion that, just before he decided to green-light the movie, he called Bob Levin, his ad chief, rather than his principal creative lieutenants.

Sony's entrepreneurial fixation on *Godzilla* was so intense that even prior to the start of principal photography the company had decided not only its release date but its opening gross. The magic date would be Memorial Day. The reason: In 1997, *The Lost World*, the sequel to *Jurassic Park*, had raised the bar for Memorial Day openings, grossing $90.2 million over the four-day period. This represented a mega-leap over the $56.8 million chalked up by *Mission: Impossible*, the Tom Cruise vehicle, a year before. And though no one at Sony was willing to admit it, their goal was not just to match the $90 million mark, but to surpass it. If the retro reptile could boast a $100 million weekend, its claim to immortality would be undisputed. It would mark the high point in the careers of all the battalions of merchandisers, marketers, PR people—yes, and even the filmmakers, Roland Emmerich and Dean Devlin.

Against this background, Sony executives mobilized their hype to such a high decibel level that they themselves became victims of their own myth-making. In so doing, they ignored many early warning signs. There were disturbing tracking studies, for example, that showed only 19 percent of the public would list *Godzilla* as their first choice to see compared with 32 percent for *The Lost World* the year before. The studies were inaccurate, Sony insisted. Thanks to the encouragement of Sony's spinmeisters, *The Hollywood Reporter*'s Box-office Preview, appearing on the eve of the Memorial Day weekend, said signals pointed to *Godzilla* matching "the best-performing pictures of all time, suggesting the potential for an awesome opening frame."

Sony also explained away the less-than-exuberant reception to the long-awaited Godzilla toys. As part of its hoopla, the studio had kept its toys out of stores until the movie was released, presumably to build excitement over the monster's look and to discourage rip-offs. This was an exercise that irritated its merchandising partners, who normally sell as much as 40 percent of the tie-in toys before the opening of a potential blockbuster. By Memorial Day weekend, when the trucks finally left the warehouses laden with Godzilla toys, Sony found itself upstaged by, of all things, the Itsy Bitsy Entertainment company, which marketed Teletubbies, based on the British cartoon series. In many stores, Itsy Bitsy's Teletubbies were outselling the reptiles by three to one.

Sony even had a quick explanation as to why Godzilla was taking such a pounding from the media—a veritable fusillade of negative reviews and carping stories. The press had been complicitous in creating the hype to begin with, said the warriors of Godzilla, Inc. Hence, it was true to form that they would turn on their own creation.

It was not until the first numbers started rolling in that reality took hold. *Godzilla* would not break the $100 million barrier, nor would it come close to matching *The Lost World*. Despite all the hype, and despite a launch budget approaching $50 million, *Godzilla* took in a disappointing $55.5 million for the four-day weekend. For its first seven days, the gross reached $74 million, slightly behind the $74.9 million registered by *Mission: Impossible*, a considerably less expensive movie that ultimately grossed $181 million in the U.S. At these levels, *Godzilla* potentially would struggle to break even, given its $200 million cost of production plus marketing.

While the industry was transfixed by the *Godzilla* numbers, the Memorial Day weekend also packed other surprises. Despite Warren Beatty's heroic efforts to stoke the media, *Bulworth* collected a drab $10.6 million on 2,046 screens. Fox's exit polls showed two key demographic support groups had effectively snubbed the movie—blacks and young men under the age of twenty-five. The notion of a mainstream white politician turning into a rapper seemingly had little impact outside of New York and Los Angeles. In small-town America, where *The Horse Whisperer* was establishing itself, the *Bulworth* theaters were empty.

Fox, the movie's distributor, tried to point to positive portents. The movie's rap soundtrack was selling briskly, reaching eighteen on the charts. Tom Sherak, the Fox executive who had become Beatty's principal backer, said that "it's easier for a movie to expand its audience downward in age and this may happen to *Bulworth*." If an older audience likes a movie, he pointed out, the young crowd may ultimately join in, while the reverse is rarely true. Beatty, who had always been suspicious that Fox would dump his movie, had taken to calling Sherak "my rabbi." To underscore that designation, Sherak had even invited Beatty, his wife, Annette Bening, and their three young children to his house to celebrate Passover. Nonetheless, no one else besides Sherak and Beatty believed that *Bulworth* was anything but dead on arrival.

Deep Impact, meanwhile, continued to defy dour forecasts, grossing $19 million on its third weekend, a drop of only 32 percent. *The Horse Whisperer* also was showing strength, sustaining a mere 18 percent loss to $13.7 million, bringing its gross to $32.2 million after only eleven days. Warner's adventure into animation, *Quest for Camelot*, dipped 23 percent for a dreary two-week total of $13.2 million.

Surveying the flood of data, Hollywood's distribution people realized they had made a serious miscalculation. Intimidated by the long shadow of *Godzilla*, they had created a competitive vacuum for the movie. The weekend after Memorial Day was devoid of possible rivals—*Hope Floats* starring Sandra Bullock was the principal new entry—and the only contender the week thereafter was *The Truman Show*, which was widely referred to in Hollywood as "the new Jim Carrey comedy with no laughs." Said the distribution chief of a rival studio: "Giving *Godzilla* a clear field was the dumbest thing I've ever done. I fell for the hype."

But if rival studios were angry that they'd bought into the *Godzilla* myth, the recriminations were minor compared with those from other sectors.

"I've been around a long time, but the mean-spiritedness of the response took me by surprise," acknowledged Sony's John Calley.

Calley found himself catching it from all sides. Some theater owners were crowing that Sony got what it deserved. Weeks earlier they'd accused Sony of bullying tactics when the studio had demanded a much more generous cut of receipts than on the typical film. One big chain, Carmike Theaters, actually predicted a sharp decline in its quarterly earnings because *Godzilla* was performing below expectations (some analysts suggested their problems had nothing to do with the limping lizard).

Meanwhile rival studios were helping to plant stories that poured salt into Sony's wounds, as if the press needed encouragement. "Hype-heavy *Godzilla* hits theaters with more of a peep than a roar," proclaimed *Entertainment Weekly*. "The ghosts of *The Last Action Hero* are haunting the Culver City lot of Sony pictures," wrote Claudia Eller in the *Los Angeles Times*, referring back to that studio's worst nightmare.

And the critics weren't helping things. Of the seventeen critics working for major media outlets in New York, twelve either panned *Godzilla* or gave it a mixed notice. In Los Angeles, seven of the nine reviews were either bad or mixed, and some radio talk show hosts ridiculed it day after day.

The studio's mania for secrecy during the weeks prior to the opening now seemed to be fueling a counterreaction. In press interviews, key cast members disclosed they had been pressed to sign documents pledging their silence before being shown photos of the monster. Reporters traveling to New York on the press junket were warned they would have to go through metal detectors and that special steps would be taken to discourage the taping of music or images. "It was the nastiest junket anywhere," said one press veteran. "The studio dictated where you went and didn't go, how and where you could take your laptop, etc."

Retailers attending the Toy Fair in New York City were told they'd need an electronic access card to gain entry to the room where Godzilla was displayed. Devlin and Emmerich admitted they'd even given out fake drawings, one slightly different from the other, to entrap potential licensees who might be leaking sketches on the Internet (they claimed they actually entrapped some suspects with this Abscam-like ploy).

Sony might have gotten away with all of this except for one consideration: The *Godzilla* that was finally unveiled to the public was a dud. It was big enough to justify the "size does matter" slogan, but it was also devoid of character or personality. From some angles it looked like a runaway raptor from *The Lost World*.

Sony had shrewdly shown only a few extremities of the monster—a footprint, then a foot, then the thundering sound of the lizard's approach. All this was effective. But the monster himself was a distinct anticlimax, and so were his myriad offspring.

In many of the earlier Japanese versions, Godzilla had turned out to be the good guy who fought off yet another giant marauder. The Devlin-Emmerich version, however, depicted Godzilla as a bad guy who meets his just desserts at the end of the film, conveniently leaving some progeny behind for a potential sequel. That is, if there ever was a sequel.

And, in the end, size *didn't* matter. The finished movie oddly lacked tension, underscoring the fact that the creature didn't become scarier as he became bigger. Yet size had been the key to the marketing effort. Starting in March 1997, the studio had dispatched three teams to crisscross the country in search of the perfect billboard. The effort was presided over by Dana Precious, senior vice president of creative advertising, who worked with McCann-Erickson and Ikon Creative Services to map out appropriate settings to show Godzilla in the context of an appropriate cityscape. The billboards were placed adjacent to landmarks with messages like "He's as tall as the Brooklyn Bridge" or "He's as long as the Hollywood sign." The message clearly got across: This was one giant lizard. That didn't mean, however, that he was really a scary lizard.

Sony's pitchmen were nonetheless superbly effective in landing their marketing partners, who came up with some $150 million to add to Sony's $50 million war chest. Taco Bell alone agreed to spend $60 million to promote the movie along with its new Gordita line of tacos. Many brands were even rewarded with advantageous placement within the film—Kodak cameras and Swatch watches, for example.

There are possibly more product placements in *Godzilla* than in any monster movie in Hollywood history.

The marketing blitz was going so swimmingly, in fact, that Sony couldn't resist boasting about it—a fact which, in the end, further fueled the antipathy. In one publication after another, the details of Sony's campaign were spotlighted as a heroic effort. ATTACK OF THE KILLER FRANCHISE bannered the *Los Angeles Times*. Even *Fortune* magazine chipped in with a detailed analysis of HOW SONY CREATED A MONSTER.

Sony executives insisted they did their best to ward off this journalistic onslaught. Bob Levin, Sony's shrewd fifty-four-year-old president of worldwide marketing, said he personally discouraged several articles on the marketing of *Godzilla*. "I was getting increasingly uneasy about the fact that we couldn't show the movie because it wasn't ready, yet there we were, seeming to boast about how brilliantly we were selling it," Levin said. "I always fear how easily the audience may turn against us if they are kept in the dark too long."

Yet Levin was quoted extensively in the *Fortune* piece and in others dealing with Sony's hard sell, most of which mentioned that he'd been the key ad man at Disney during the days of *The Lion King* and had also presided over Sony's inspired campaign for *Men in Black* the summer before. All this only further heightened expectations. "The normal movie business consists of skirmishes," Levin was quoted as saying in the *Los Angeles Times*. "But this is full-fledged D-Day warfare."

As of Week Three, however, there were indications that it was a war he would ultimately not win. And clearly the warfare already had claimed its share of casualties. Some workers at Sony reported that the atmosphere inside the studio was one of "fear and loathing." During the days in and around the opening "everybody was mad at everybody," reported one Sony executive. "Devlin and Emmerich suddenly became monsters with their demands and complaints." By the time the movie was finally declared ready, there was no room for test screenings or previews. When Calley finally saw the finished version, he was furious that he had no time to make his changes. "John wanted to revoice the girl," said one associate. "He had a list of changes that he felt would have vastly improved the movie, but he had no time to do anything." Though the Sony chief was usually calm and jocular, he turned angry after *Godzilla* opened. When I had lunch with him four weeks later, he burst into an angry peroration about the press, claiming that *Godzilla* had been singled out for unfair criticism. "What John was really pissed off about wasn't the press, but rather that he'd never had his shot at improving the movie," said a top aide. Indeed, Calley on several occasions had even suggested surrendering the Memorial Day opening in order to gain more postproduction time, but Devlin and Emmerich had protested, insisting that they would be ready on time.

"I learned my lesson," Devlin acknowledged later. "Never again will I allow a movie of mine to open without time to test and make fixes. You can't live that way. You can't make good movies that way."

WEEK FOUR Monday, June 1

Following a blizzard of opening-week criticism, the hapless lizard was picking up sympathizers. *Godzilla* had been a victim of a "rush to judgment," some film executives felt. Its shortcomings had been exaggerated—certainly *Independence Day*, from the same filmmakers, had exhibited the same arch, quick-and-dirty style of filmmaking, with the same slapdash performances, yet it escaped the savage critiques accorded *Godzilla*. Sony had never tried to present *Godzilla* as an artistic triumph, but rather as a big, brash, summer popcorn picture. And its opening gross of $55 million would qualify it as a hit by any normal standard.

This revisionist thinking about *Godzilla* was short-circuited by a succession of second-week setbacks, however. From around the country, the audience's response to the movie mirrored that of most critics.

Godzilla's second weekend reflected a drastic 60 percent drop to $17 million—an extremely weak return. After thirteen days the movie was still just shy of the $100 million benchmark that Sony had hoped to achieve by the first weekend.

For Sony, the issue now became one of damage control. Because anemic box office returns and negative reviews can also reduce ancillary income streams such as video and TV sales, Sony hurriedly dispatched its negotiators to the television networks with the mission of establishing a floor for an eventual sale. Sony hoped that $35 million would be a tenable number, but at one meeting after another, the Sony representatives were rebuffed. Word of mouth was weak, they were told, and box office was dropping off quickly. Stung, Sony decided to accept a less-than-thrilling offer from NBC: $25 million for five showings over five years, with an additional sliding-scale bonus if the movie grossed over $125 million in the U.S. (the sliding scale would ultimately yield Sony a paltry $1.5 million). This was hardly the deal Sony had hoped for.

On *The Lost World* Spielberg's operatives had swung a beneficent $80 million TV deal with Fox, though it included more runs and an additional window for pay TV.

Sony seemed mired in a defensive posture. Though still complaining about a negative press and hostile critics, the company nonetheless had to come to terms with the reality that *Godzilla* would not be a megahit after all. Indeed, to transform the movie into even a modest moneymaker would require some realistic planning and shrewd cost controls on the marketing side from here on in.

But the bad news kept coming. At the American Booksellers Association meeting in Chicago, the initial hype about *Godzilla* had induced book publishers to market an array of *Godzilla* tie-ins, including the usual novelization of the movie, a book about the making of the film, a poster book, and even a line of children's books from Scholastic. However, buyers were now turning a cold shoulder to these offerings.

The overall box office results only added to Sony's frustration.

Even as *Godzilla* was stalled short of the $100 million mark, *Deep Impact* briskly soared past that milestone over the weekend. The absence of hoopla surrounding *Deep Impact*, observed the *Los Angeles Times*, "gave the public the impression that it had discovered the movie rather than having it stuffed down their throats." The *Times* went on to quote an unidentified Sony executive as stating, "I'd be the first to admit that maybe we were too aggressive in promoting the film, but that still doesn't explain the constant and mean-spirited attention that's been directed at the movie since it opened."

While *Deep Impact* continued to hold its own remarkably well (its $10 million weekend on 3,280 screens lifted its total to $112 million), *Hope Floats*, a slender love story starring Sandra Bullock, surprised observers with a buoyant $14.6 million opening. Exit polls revealed that its audience was predominantly female, leading its distributor, Twentieth Century Fox, to speculate that the movie would be summer '98's version of the 1997 sleeper *My Best Friend's Wedding*. The opening represented a personal triumph for its star, Sandra Bullock, who got Fox to commit to make the movie in exchange for her participation in the studio's supposedly more commercial film, *Speed 2: Cruise Control. Speed 2*, of course, sank in red ink, nonetheless yielding Bullock a $12 million payday and a chance to make a movie she vastly preferred.

Fox's returns from *Bulworth* continued to be disappointing, however. Warren Beatty's movie plunged another 38 percent, registering a $5.1 million gross on 2,051 screens. Its cumulative gross now totaled $17.6 million after two weeks in wide release compared with $43.5 million for *The Horse Whisperer* after three (the Redford movie grossed $7.4 million on its first weekend). The other major loser of the summer, *Quest for Camelot*, the animated feature from Warner Bros., sank another 50 percent with a weekend gross of $2.3 million, yielding it a mere $17 million after three weeks.

Having chewed over every bit of gossip about *Godzilla* and *Bulworth*, Hollywood was finding fresh fodder in two new movies that had managed until now to stay below the radar. Disney's reticence about screening *Six Days, Seven Nights* had fueled rumors that this $70 million production was in trouble. The studio insisted that the film simply was not ready to be shown, yet word leaked that exhibitors had seen a virtually complete version a few weeks earlier. The less than steamy on-screen relationship between Harrison Ford and Anne Heche was starting to become grist for the rumor mill, as was Heche's very public lesbian relationship with Ellen DeGeneres. Disney spokesmen nonetheless insisted the film was testing well and would find its audience.

By contrast, the buzz on *The Truman Show,* Paramount's movie scheduled to open in a week, had done a complete 180-degree shift. Two incidents had earlier sent up warning flags. When Dennis Hopper was abruptly fired from a costarring role (eventually filled by Ed Harris) the gossip suggested that Peter Weir, the Australian director, was at odds with Paramount. These rumors started circulating again many weeks later, after Weir had shown his cut to the senior Paramount executives, only to receive some very blunt demands for editing changes. "The studio hated the picture" was the rumor, and it was pervasive.

To combat this negativism, Scott Rudin, the combative young producer, urged Paramount to take the unusual step of screening the film one-on-one for a few critics and reporters. Let the movie speak for itself, he argued. Even in making his proposal, Rudin knew Paramount would be resistant. "Most studios are used to running scared," he pointed out. One or two bad reactions, they reasoned, could only further poison the atmosphere.

The argument continued for several weeks. Then, in mid-April, I got a phone call from Rudin. "I'd like you to see my movie," he said. "It's a very different sort of movie. I hope you'll like it. If you hate it, I would appreciate it if you wouldn't tell anyone. If you like it, tell as many people as you'd like. Tell the whole fucking world."

"Will this be some sort of press screening?" I asked.

"No, this is you. You and your wife, if she'd like to come."

Two days later, my wife and I walked into the Paramount Studio

theater, a superbly comfortable, well-engineered structure built a decade ago as part of the overall makeover of the seventy-year-old lot.
The empty theater seemed chilly and cavernous with no other bodies
present. We seated ourselves precisely at the center of the theater,
then heard a disembodied voice behind us ask, "Would you like to
start now?"

Even as the room darkened, I pondered the arguments that must
have been made by Paramount against this screening. I had heard
them all during my own studio days. People were spooked when they
sat in an empty theater, it was said. Moviegoers worked off each
other's responses—the laughs, the tension are all contagious.

In point of fact, *The Truman Show* played all the better under
these conditions. The movie's off-center style, its paranoia-inducing
point of view, seemed even more effective in this chilly environment.
Roughly a third of the way into the movie I found myself asking, What
is this movie trying to tell me? Ten to fifteen minutes later, I was
telling myself that this was one of the most original, brilliantly conceived films I had seen in years, and also that it was a peculiar film
to release in midsummer. It wasn't funny. There was relatively little
in the way of action.

The next morning I telephoned Rudin. "Okay, you got me," I told
him. "The movie is brilliant. I would hate to be the man in charge of
dreaming up an ad campaign, however—to try and grab attention
away from the *Godzilla*s and the *Armageddon*s. Who else are you
showing it to?"

"I showed it to David Thomson of *Esquire*. He liked it. And you
liked it, so maybe I'll keep showing it."

From Rudin's tone, it was clear that he knew full well what he
was up against. This was a movie that would require not just favorable
nods from the critics. It would need absolute raves—veritable clarion
calls of praise.

Within a couple of days I was faxed Thomson's review. "*The Truman Show,*" he wrote, was "the movie of the decade. It may be the
most frightening film you'll see this year. It's not violent. There's no

torture. No leering sex. And no creatures more horrific than the kinds of people who run the show at Disney World."

Thomson had clearly written a review that could be quoted. Good for him, I thought. But the questions persisted: How do you sell a Jim Carrey movie that has no laughs?

The top people at Paramount, of course, were asking the same question. A few days later I ran into a senior marketing official and asked about the internal projections on the movie. "I'll be frank," he offered. "I think that the movie could open to $7 million and disappear. That's what I think. We'll all get our heads handed to us." He was silent for a moment, then added: "On the other hand, there's a damned good chance this movie could be the sleeper of the summer."

Now that, I told myself, was a man with conviction.

WEEK FIVE Monday, June 8

"There must be something in the water. *Godzilla* tanks. *The Truman Show* opens huge. What's going on here?"

The person asking me these questions over dinner was Terry Press, the imaginative and irreverent head of marketing for Dream-Works. Press, who had held a similar job at Disney for many years, had long since steeled herself to surprises. The only thing one can expect is the unexpected, she liked to say. And summer '98 thus far was bearing her out.

Industry screenings of *The Truman Show* had produced a pervasive sense of the surreal for those in the movie business. Not only was the movie itself disorienting, the notion of opening it wide in early June was in itself even more outlandish. First *Bulworth* and now this.

To be sure, Terry Press had her own little secret. Having worked on *Saving Private Ryan*, she knew she was sitting on what would likely be the biggest surprise of all—a movie that also would seem utterly inconsistent with the effects-laden action movies that had become de rigueur during summer. Spielberg's crushingly realistic movie was anything but an orthodox summer entertainment. And, in response to this, Spielberg and Press had crafted a deliberately understated, low-key campaign that would contrast dramatically with the *Godzilla*-style hype. If *Godzilla* was the most oversold movie of the decade, *Saving Private Ryan* would be the most undersold.

But that campaign was still under wraps. The ads for *The Truman Show*, stacked with the best critics' quotes in years, were festooned across the pages of every major newspaper. And the box office business was booming.

Days before the opening, there'd been a sudden buzz that the movie's last-minute tracking had been erratic, that young Jim Carrey fans felt let down because the movie was "too serious," but the opening weekend numbers ended all the carping. *The Truman Show* rang up $31.6 million for the weekend, or an impressive $16,300 per-screen average. "The makeup of the audience is even broader than we expected," said Wayne Lewellen, the distribution chief at Paramount. "We had a lot of young males as well as many older people who normally wouldn't come to a Jim Carrey picture."

Lewellen reported that theaters were packed in small markets as well as the big cities. The only possible cloud on the horizon: According to the exit polls, kids considered this to be "a serious picture." The big question: Did they still like it enough to challenge their friends to see it?

The buoyant opening numbers for *The Truman Show* would all but guarantee the movie's admission to the Hundred Million Club. Only one nonsequel in history, *Bram Stoker's Dracula*, had ever opened to more than $30 million and failed to crack the $100 million mark (sequels tend to open strong and fade fast).

According to Paramount, 78 percent of the people who had seen the movie described it as excellent or very good. On the morning talk shows, critics were comparing *The Truman Show* to *Forrest Gump*, but Paramount's marketing people were nervous about that. *Gump* registered an amazing $330 million gross in the U.S. *The Truman*

Show, said the experts, had a reasonably good chance of approaching $125 million. Paramount's marketers didn't want to raise unrealistic and unattainable expectations.

Though *The Truman Show* dominated media attention, there was still room on the weekend for the Michael Douglas picture *A Perfect Murder* to roll up a respectable $16.3 million opening. While this was hardly a spectacular debut, Warner's marketing executives offered a convenient rationalization. Some 95 percent of the audience, they reported, was over the age of twenty-five, and older audiences were less likely to rush out to see movies on the opening weekend. Hence the thriller, a rather pedestrian remake of *Dial M for Murder,* might have solid legs.

Other numbers followed true to form. The fast decline of *Godzilla* continued unabated: Its $10 million weekend represented a drop of 45 percent, meaning the movie had grossed $114 million in three weeks. The Sandra Bullock movie, *Hope Floats,* also fell sharply to $8.5 million, a drop of 40 percent, putting an end to the notion that it would replicate *My Best Friend's Wedding. Deep Impact* continued to hold up surprisingly well at $6.7 million, with its total now approaching the $125 million mark. "The *Armageddon* folks are getting crazy over the way this movie is holding," said a senior Paramount executive cheerily.

Indeed, the once-subtle propaganda wars between the asteroid movies had moved into the open. Mimi Leder and others who had steered *Deep Impact* had been stung by complaints from Michael Bay, the petulant young director of *Armageddon,* that they had stolen plot points and even dialogue from his move. Firing back, the Paramount forces were gleefully reporting that *Armageddon* was deep into reshoots after two inauspicious test screenings. "The ending of *Armageddon* is a mess," confided one Paramount spinmeister. "They're shooting in Paris and other places. You know damned well if they need more footage of asteroid damage they must be in deep trouble."

The response from Joe Roth was predictably adamant. Not only were the screenings a success, he assured me, but the studio was now convinced that the *Deep Impact* audience would return to see *Armageddon*—the movies were that different. Further, he said, the reshoots had been planned from the outset. Everything was going according to plan.

With Paramount and Disney exchanging shots, Dean Devlin, the normally taciturn producer and cowriter of *Godzilla*, now decided to take up the cudgels in defense of his movie.

Weeks prior to the release of *Godzilla*, an online bulletin board had been established to hype the movie. Though it had worked well for the movie at first, the chat in the chat room had started to grow ugly once the film was out in the theaters, with one self-appointed cyber-critic after another launching an assault.

The criticism became so personal that Devlin could no longer restrain himself. When one moviegoer called the movie a flop, Devlin responded: "Please tell me how you figure that a movie that will make a studio over a hundred million dollars in profit is a flop? Where did you learn your math?" To another of the boo-birds, he replied: "Our movie did what it was supposed to do and we're happy about it. If you don't like that, to hell with you."

Soon wearying of this exercise, Devlin admitted to friends that it was "just stupid" to take the bait. Three weeks after *Godzilla*'s grand opening, the online bulletin board suddenly went blank.

Still, there was no quashing the peripheral nastiness that surrounded the movie, much of it now focusing on Sony management. The *New York Post* reported solemnly that "Hollywood insiders are pointing fingers at the sixty-seven-year-old John Calley, saying he's lost his management touch with *Godzilla*. They say he gave too much freedom to underlings to blow money on a costly film that wasn't tested in focus groups to measure its appeal. The monster movie wasn't even previewed by executives until a week before its release." Sony stock, the *Post* added, had fallen nearly 5 percent this year while the Dow overall had climbed 14 percent.

Not only was the disappointing network TV sale of *Godzilla* being cited, but even video dealers seemed to feel threatened, arguing suddenly that a tiered pricing policy should be introduced to protect against overhyped movies that failed to perform. Under the existing rigid structure, the wholesale price of a cassette was pegged at $70, give or take a few dollars, with that price prevailing whether a movie grossed $10 million or $100 million. The performance of *Godzilla,* it was said, pointed up the need for flexible pricing from $30 to $70. This notion did not sit well with the studios.

Sony management had hoped that the success of *The Truman Show* might shift the attention away from *Godzilla,* and, to a degree, that hope was realized. Still another distraction was looming: *Six Days, Seven Nights.* Maintaining a brave face, Disney tossed a premiere party for the movie, but the audience reaction was politely tepid. The movie seemed oddly spiritless, as though the filmmakers had been compelled to make the film against their wills. "It's all so predictable you begin to wonder, why did they bother?" asked Richard Schickel of *Time* magazine in an advance review.

Surely the only element of the movie that held the audience's attention lay in the chemistry, or lack of it, between its costars. Would Anne Heche project any credible interest in Harrison Ford? Not only was the audience fixated on this question—the studio was, too. Indeed, $70 million was resting on it. A stubbornly idealistic man, Ford had put himself on the line in refusing to replace the actress even when the preproduction publicity became intrusive.

In the middle of the movie, while Ford and Heche were locked in a blissful kiss, my wife fled to the ladies' room only to confront Heche's best friend, Ellen DeGeneres, feverishly fixing her makeup, a tortured look on her face. "Ellen looked more than uncomfortable," my wife whispered in my ear as she returned to her seat. "This movie must be like root canal to her." DeGeneres later confided to a reporter that she found it sheer agony to watch romantic scenes involving her lover.

When the movie had ended, Heche herself put on an insistently happy face, however. "I like this movie," she told me with a fixed deer-in-the-headlights smile. "It's an old-fashioned movie with an

old-fashioned story. My life is an old-fashioned story, too." I took her
word for it.

Ivan Reitman, the director, clearly admired her postscreening performance. "There's this great fearless quality about Anne," he remarked at the South Seas–themed party. "You have a sense of
someone who's been knocked around a lot and who has risen above
it."

Not famed for subtlety, Disney's marketers were pinning their
"sell" on Heche's sex appeal, with posters showing her shirt hanging
open just enough to reveal a skimpy bikini and ample cleavage. And
indeed Heche was sexy in the movie, most people at the premiere
agreed. Cast as a writer for a magazine, she was playful and endearing. Ford, however, was relegated to the Bogart-like role of an island
drifter who piloted his small plane between resorts, and he seemed
distinctly uncomfortable. "At this point in his career, Ford can be
believable as the CEO of a corporation or the president of the United
States as in *Air Force One,* but he looks ridiculous in this movie," said
one of the town's most senior agents at the premiere. "When actors
get the muscle to choose their own roles, it's always amazing to me
the mistakes they make. It's downright perverse." Of course, the other
reason that major Hollywood agents remained critical of Ford was that
he'd always snubbed the big agencies, preferring to work with a low-
profile manager. To the Hollywood establishment, that was easily a
greater heresy than Anne Heche declaring her eternal love for Ellen
DeGeneres.

WEEK SIX Monday, June 15

Putting aside the individual triumphs and debacles, one overriding
fact seemed to be emerging from the melee of summer '98. Unless the
signs thus far were extraordinarily misleading, the season would spell
good news both for Hollywood and for the average filmgoer. On one

hand, overall ticket sales were running considerably ahead of last year. At the same time, moviegoers were being given a far wider range of choices. By the sixth week of summer '97, the dreadful *Speed 2* dominated the malls, along with a by-the-numbers comedy thriller, *Con Air*. This summer the choices included *The Truman Show, Six Days, Seven Nights, A Perfect Murder,* the teen comedy *Can't Hardly Wait,* and, soon to open, *Mulan* and *The X-Files.* And of course *Deep Impact* and *Godzilla,* the big effects megamovies, were still playing widely.

The box office numbers reflected this phenomenon. While *The Truman Show* had a very respectable $20 million second weekend, off 36 percent (hurt somewhat by the NBA finals), *Six Weeks, Seven Nights* also registered a solid $16 million. *A Perfect Murder* grossed $11.2 million, down 32 percent, while *Can't Hardly Wait* had a weak debut of $8.2 million. *Godzilla,* meanwhile, faded still further to $6.5 million and the studio acknowledged for the first time that it would be pleased with a domestic total of $140 million, roughly half of what it had once fantasized.

Judging from TV spots and from the Sunday newspapers, however, the big money was riding on the two movies set to open a week hence, Disney's *Mulan* and Fox's *The X-Files.* Each project represented an important gamble for its studio, and each had to overcome, yet again, some negative word of mouth.

In part, the skepticism over *Mulan* stemmed from its basic story line. It was the first animated movie ever made about a cross-dresser, and an Asian cross-dresser at that. The central character was a Chinese teenager who disguised herself as a man to go to war in place of her ill father and save her country from the evil Huns.

To be sure, *Mulan* embodied all the standard Disney values— superb animated artistry, a lush musical score, and an assortment of sight gags involving a miniature dragon voiced by Eddie Murphy. Much of the animation work came out of Disney's new studio in Orlando, Florida, which CEO Michael Eisner had willed into existence only a few years ago.

Given its off-center subject matter, the question facing *Mulan* was whether it could battle the downward cycle of Disney's animated features in the years since *The Lion King*. Though still the stalwart leader in animation, Disney's recent entries, *Pocahontas, The Hunchback of Notre Dame*, and *Hercules*, had shown progressive declines not only in the box office but also in ancillary revenues. *The Lion King* had been a financial geyser generating $751 million in worldwide box office revenue, $500 million in home video income, and $250 million from consumer products. By contrast, *Hercules* and *Hunchback* had each hit the wall at about $100 million in domestic gross. *Hercules* generated only about one third of the video income of *The Lion King*.

The official Disney line on this downtrend was that *The Lion King* was an anomaly, that it was useless to measure other animated features against it. At the same time, this weekend's first double-page ads for *Mulan* bannered the following quote: "Disney's greatest achievement since *The Lion King*." If one searched for the source of the quote, the small print explained that it represented the opinion of WOKR, an obscure TV station in Rochester, New York. A second quote, "An amazing triumph," had even more obscure origins—an organization I had never heard of called Hangin' in Hollywood.

When I had lunch with Peter Schneider, Disney's animation chief, shortly before the opening of *Mulan,* he, too, had gone to pains to emphasize that *The Lion King* had become a millstone for his people. An elfin man with a ready smile and reedy voice, Schneider came out of the theater scene in Chicago with interests stretching well beyond animation. Placed in charge of Disney's theater program, Schneider was principally responsible for bringing in the gifted off-Broadway director, Julie Taymor, to stage *The Lion King* on Broadway.

Mulan was not another *Lion King*, Schneider told me with a wary smile. "Not that either of *The Lion King*s represented perfection, mind you. I wished the Broadway version had consistently better music, for example. I am sure *Mulan* is not perfection either, but I feel the story works on an emotional level. I feel confident Asian Americans will love it. I also think the general audience will love it."

Certainly *Mulan* offered the elements of myth, legend, and whimsy that Schneider favored in his work. Disney colleagues say there had been growing friction between Schneider's approach to animation and that of then Disney president Jeffrey Katzenberg, now a partner in DreamWorks. Schneider reportedly felt Katzenberg had sought to replicate live action in his animated features rather than letting them reside in a more mythic landscape. Katzenberg's contributions to *Hunchback* had been especially divisive—"that movie was harsh and on-the-nose," said one Disney animation veteran. Katzenberg's defenders at Disney insisted he had not been didactic on the creative level and that his main contributions had been in the area of marketing, where he was a fervent supporter of Disney's animation effort. Indeed, Katzenberg had tried to recruit Schneider to join Dream-Works—an offer which Schneider resisted. Undaunted, Katzenberg had put his new company on a course to become a key rival of Disney in the animation arena, with *The Prince of Egypt* as that company's most heavily promoted release. The Disney troops made clear that they intended to toss as many obstacles as possible in Katzenberg's way.

The presence of DreamWorks in the marketplace in summer '98 also gave an added competitive impetus to Disney's top managers. Though no member of Disney's executive corps would talk about it on the record, the tension between Eisner and Katzenberg was still a palpable force. In conversations with friends, neither Eisner nor Katzenberg made any effort to conceal his animosity toward the other. To Eisner, his former president remained an ungrateful, habitually discourteous gnat who had been given too much authority at Disney and was carried away by his own importance. To Katzenberg, Eisner represented the ultimate power-crazed corporate bully who manipulated his executives but ultimately feared them as potential rivals. Katzenberg had lost this battle, had filed his lawsuit against Eisner over his dismissal, and now had gone on to become his former boss's bitterest rival.

With *Deep Impact, Saving Private Ryan,* and *Small Soldiers* as

DreamWorks' first summer releases, the Disney soldiers knew that this was not a season where failure would be forgiven. And the marketing of *Mulan* represented the first key test of summer '98. No one understood this better than Richard Cook, the calm, moon-faced man who, as chairman of the Walt Disney Motion Picture Group, was ultimately responsible for the studio's marketing effort. When Cook first joined Disney as a ride operator at Disneyland two decades earlier, Disney was still a somnolent enterprise run by the immediate heirs of the Disney family. Moving into distribution, Cook discovered there was essentially no market for the tired, old-style family product Disney was producing. He remained the lone survivor as Michael Eisner and his then partner, Frank Wells, reinvented the company, replacing dispirited, tired veterans with fiercely ambitious new recruits. Suddenly the parking lots were filled every morning before eight A.M. and no one left to play golf after lunch. And Dick Cook, a born survivor, adapted to the new rhythms and personalities.

It was a rough-and-tumble world in which Cook now found himself. Most of the theater owners with whom he did business were Jewish, and so were his rivals at other studios. The courtly, soft-spoken Cook, who'd been educated at the University of Southern California, where he'd played on the baseball team, was the last symbol of WASP-dominated Disney. "There were some pretty hard-dealing older guys among the exhibitors, but I would sit down with them and say, 'I need your help,' and they would come through for me," Cook recalled. When Joe Roth joined Disney, there was once again speculation about Cook's future, but again he beat the odds.

When I visited Cook at the studio in mid-April, he was mobilizing his final assault on the summer, yet as usual his demeanor was downright serene. Though Cook worked in Disney's radical-looking new administration building, his suite of offices remained prototypically old Disney, with its bulky wooden furniture and its walls crowded with photos of studio old-timers. In these vintage photos, the early Disney staff looked as if they'd just got off the bus from Nebraska. Even old Walt, in his framed photograph, could have been operating a filling station in Topeka rather than a studio in Burbank. He had tended to speak that way, too: I remember lunching with Walt in the mid-sixties in the somewhat rudimentary studio commissary and asking a question that required some financial input. Old Walt pondered it for a beat, then asked me, "Do you mind if I call over my Jew to help answer that?" He motioned toward his dark-suited chief financial officer, who was dining at a nearby table. I told him that wouldn't be necessary—it wasn't an important question.

Entering his waiting room now, Cook, in shirtsleeves, saw me peering at his photos. "Those were different times," he said with his usual gentle smile. "I don't think those guys would feel much at home around the industry today."

As we reviewed the summer campaigns, it was clear Cook felt oddly confident about his competitive edge. "This summer will be one of unprecedented hype, and I think the smartest thing to do with *Mulan* would be to go counter to it," he observed. In line with this notion, Cook said, the campaign for *Mulan* would start late and be restrained in tone, unlike previous animation openings; there would be no shutting down of Times Square, no Central Park premieres. "We're taking down the noise level," he said. "It feels right this summer." At the annual retreat of the animation studio in Vermont, several officials had brought up what they termed "the sincerity issue." Disney had so overhyped its animation that the public had grown cynical, it was asserted. It was time to reverse the trend.

In part, this strategy of restraint reflected the studio's faith in its film, Cook explained. Though not yet complete, *Mulan* had been tested a number of times with audiences over a period of six months. The results were the strongest for any animated film going back to *Beauty and the Beast*. Even Michael Eisner, when discussing *Mulan* with me one day, flashed a coy smile and predicted, "We're going to surprise a lot of people with this one."

The initial ads for *Mulan* broke just prior to the opening and were aimed at adults, not kids. The only TV promo a week before the premiere consisted of an ice show on ABC-TV in which Michelle Kwan,

the Olympic medalist, skated to the music of *Mulan*. In subsequent
TV spots, shows aimed at boys got ads depicting action scenes, while
those favoring girls showed father-and-daughter scenes.

Though determined to remain within politically correct bounds,
Disney's venture with McDonald's, which didn't break until the premiere, stepped on a few Asian toes. Chicken McNugget containers
were emblazoned with puns like "Run, don't wok" and "McNuggets
are Chinamite." McDonald's TV spots aimed some aggressively
"cute" jokes at Asian customs, such as sitting on the floor to eat.
"Offensive caricatures," complained Jeff Yang, publisher of *A.* magazine, geared to Asian Americans.

Again aiming at restraint, Disney staged its premiere of *Mulan* at
the Hollywood Bowl. A rather austere basket of Chinese food came
first, the lukewarm egg rolls followed by a concert reprising the musical themes of Disney animated movies. I looked over at Michael Eisner's box, saw him sitting, face frozen, and I couldn't help but wonder
how many times he'd sat through these leaden melodies, ever the
dutiful CEO. By the time the movie had begun, darkness had fallen
and a chill seized the night air. There were many children at the
Bowl, who had accompanied their celebrity parents to this evening's
adventure, and even as their teeth began to chatter, they were trans-
ported into yet another of Disney's magic kingdoms. *Mulan* was as
Peter Schneider ordered it up: a movie of myth, legend, and whimsy.

WEEK SEVEN Monday, June 21

"School's Out—Forever." That was the apocalyptic banner atop the
first advertisting blast from *Armageddon*. The red-and-black eight-
page insert that appeared in major newspapers across the country described in shorthand each character's motivation for participating in
the mission ("He's doing it for honor. . . . She's doing it for love. . . ."").
"The End Is Near," the ad concluded.

All of which seemed an appropriate overture for *Armageddon,* scheduled to open on July 1. College commencements were taking place that weekend and, by Hollywood's calendar, summer had reached that soft middle stage that felt like an intermission. The first onslaught led by *Godzilla* had arrived and sputtered. The second, led by *Armageddon,* was still two weeks away. And the movies arriving on the scene in between seemed more like stealth missiles than rockets, distributors launching them tentatively to see how high they could fly.

Given this atmosphere, *Mulan* had responded respectably but unspectacularly. With its soft-sell ads finally kicking in, the movie grossed $23 million over the weekend, 10 percent better than either *Hercules* and *Hunchback of Notre Dame.* Disney professed its delight. "We're walking on air," exulted Philip Barlow, the studio's distribution president, pointing out that the story and setting of *Mulan* remained a mystery to many young moviegoers while *Hercules* had been a known quantity.

Fox expressed similar satisfaction with the opening of *The X-Files,* which grossed a robust $31 million over the weekend. The studio claimed that the movie already had exceeded the scope of its TV audience. Box office analysts remained skeptical, however. Ticket sales had declined some 18 percent between Friday and Saturday, they noted, suggesting that the audience could in fact be limited to the fans of the TV show. If this scenario proved correct, *The X-Files* might replicate Paramount's 1996 experience with *Star Trek: First Contact,* which opened to $30.7 million, but wound up at $92 million.

Holdover releases also seemed to be suffering a slight malaise. *The Truman Show* declined 38 percent, a sharper dip than Paramount had predicted, registering only $12.4 million over the weekend. *Six Days, Seven Nights* from Disney also fell 38 percent to $10.5 million, while *A Perfect Murder* had dwindled to $7.3 million.

But again, the sheer range of choice seemed to be helping. Ticket sales for the weekend climbed to $106 million, or 2 percent higher than the same week of 1997 when the quick-to-fade *Batman and Robin* had a flashy $42.9 million debut. On the same weekend, *My*

Best Friend's Wedding had opened quietly, but ultimately showed vastly more staying power, becoming the sleeper of the summer.

Would this week's openings display similar legs? While neither *Mulan* nor *The X-Files* seemed to have hit a hot button, no major competition loomed in the immediate weeks ahead. Universal's ad campaign for *Out of Sight*, starring Jennifer Lopez and George Clooney, seemed lifeless, and the one for *Dr. Dolittle* was simply baffling.

The flaccidity of the *Dolittle* campaign reflected the mixed signals sent out by the studio. In deciding to make *Dolittle*, Fox's production team had bought producer John Davis's argument that this was a "presold title"—that parents around the world venerated the *Dolittle* stories and would rush to take their kids to see the movie adaptation. Once the film was delivered into the hands of Fox's ad department, however, its research prompted an abrupt U-turn. "Kids don't want to be known as kids," concluded Bob Harper, the cautious, buttoned-up corporate player who presided over advertising. "If you're going to attract kids to a movie, that movie's got to be cool." Translated, this meant that once a film became stigmatized as a family picture, no one over the age of nine would agree to see it. Hence the *Dolittle* campaign would be geared not to the legacy of the book but to Eddie Murphy, who was pictured in ads improbably attired as a doctor, bending over a bunch of squawking animals. "The funniest movie of the year," proclaimed a banner attributed to Bill Zwecker of NBC-TV, who, it turned out, worked at the network's Chicago affiliate.

Given these other movies' apparent problems, both Disney and Fox felt they had a solid opportunity to expand their audiences for *Mulan* and *The X-Files*. Once *Mulan* had opened, the baton had been passed from the studio to Disney's marketing partners, led by omnipresent McDonald's. That company would now foot the bill for most of the campaign—a setup that had worked well for *George of the Jungle* in summer '97. *Mulan*, however, was neither as mainstream nor as accessible as *George*. There were the subtleties of political correctness to be observed, and the depth of the market had not as yet been tested:

Would the audience stretch to teenage boys? Still, Disney's partner understood one thing—even if *Mulan* "failed," it would still be a $100 million failure, which was nothing to cry about. It would still help sell a lot of burgers.

That sort of equanimity did not prevail at Fox. While *Mulan* represented a virtual oligopoly, *The X-Files* hopefully would mark the inception of a new franchise built on a TV constituency. Over the course of five years, "The X-Files" had built up what appeared to be a devoted audience of about 20 million. Now that loyalty was to be tested.

It seemed like an intelligent business risk, and Fox's regime was eager to appear businesslike. The motion picture group, operating within the framework of a hard-edged multinational corporation run by the notoriously unsentimental Rupert Murdoch, had clearly gone out on a limb the year before. With *Speed 2* and *Titanic*, among others, they had committed vast resources to movies that were, on the face of it, uncontrollable. They had been bailed out, to historic proportions, by *Titanic*, but they could not risk that sort of madness again. Hence every decision of summer '98 had to be defensible on a bottom-line, corporate level. They had to make decisions that the suits in upper management could understand.

The X-Files, however, also carried serious risks, which the suits probably wouldn't have understood. No one could remember a studio ever making a movie based on an ongoing TV series other than "Star Trek." Why would a moviegoer pay seven or eight dollars to see something they could watch for nothing on the small screen? Moreover, this would be no low-budget caper. Chris Carter, the show's egocentric creator, firmly believed that his darkly moody, fuzzy-brained series, which *Newsweek* once said was aimed at "seriously paranoid geeks," was more than a TV hit—it was art. Bill Mechanic and his colleagues at Fox knew that Carter would demand a production budget of at least $60 million and possibly more for his wide-screen debut, and that it would be a day-to-day battle to contain him. Given Carter's ego, Fox also knew he would resist reaching outside of his TV family for assistance from people who were savvy at big-screen filmmaking.

His director would be Rob Bowman, a TV veteran who had directed twenty-five episodes of "The X-Files." The cast would be that of the TV show and, of course, the principal writer would be Carter.

The two protagonists, who insisted on calling each other Mulder and Scully, were played by David Duchovny and Gillian Anderson, respectively an FBI man who believed in paranormal phenomena and a cool-headed scientist who holds an M.D.

Carter had come to TV after a undistinguished career in journalism (he was a staff editor at *Surfing* magazine). With his broad forehead, jutting chin, and swath of silver hair, Carter was an intimidating figure on his set, where he fulfilled the role of classic control freak. "Carter is a reasonable reflection of his show," said one who worked closely with him. "He is somewhat paranoid and vaguely nasty." When *Newsweek* wanted to do a story on him, he proposed a cover presenting him as a Svengali-like puppeteer dangling characters in his show on a string.

As the man who liked to pull strings, Carter was respected by his fellow TV producers for sustaining a well-crafted show with strong production values. In transferring his creation to film, however, he seemed to lose track of his priorities, possibly because he started with two potentially contradictory objectives. On the one hand he was determined not to confuse his TV loyalists by altering the vocabulary or mood of the show; on the other hand, he knew he had to open it up to utilize the advantages of the big screen. Possibly as a result, the movie version of "The X-Files" that ultimately emerged was stultified by numbing dialogue and riddled with convenient coincidences and set pieces that seem to go unresolved. The climactic scene in Antarctica—an oddly staged piece that was at once grand yet claustrophobic—was itself the source of a furious budgetary battle between Carter and Mechanic.

Carter's battles were not limited to the production. Intent on preserving the secrecy of his plot, he demanded a complete media blackout—one that came as a surprise to the studio.

This created a *Godzilla*-like confusion at the Toy Fair for toy store buyers in New York City, where all *X-Files* action figures had to be removed at the last minute with the exception of those representing the two main characters, Mulder and Scully. Another Carter dictum: Licensees making *X-Files* apparel were warned that the X-Files logos would have to be printed on the inside—peculiar for anyone trying to promote a show, but true to form for anyone hoping to create an aura of paranoia.

As the premiere date approached, this mysterioso atmosphere seemed to intensify. Fox had originally planned an opening salvo of ads with positive quotes to legitimize the show as a true feature, but none of the quotes, even from established blurbmeisters, satisfied Carter. Hence, the picture was launched with a rather fuzzy gray photo intended to denote mystery and danger. "In Five Days the Fight for the Future Begins," screamed the banner, which sounded vaguely reminiscent of *Armageddon*.

Fox also planned a massive TV campaign designed to characterize *The X-Files* as an event picture, even though the event was also running on TV every week. Bravely the studio initiated one campaign of TV spots to run on "The X-Files" show itself, and another for other time slots. The first spots employed "X-Files shorthand"—they preached to the converted while trying to convey a sense of urgency. Those spots aimed at the general audience sought to frame the movie as an exotic sci-fi epic that couldn't be missed.

Said one Fox ad man: "There were theoretically two audiences for this movie and we needed two campaigns, one for the loyalists and another for the I-don't-cares."

To dramatize its support for its *X-Files* adventure, Fox opened its coffers to underwrite a major premiere in Westwood, replete with red carpets, klieg lights, and a postscreening party. Westwood had witnessed decades of glitzy premieres, to be sure, but the crowds still turned out for a glimpse of a Tom Cruise or a Harrison Ford. With *The X-Files*, however, one could sense a certain letdown in the crowd as the parade of TV actors, including Gillian Anderson and David Duchovny, paraded along the red carpet. Even as the studio-paid photographers snapped their shots and studio-paid TV interviewers did their sound bites for delivery to the late-night local news, some of the spectators began to wander off in puzzled disappointment. A die-hard cluster of "X-Files" fans nonetheless pressed forward as Duchovny strode by, wearing his usual ambiguously blasé expression, but neither he nor the other cast members moved with that bigger-than-life, movie-star swagger. One reason was that they were *not* movie stars. They were instead TV personalities who, though gifted, displayed a more introverted, almost fragile charisma.

The postpremiere party was staged in a cavernous hangar at Santa Monica airport, where guests were suffused in an eerie white fluorescence apparently intended to suggest a futuristic setting. Cocktail waitresses in skin-tight white costumes distributed beverages and snacks. Studio executives looked on tensely, as though they sensed that the response to the movie was at best mixed. "What do you think of it?" Fox's chairman, Bill Mechanic, asked one reporter. "You don't want to know," replied the writer. One *Variety* reporter tried to conduct an instant minipoll and was puzzled by his results. "Fans of the TV show seemed more disappointed than those who never watched the show," he said. "They had expected more, but all they got was another long episode."

Carter himself was not the sort who would be troubled by any of this. Nor would he likely pour over his reviews, which were by and large tepid. "Only those familiar with the small-screen series will get many of the film's characters and references," warned Kenneth Turan of the *Los Angeles Times*. Said Janet Maslin of *The New York Times*, "The cult fascination with 'The X-Files' may itself be more remarkable than the material. . . . The movie teasingly offers the prospect of big developments . . . but all it really does is create a vague omnibus format for future movie spin-offs." Even Richard Corliss of *Time* magazine, a self-proclaimed fan of the show—"a terrific series"—found himself let down. "If the movie declines to enthrall it is because its creators forgot what makes the show shine. . . . Carter has turned this complex talk show into an action movie. . . . It's as if the cleverest grind in class were told he had to retake PE before he could graduate. And that's enough to turn an X-phile into an ex-phile."

The Internet also crackled with *X-Files* debate. Steven Harris, president of the X-Files Fan Club, tried to take the high road in a posting on the "X-Files" web site by declaring, "The movie is a major-league hit." His conclusion: "I thought they kept the conspiracy theory–mythology material to a minimum for nonfans while offering some new details for regular watchers."

His views were widely challenged by other "X-Files" fans, however. "It's nothing but a two-hour TV movie you have to pay for," said one disgruntled fan. "Hard-core fans will be disappointed with the movie because they expected five years worth of well-thought-out questions would be answered in a two-hour movie."

The clash of opinion was so pervasive that, instead of writing my customary column in *Variety*, I decided to share the forum with my television editor, Jenny Hontz, a bright young woman who greatly admired the show. A portion of our jointly offered testimony was as follows:

BART: The most interesting aspect of *The X-Files* movie is that it isn't a movie. Chris Carter, renowned as the most arrogant writer-producer in television, has lived up to his reputation by blowing up a TV episode and calling it a movie—one that only his cultlike TV following could either understand or appreciate. If his curious exercise succeeds, the mind boggles where it will lead. Next summer our multiplexes will be showing expanded episodes of "Touched by an Angel," "Xena," and "Dawson's Creek." Maybe Jerry Springer will become a movie star after all.

HONTZ: *While viewers who have never seen "The X-Files" TV show will probably be a bit confused by the movie, fans of the series will love it. It's a chance to see two of their favorite char-*

acters, Mulder and Scully, on the big screen, like one supersized
episode with more action and better effects.

Because the film is dropped in the middle of a continuing
story line linking last season's finale and this fall's opener, it
doesn't stand alone like most films. The result is similar to that
of the second Star Wars *movie, where Han Solo is frozen and*
you have to watch the sequel to find out what happens. Fox is
hoping this cliffhanger will force "X-Files" novices to tune in to
the series, but it could backfire by frustrating some moviegoers.

BART: Well, it backfired as far as I'm concerned. The very elements that allegedly lend the TV show its noirish character
don't work on the big screen—the flat dialogue, the TV-style
close-ups, the incessant clangorous music. And, most of all,
the cast. I realize that "X-Files" fans accept the fact that
Scully and Mulder, the two leads, never change either their
facial expressions or their tone of voice, but on the big screen
they tend to disappear altogether. It's little wonder that Janet
Maslin, *The New York Times'* meticulous film critic, starts referring to Gillian Anderson, who plays Scully, as "Ms. Arm-
strong."

HONTZ: *At the center of the film is the platonic love between*
Mulder and Scully that stems from sharing intense experiences
that no one else believes or understands. The chemistry is pal-
pable, but, as usual, you leave wanting more than you get.

The film answers many of the puzzling questions posed by
the series, but it raises new ones, too. And while much is re-
vealed, X-philes know that the show always has a way of taking
things you thought you knew and turning them completely up-
side down a week later. If you want all the answers, you'll
go nuts. But if you sit back and enjoy the ride, you won't be
disappointed.

BART: Well, I was disappointed. Also perplexed. I realize that "X-Files" is designed to appease conspiracy theorists and government-haters. What other show would depict as its ultimate heavy the Federal Emergency Management Agency—those "dangerous" folk who turn up in times of disaster? With his customary modesty, Chris Carter declares, "The show's original spirit has become kind of the spirit of the country, if not the world." Sure. What this really means is that the show fosters paranoia by sowing confusion. It weaves a plot that is essentially unintelligible and therefore encourages unintelligible analysis. Charles McGrath, editor of *The New York Times Book Review*, no less, concluded his essay on *X-Files* last week with the following pithy analysis: *The X-Files* has taught us that it's more entertaining, and probably more epistemologically sound, to believe in everything and in nothing at all."

I knew I could count on *The Times* to clear things up.

HONTZ: *The thing to remember is the movie carries little risk for Fox because "The X-Files" has 20 million fans who tune in to the show each week. Even if half of those viewers see the film, Fox will likely recoup its investment.*

But perhaps the most trenchant comment on the *X-Files* movie came from Joe Morgenstern in the *Wall Street Journal*. "The most intriguing conspiracy here," he wrote, "is the one cooked up by Twentieth Century Fox and Fox TV."

WEEK EIGHT Monday, June 29

There are some weeks when the box office results fulfill expectations and others when they simply confound. Such had been the case the previous weekend when *Dr. Dolittle*, a movie that was hard to love, emerged as a hit while *Out of Sight*, a witty film that was downright lovable, emerged as a flop. "How could this happen?" muttered a devastated Danny DeVito, the bantam-sized actor-producer whose company, Jersey Films, was responsible for both *Out of Sight* and its predecessor, *Get Shorty*. Yet happen it did, with *Dolittle* grossing an impressive $29 million, better even than last year's Eddie Murphy remake of *The Nutty Professor*. Since that film went on to gross nearly $129 million in the U.S., Fox, the distributor of *Dolittle*, was in a festive mood. By contrast, a palpable gloom settled over Universal as a result of the dim $12.7 million opening for *Out of Sight*, which starred George Clooney and Jennifer Lopez. Universal's summer schedule was meager compared with Fox's, and the studio had moved the film to a prime June date in the hope that it could find a broad audience. Both *Out of Sight* and *Get Shorty* had been adapted from quirky novels by Elmore Leonard, with *Get Shorty* going on to gross $72.1 million in the U.S. That total now seemed unattainable for *Out of Sight*.

Given *Dolittle*'s fixation on butt jokes and toilet humor, Fox had feared that its audience might be limited to preadolescent boys, but exit polls revealed some surprises. Not only were girls embracing the film, but Eddie Murphy was pulling in a very considerable black family audience.

Murphy was a star who always had made studios nervous, having cultivated an ability to dart in and out of fashion with great alacrity. Despite his spotty record, he was also a reluctant promoter of his own work. On *Dolittle*, Murphy had showed up as promised for interviews connected with a press junket, only to pull a disappearing act shortly thereafter. The studio was not surprised, given the mounting gossip about the comic. The rumors were triggered when a twenty-one-year-old transsexual hooker named Atison Ken Seiuli fell to his-her death from a window in a downtown Los Angeles apartment house. A year earlier, police had pulled Murphy over in West Hollywood while he was driving with the very same hooker. He said he was just giving her a ride home and was not charged with any crime, but given Seiuli's death, neither Murphy nor the studio felt the actor's presence at that time would be of value in promoting a family movie. (Murphy was also the voice of the key comic character in *Mulan*, but was absent from Disney's promotional plans as well.)

Though delighted by *Dolittle*, Fox was dismayed by the wobbly legs of its other expensive summer picture. *The X-Files* fell sharply during its second weekend, grossing $13.6 million for a 55 percent drop. While its core audience initially had rushed to its support, there was little evidence that the buzz was crossing over to non-TV fans. By contrast, *Mulan* fell only 24 percent in its second week, grossing a solid $17.3 million. Studio statisticians were quick to point out that this represented the best second weekend, excluding holidays, for any Disney animated feature.

While pleased with *Mulan*, the attention of Disney's hard-driving, free-spending marketing team had clearly shifted to their highest-risk movie of the summer, *Armageddon*. From Joe Roth on down, Disney executives were angered and frustrated by the reaction of the press to this week's packed media screenings. While they were by no means as dismissive as with *Godzilla*, the critics felt that *Armageddon*, too, had failed to deliver. Todd McCarthy, *Variety*'s chief film reviewer, usually a reliable indicator of critical response, opened his review by stating, "Bruce Willis saves the world, but can't save *Armageddon*." McCarthy criticized the "frequently incoherent staging and an editing style that amounts to a two-and-a-half hour sensory pummeling." *Deep Impact*, by comparison, seemed like "a humanistic masterpiece," he concluded.

Not surprisingly, McCarthy's review produced some irate phone calls, one of them from Michael Bay, the director, to McCarthy, and another from Joe Roth to me. Bay and McCarthy played phone tag for much of the day, and when they finally connected, the filmmaker protested the treatment he had received, vaguely suggesting that McCarthy had a personal agenda. McCarthy couldn't figure out what he meant, but Roth, in his call to me, spelled it out. It was Bay's recollection that, while both were students at Wesleyan University,

Bay had dated a girl who'd been going with McCarthy, and that the critic was still peeved. "It's an interesting theory," I told Roth, "but there are at least two holes in it." For one thing, McCarthy was about fifteen years older than Bay. Secondly, he had gone to Stanford and had never set foot at Wesleyan.

That aside, Roth nonetheless felt that criticisms such as McCarthy's represented a generational divide. The young audience, weaned on MTV and other video fare, was conditioned to lightning-paced, quick-cut rhythms that reduced narrative to shorthand while the older generation found this confusing, if not downright annoying. Indeed, some of the older film editors, among others, termed Bay's style "frame-fucking," referring to the fact that the beginning and end of most scenes were eviscerated in an effort to speed the storytelling. Cumulatively the result could be off-putting since the viewer was always plunging into the middle of a conversation, often without understanding even the locale. Given the lengthy running time of *Armageddon*, Bay and his editors had indulged so heavily in "frame-fucking" that even the veteran producer, Jerry Bruckheimer, felt it excessive. Bruckheimer, whose past credits included *Beverly Hills Cop* and *Top Gun*—neither of them exactly slow-paced—had wanted time to smooth the rough edges on Bay's cut, but with special-effects work running behind schedule he never had the opportunity.

In discussing the issue with Roth, I couldn't tell whether he really admired *Armageddon* stylistically or simply felt obliged to defend the work of his filmmakers. Roth argued his case in his customary controlled, even-tempered manner, though his tone became almost plaintive as he complained, "These *Armageddon* reviews are the worst I have ever received on a big-budget picture." In part, Roth felt, the reviews reflected a continuation of the *Godzilla* syndrome. *Armageddon*, too, had been served up not as an ordinary action movie but as a surefire megahit, anointed as such by the press as well as the studio, and now the media was turning on it. That plus the generational issue meant that *Armageddon* was doubly cursed, and Roth was unhappy about that. "It's not being given a fair shake," he insisted.

Stung by this, Roth was taking aggressive steps to ensure that his movie became critic-proof through the sheer magnitude of the promotional spending. Though Disney declined to disclose its launch budget, rivals guessed that something in the neighborhood of $100 million had been allocated for the opening alone. About half of this was advanced by Disney, with the rest coming from partners like McDonald's, Nestlé, and Nokia. The *Armageddon* logo seemed to be emblazoned on virtually every billboard in America. Commercials on the Superbowl had set the studio back some $2.6 million. Hundreds of journalists and a few stars were set to be flown to Cape Canaveral for the June 29 premiere in what would be a sort of combination coronation and coming-out party.

The strategy behind all this was to position *Armageddon* as the number one movie in the country, the event of the summer, a movie people felt they had to see. *Godzilla* had allowed itself to fizzle from the outset, but Disney was not simply going to open the movie and wait for the results. It was going to predetermine the results, even if that meant buying virtually every ticket.

In doing so, Disney knew it would come under fire once again from rival studios. There'd been a growing sense in Hollywood that Disney was dangerously raising the bar on ad spending—indeed, on spending in general. In the first half of 1998, the five top movies had collectively cost some $620 million to produce, almost twice the $350 million tab for the top five pictures of 1997. While summer box office totals were running a healthy 11 percent ahead of the previous year, the cost of making and marketing these movies was rising exponentially. Moreover, the studios' efforts to build new franchises, as with *Godzilla* and *The X-Files*, simply weren't panning out. And while several films were rolling up strong grosses, there now seemed a strong possibility that no summer '98 movie would reach the $200 million milestone. *Armageddon* had been given the best shot, but the initial screenings had now stirred much skepticism.

Hence, even as Hollywood braced for the second half of its summer, there was growing concern that the numbers were getting out of whack, and that the underlying economics of show business needed careful reexamination.

There's an axiom in the movie business that it's the nightmare projects that turn out to be the biggest hits—those that are all but impossible to pull together and that are fraught with controversy. Early in my career I assembled just such a project. It was called *The Godfather*, and there was not a moment when pitched battles were not being fought over the casting, editing, even the music. By contrast, trouble-free projects, like *Out of Sight*, seem to sail along effortlessly until the final moment of truth when the movie opens. Then there's rarely a happy ending.

The production team responsible for *Out of Sight*, consisting of Danny DeVito and his two producer partners, Michael Shamberg and Stacey Sher, had been working together since 1990 as Jersey Films. One of the first projects they had managed to cobble together was *Pulp Fiction*, which, unique among low-budget "art" pictures, had gone on to gross slightly over $200 million around the world. The team also had seen its share of clunkers: *Fierce Creatures*, starring John Cleese, was barely releasable, even after extensive reshooting.

In 1996, Jersey Films returned to winning form with an oddball film called *Get Shorty*, based on the Elmore Leonard novel and starring John Travolta, Gene Hackman, Rene Russo, and DeVito. The movie grossed $120 million worldwide and helped establish Barry Sonnenfeld as a major-league director. When the manuscript of Leonard's *Out of Sight* appeared on the market in 1997, the Jersey partners jumped at the opportunity. By this time Jersey had made a new deal at Universal, and that studio agreed to put up the $2.5 million to acquire the novel. Both Jersey and Casey Silver, Universal's production chief, were aware that *Out of Sight* was strong on idiosyncratic dialogue while limited in terms of plot, but the lure of reinventing *Get Shorty* was too great.

So was the prospect of reassembling the creative elements. Scott Frank, the brilliant young screenwriter who'd adapted *Get Shorty*, signed on. However, Barry Sonnenfeld, its director, by now had vaulted to superstar status as a result of *Men in Black* and was not interested in directing what would be by his new standards a small picture.

Besides, Casey Silver had come up with what he considered to be a better idea. Steven Soderbergh had scored a major success with his first film, *Sex, Lies, and Videotape,* in 1989, but his five movies since then had failed to find an audience. The Universal executive was persuaded that *Out of Sight* would demonstrate Soderbergh's ability to connect with more commercial material. Silver had similar expectations of the actor he selected to star in the movie, George Clooney, who had established himself as a TV star on "ER" but had fizzled on the big screen. Again, in Silver's mind, *Out of Sight* would reverse Clooney's slide.

These choices were readily accepted by DeVito and his two partners. Within eighteen months of the acquisition of the novel, the movie was ready to start production—a remarkably swift process by Hollywood standards. Shot in sixty days, *Out of Sight* came in slightly under its $50 million budget. The director and his two stars, Clooney and Jennifer Lopez, were electric together, and the producers admired the discipline and energy with which Soderbergh approached his work. Even during the lunch break, the director almost never left his camera, planning his setups and conferring with crew.

Not until the editing process did the producers hear the words from the studio that would abruptly end their euphoria. The movie had turned out so well, they were told, that it would be awarded a prime summer date. *Out of Sight* would open on the July 4 weekend. It would be Universal's major summer release.

DeVito and his colleagues were at once delighted and appalled. It was gratifying to be informed that their movie was so well thought of, yet the July 4 date seemed an obvious trap. *Get Shorty* had opened in October and *Out of Sight,* they reasoned, would similarly benefit from a less pressure-packed date. Further, it was downright intimidating to open against Disney's well-plotted *Armageddon* onslaught. Though studio executives claimed that *Out of Sight* represented superb counter-programming, DeVito and Shamberg considered it more like suicide. This was especially true since July 4, 1998, fell on a Saturday, a day of barbecues and other distractions.

It didn't take long for the Jersey partners to figure out Universal's true motivation for slotting *Out of Sight* as a summer picture. Casey Silver had always planned on the Brad Pitt picture, *Meet Joe Black*, as his big summer movie, but that film had fallen behind schedule. Silver and Martin Brest, its director, were longtime friends, and the Universal production chief was not disposed to pressure Brest or to take him off the movie. Still, Universal was desperate for a summer replacement, and that's where *Out of Sight* came in.

So while postproduction pressure was taken off Brest, it was now applied to *Out of Sight*. Not only was Soderbergh rushing his work in the editing room, but suddenly the producers felt they were being given short shrift by the marketing department. Their film was being handled by Buffy Shutt and Kathy Jones, the two ad chiefs who had just been dismissed by Edgar Bronfman, Jr., and who were putting in their last months at the studio supposedly under a producing deal. Even at the initial meetings on the trailer and the campaign, the two lame-duck executives seemed unwilling to listen to new ideas or even to test existing materials. Jersey Films' Shamberg in particular felt the studio's trailer was "just plain dull" and demanded that it be tested in theaters before live audiences alongside trailers for other summer movies like *Zorro* or *Lethal Weapon IV*. The response: "There's not enough time."

Shamberg's frustration was so great that, even as the movie opened, he wrote an indignant memo to Silver protesting the treatment that he and his partners had received. According to the three-page, single-spaced memo, Universal had been guilty of the following:

• The decision to open opposite *Armageddon* with a "rudimentary" campaign was absurd.

- There was no master plan for the campaign; it was all improvised as things went along.

- No meetings had been set up with the publicity department to plan media strategy. As a result, several magazines, like *Entertainment Weekly*, killed potential cover stories because "there's no buzz on your film."

- While a *Zorro* trailer played with *Godzilla*, Universal could only deliver a thirty-second spot on *Out of Sight*, which ran with *BASEketball*, a movie no one went to see. "Our spot was such a disaster it instantly got trashed on the Internet," Shamberg wrote.

As a result of all this, *Out of Sight* managed to receive outstanding reviews, but failed to capitalize on them. The final indignity was when *Entertainment Weekly*, though giving it a rave, called it "the perfect fall film."

"The whole experience with *Out of Sight* was a study in supreme frustration," Shamberg reflected. "It seemed all the more so because I found myself fighting with people I basically liked. Casey Silver is a terrific guy who keeps his word. So is Ron Meyer. Somehow it hurts all the more when you feel you've been screwed by friends, not enemies."

With the movie scheduled to open, Shamberg couldn't take it anymore. He gathered up his family and flew to Hawaii. His colleagues also vanished. They felt they had done their job. They had delivered a good movie. Why, they wondered, did it have to end like this?

July

WEEK NINE Monday, July 6

Joe Roth is first and foremost a family man and, as such, decided to spend the July 4 weekend with his wife and children in Savannah, Georgia, where Donna Roth, his wife of eighteen years, was producing a movie for DreamWorks called *Forces of Nature*, starring Sandra Bullock and Ben Affleck. Roth was proud that his wife's producing career was blossoming. By midday Sunday, however, the phone calls from Disney had started rolling in and Roth felt under siege. The *Armageddon* numbers for Friday night had been good but not great, and Saturday, July 4, was not much of an improvement. Nonetheless, the exit polls indicated the predominantly young male audience liked the movie and would recommend it to friends. Back at the studio, however, the marketing and PR staff was fielding calls from the press demanding to know how the studio would respond to its mediocre opening, whether the campaign would be changed and more dollars allocated. This was *Godzilla* all over again, the reporters said, only the results weren't even that good.

"I felt I was caught in a feeding frenzy," Roth said later. "I had known all summer that the press was in an attack mode, but I never expected anything like this. By Monday morning when I looked at the numbers for the entire weekend, I knew we had a hit. A big hit. But there I was, taking call after call from reporters who had decided it was a flop."

Monday's stories about the box office confirmed Roth's worst fears. The headline in *Daily Variety* trumpeted B.O. KICKED IN THE

ASTEROID, and its story reported that *Armageddon* had grossed $34.8 million for the three-day weekend compared with *Godzilla*'s opening of $44 million. In its first five days *Armageddon* had grossed $52.9 million, which seemed paltry compared with the $96 million registered by *Independence Day* in its first six days or $84.1 million for the first six days of *Men in Black*.

Though forecasting a movie's ultimate results based on its opening weekend is a dicey exercise, dire predictions for *Armageddon* already were being advanced. The movie would do somewhere between $125 million and $150 million in the U.S., according to the brave prognosticators. And as such, this would certainly not be the profit center Disney had hoped for.

"To be completely honest, I was sweating bullets," Roth said. "I was sitting there with my own numbers and predictions. Based on everything I knew, and the sum total of my experience, I felt I had a movie on my hands that would approach $200 million in the U.S. alone and do easily that well overseas. But listening to all these theories, I said to myself, either I'm crazy or everybody out there is misreading the situation."

If Roth seemed perplexed, so, at least briefly, were Disney's spinmeisters. Only a week earlier, Disney's PR team had enjoyed a rare moment in the sun. The *Wall Street Journal* had run a page-one story about the effectiveness with which Disney had implanted the notion in the public psyche that *Armageddon* would be "the movie of the summer." When Bruce Willis's marital problems with Demi Moore became an issue, the PR team shifted their spotlight to the film's younger stars, Liv Tyler and Ben Affleck. According to the *Journal*, Terry Curtin, Disney's shrewd senior vice president for publicity, had cautioned everyone involved in the movie not to get trapped into making box office predictions. This, to be sure, turned out to be smart advice. For Disney, the only glitch in the *Journal* article was a quote attributed to Oren Aviv, senior vice president of marketing, who had supervised preparation of the *Armageddon* trailers. In preparing the trailer and other advertising materials, Aviv said, he and his aides reminded themselves that their aim was not to get a mere $25 million or $30 million opening. *Armageddon* was not like normal Disney releases; it was destined to be a blockbuster.

Though Disney's flacks looked good in the pages of the *Wall Street Journal*, just one week later they were struggling to get their voice heard above the media din. Their lone champion turned out to be James Sterngold of *The New York Times*, who was new on the Hollywood beat as an occasional backup to Bernard Weinraub (Weinraub's writings increasingly had been inhibited by the fact that his new wife, Amy Pascal, had ascended to production chief at Sony under John Calley, thus inadvertently placing her husband in an occasional conflict of interest). Writing about *Armageddon*, Sterngold warned readers to lend a deaf ear to film critics or to those who claimed that "movie audiences are losing their appetites for vacuous, special effects–laden thrill rides." *Armageddon* was destined to become a big hit, Sterngold wrote, quoting Joe Roth as stating: "I really don't understand the reviews, seeing how the audiences reacted. The reviews were generational. They attacked the style in which the movie was made, not the substance."

Rather than argue about the *Armageddon* box office numbers, Disney spokesmen instead tried to shift attention to *Mulan*, which continued to be tracking well ahead of *Hercules* and *Hunchback of Notre Dame*. The movie would clearly become the most successful Disney animated feature in years, they pointed out. Also performing well over the July 4 weekend was *Dr. Dolittle*, which grossed $19.8 million on its second weekend.

Not surprisingly, the big disappointment of the weekend turned out to be *Out of Sight*, despite its felicitous reviews. Writing in *Variety*, Emanuel Levy called it "a sly, sexy, vastly entertaining film . . . that represents Steven Soderbergh's most accomplished work to date." *Out of Sight* finished in fourth place with an uninspiring $6.5 million and was instantly written off as a disaster.

———

The controversial opening of *Armageddon* provided a vivid reminder that special-effects movies had arrived as a distinct genre. Nearly all of the major summer movies were effects-oriented, the most prominent examples being *Armageddon*, *Godzilla*, *Deep Impact*, and *Small Soldiers*. Even those films that didn't seem like effects movies were totally dependent on newly emerging technology. Without the computer-generated animals chattering away, *Dr. Dolittle* would have been utterly flat as a movie. Even those movies that fell below the radar were effects movies. *Species II*, which represented MGM's lone summer hope, had disappeared quickly despite its impressive effects. The special effects on the $85 million Robin Williams movie, *What Dreams May Come*, proved so complex that the movie couldn't even make its summer dates, getting pushed back until late September.

To be sure, two movies of summer '98 were downright retro in their resistance to the new technology. Even as he was shooting *Lethal Weapon IV*, Dick Donner boasted about the fact that there would be no computer-generated tricks in his film. The chases and fights would represent old-fashioned Hollywood stunt work. Similarly, the Farrelly brothers, as they were shooting *There's Something About Mary*, took pride in the fact that they had absolutely no knowledge of special effects—indeed, they said they were still figuring out which way to point the camera.

Whatever their subject matter, however, all the movies of summer '98 were dependent on the digital revolution when it came to postproduction. Filmmakers were able to shoot their scenes with impunity because they knew they would have the opportunity to "fix it in post," as the battle cry went. This would usually entail enhancing the imagery but also could be called on to alter a setting or even eliminate a character. Perhaps a catering truck had found its way into the corner of a shot in a period movie, or the sound man's equipment had cast a shadow. To the digital wizards, these were easy fixes. The problem was that most directors had become dependent on their work, and the postproduction budgets had started to balloon.

"The quality of the CGI [computer-generated imagery] work is so high that the natural temptation is to ask for everything," noted Robert Relyea, the veteran chief of physical production at MGM. "But when we start changing the actor's hairline, or things like that, then we're getting into the area where the technology becomes a toy and not a tool."

Clearly *Titanic* had changed all the rules about special-effects films. The James Cameron film was the first major effects hit that used technology to help enhance emotions, not just physical action. *Twister* and *Independence Day* had been huge hits, but they were more like theme-park rides. They made no pretense of relating a personal story. In *Titanic*, for all its simplistic dialogue and flimsy characterization, the director did not appear to design his story for the sole purpose of showing off technology. Instead, the technology served the narrative.

Deep Impact tried to take all this a step further but with limited results. The star of the movie still ended up being the big wave enveloping the coastal communities. "When I saw their TV spots featuring that wave, I knew they would have a hit on their hands," said Joe Roth.

Some of the cast and crew who worked on *Deep Impact* felt that the demands of the physical production weighed so heavily on director Mimi Leder that they distracted her from directing her actors. Industrial Light and Magic (ILM), for example, created 129 effects shots depicting the tidal wave, the asteroid, and the spaceship dispatched to destroy it. Though the spaceships were largely miniatures, the comet itself was purely a computer creation, as was its long tail. Leder had to spend tremendous amount of time on these aspects of the film.

ILM also played a key role in *Small Soldiers* where its CGI effects had to encompass the animatronic movements of the little military figures created by Stan Winston Studios. Winston and Hasbro Toys designed the live-action militaristic dolls that were to run amok in a suburban neighborhood, but the digital wizards also had to create an entire environment for these perverse little figures.

In *Dr. Dolittle* the CGI troops were assigned to enhance the actual movements of the various animals. The dog and other beasts were trained to move their mouths up and down on cue, with these movements then computer enhanced so that the animals would seem to be talking—a considerable advance over the techniques utilized in *Babe*. The job became more complex with the smaller animals. In the case of the rats, for example, the top half of the rat bodies were computer-generated; the computers then tracked them along with the lower bodies of real rats. Creation of the composite rodents took roughly six months to master.

A key test of the CGI crew on *Armageddon* was to invent "the heavy"—the giant asteroid that would threaten humanity. That job was assigned to a company called DreamQuest Images, which set about designing something that would be at once menacing, gothic, and moody—and which also seemed somehow alive, spewing gases and showing its spikes as it rotated. The rock itself was real, but the gases and vapors were digitally created. Given the fact that asteroids have their own atmospheres and leave a milky field as they hurtle through the sky, the key problem was to create the illusion of depth.

Paradoxically, *Godzilla*'s "Size does matter" slogan resonated rather sourly among the myriad technicians who labored on that film. It was Godzilla's unruly measurements that caused the biggest headache for the cinematographer, who desperately struggled to sustain a sense of sale, and for the technicians, who had to juggle some four hundred special-effects shots and integrate them with miniatures. Indeed, Godzilla's sheer dimensions reduced his sense of menace. The sight of the massive foot was immensely effective, and the audience responded to the thunder of his movements as the sound reverberated through the theater. But when the beast appeared in all its glory, its relationship with real characters and with a realistic landscape was compromised. Exacerbating this was the director's decision to shoot his movie against a pervasively dark, rainy landscape. Director Roland Emmerich explained that it was all in the interest of creating an ominous mood, but it struck many as an artifice to conceal the limitations of the effects.

Given the ubiquitousness of the effects genre, industry executives early in the summer were furtively consulting dweeb glossaries so as to appear literate in the new digital technology. Hence studio bureaucrats who had no knowledge whatsoever of the effects business were commonly dropping terms like *compositing* (combining two or more images), *rotoscoping* (removing an image from the background), or *motion control* (tracking the camera and lens so that a shot can be replicated time and again).

Despite the techie talk, a mounting uneasiness about the new effects genre was gripping the executive offices. As spring flowed into summer, it was alarmingly clear that the process of budgeting special effects was completely out of control. Over and over estimates of both money and time proved woefully inadequate and filmmakers were shrewdly manipulating delays to maintain control over their work. Intrusive studio chiefs couldn't see the movies if they weren't finished and hence couldn't advance suggestions. More important, it was becoming increasingly clear that effects movies were subject to the same artistic constraints as conventional ones. If the story worked, the movie worked. Audiences proved unforgiving, even if the effects were lavish.

As if to dramatize this point, midway through summer '98 George Lucas let it be known that he had completed work on his *Star Wars* prequel—a disclosure that raised the pulse rate of exhibitors and toymakers, not to mention Fox, which had acquired distribution rights. *Star Wars* had become more than a series, more even than a franchise. Lucas's movies had been mythologized by two generations of moviegoers, and since he owned the negative, and owned the company which financed it, he was in control of his release dates. Lucas would not be rushing helter-skelter through makeshift test screenings. He would have nearly a year to massage his film before making it available to the public.

The sheer mention of *Star Wars* seemed to cast a shadow over *Godzilla* and *The X-Files*, two projects that aspired to the *Star Wars* aura. While Lucas's original film had been made on a slender budget and had arrived with little hoopla, it had nonetheless carved out a degree of immortality. And by midsummer 1998, *Godzilla* and *The X-Files* had already receded from memory.

WEEK TEN Monday, July 13

"A guns 'n ammo weekend," heralded the *Los Angeles Times*. "The boys are back," said *Daily Variety*. This was supposed to be the ill-planned, crash-and-burn weekend when three male-oriented action pictures were going to shoot one another in the foot. It didn't work out that way. As often happens when movies with wide audience appeal open up against one another, the market expands to accommodate all of them. In this case, the three were *Lethal Weapon IV*, which grossed $34.8 million; *Armageddon*, which grossed $23.1 million in its second week; and *Small Soldiers*, which did a respectable but unexciting $14.4 million. In every case, competing studios felt that the numbers supplied by their rivals were exaggerated. *Lethal's* real numbers were more like $32.5 million rather than the professed $34.8 million but, as the *Los Angeles Times* put it, "What's a million or two between friends?"

There was also enough room in the marketplace for two family-oriented movies to perform well. *Dr. Dolittle* continued its surge by grossing $12.8 million while *Mulan* ran up $7 million. *Dolittle*, at this point, seemed to be on a track to surpass *The Nutty Professor* and become perhaps the surprise hit of the summer. Somewhat lost in the shuffle was *Madeline*, a picture targeted at young girls that registered a passive $6.6 million after receiving tepid reviews. In addition, an independent movie called π (*Pi*) rolled up the biggest single-screen debut of any film within memory, grossing $33,000 at New York's Angelica Theater on its opening weekend. This represented quite a triumph for a small movie that raised its money from a variety of contributors.

The enormously successful debut of *Lethal Weapon*'s fourth episode testified not only to the durability of the "buddy" cop genre, but also represented an implicit poke in the eye to the summer's special effects–laden movies. "There were two reasons we had no effects in our movie," Joel Silver, the producer, explained. "We had no time and we had no money." Clearly, the audience didn't miss them.

Armageddon, meanwhile, was performing far better than pundits had forecasted. The movie's first week's results totaled $76 million, compared with $110 million for *Men in Black* and $125 million for *Independence Day*. The movie's second week numbers seemed to support Joe Roth's belief that moviegoers liked the movie a lot better than the critics did.

According to *Weekly Variety*'s Crix Pix tally, the combined critics' vote in New York, Los Angeles, and Chicago for *Armageddon* was nine pro reviews, sixteen con reviews, and sixteen mixed. The big summer action pictures have always been notoriously critic-proof, which means that audiences embrace or reject them irrespective of what the media says. Yet an unusual number of letters were published by newspapers singling out *Armageddon* as representing an ominous trend in filmmaking. One letter printed Monday, July 13, in the *Los Angeles Times* and written by a reader named David Fieber stated: "For years I have believed that the introduction of MTV marked the beginning of the end for movies and now I am convinced that the end is finally here. Gone are human characters and coherent storytelling, replaced by obnoxious morons spouting stupid one-liners and visual style that caters to adolescents with an attention span of about three seconds."

Small Soldiers had also triggered negative responses, but on quite different grounds. Some moviegoers expressed anger at the degree of violence in the DreamWorks movie. Also upset was DreamWorks' biggest licensee, Burger King, which, upon realizing that *Small Soldiers* would get a PG-13 rating, had to scramble at the eleventh hour to alter its kiddie promotions and pull its TV campaign out of Saturday morning. Burger King employees were given the complex assignment, even as they were handing out toys at drive-through windows, of advising parents that the movie associated with the toys might not be appropriate for small children. Indeed, they could trade their *Small Soldiers* toys for more benign products such as Mister Potato Head. The experience underscored the risk for a Burger King or a McDonald's of committing to a movie without seeing it. Indeed, given the nature of most deals, the marketing partner must make a commitment before the movie even goes before the camera.

The long lines outside the theaters showing *Lethal Weapon IV* were particularly gratifying for Warner Bros., which otherwise had endured a pretty bad week. The *Pinocchio* trial, which pitted the studio against Francis Ford Coppola had ended earlier in the week, with the jury slapping a stiff $80 million judgment against Warner Bros.

And while the studio wallowed in the favorable coverage of the box office results of *Lethal Weapon IV*, Warner's Semel and Daly had been irritated by stories questioning whether the movie would ever turn a profit. In their opinion, it was nobody's business how much their movies cost, or what percentage of the gross they chose to give to the cast. Deflecting questions, Semel had repeatedly said that talent had been very cooperative and that back-end deals had been modified to accommodate an ensemble cast. Even Mel Gibson had lowered his normal demands, Semel said, in recognition of the extraordinary money he had gleaned from his gross participations on the first three *Lethal*s. "Everyone has made money from this franchise," Semel told me. "It was in their interest to accommodate."

This line of reasoning was dutifully reported by the *Wall Street Journal*, which stated, "Warner Bros. executives say that *Lethal* will be profitable and that its principals agreed to lower their fees and profit participations because, explained one executive, 'less of more is more.'" At the same time the *Journal* estimated that the movie ended up costing about $120 million and that "about one third" of its revenues would go to its profit participants.

Studio PR representatives were unhappy with this report, and reiterated the official line that *Lethal Weapon IV* had cost $90 million, not $120 million, and that the *Journal* had inflated the gross participations. This was privileged information in any case, Daly and Semel said, and it was nobody's damned business.

All of which only intensified the guessing game. A few select phone calls to the principal agents involved in making the key deals on the movie revealed that they uniformly scoffed at the "less is more" line. Consistent with normal practice on sequels, they had asked and received richer deals, not lesser ones—no accommodations had been made for the greater good.

As for the overall negative cost of the movie, sources at the studio again declined to support the official $90 million estimate. "It was a $125 million picture, and that's without overhead," blurted one studio executive. For accounting purposes, he added, that number could be adjusted upward or downward in several ways. Some of the gross participants had overall deals at the studio, for example, and part of their compensation could be assigned to those accounts. Cosmetic bookkeeping aside, however, another studio executive volunteered, "I don't see the studio making money from this movie."

WEEK ELEVEN Monday, July 20

The *Los Angeles Times* put it succinctly: "There are plenty of hit movies but no runaway success." As a result, the numbers looked bright week after week during the summer, but the studios couldn't find that one runaway blockbuster that would wipe away all the small mistakes.

This weekend's grosses further underscored this concern. *The Mask of Zorro* grossed a very respectable $23 million over the weekend, opening the prospect that it could ultimately edge toward the $100 million mark. But the early numbers suggested that *Zorro*, which cost over $70 million to produce, would not qualify as a blockbuster.

Something About Mary also opened to an encouraging $13 million, and Saturday night business showed the sort of bump that might portend resiliency. Again, encouraging, but not yet a runaway hit.

On the other hand, *Lethal Weapon IV* dipped only 38 percent to gross $21.2 million, indicating anew that this would be a solid performer. *Armageddon*, too, held well at $16 million, off 32 percent, again quieting the naysayers. *Small Soldiers*, developed by Steven Spielberg's company for DreamWorks, all but disappeared from the charts, hinting that it would struggle to get to $50 million. The movie's apparent failure reflected the reservations of critics and exhibitors alike that the project got its demos scrambled. The movie was too violent and nasty for small children, yet not hip enough for teenagers.

The most urgent speculation surrounded a movie that had not yet opened, however—*Saving Private Ryan*. Tracking on the film had concerned some DreamWorks executives because the project showed insufficient strength among young males. Do the kids out there who saw *Armageddon* manifest any appetite for World War II movies? Do they even know what the war represented? Imposing three-page ads ran in the major newspapers over the weekend, carrying this legend: "In the last great invasion of the last great war, the greatest danger for eight men . . . was saving one." While there were no initial quote ads, the cover of *Entertainment Weekly* spoke for itself: "A masterpiece of terror, chaos, blood and courage."

Despite Steven Spielberg's press tour and the encouraging advance buzz, exhibitors were keenly aware of the movie's underlying problems: nearly three hours long, R-rated, and about a war that ended before 80 percent of the U.S. population was born. Also, few serious movies ever had achieved blockbuster status. Indeed, among the top one hundred domestic grossing movies of all time, only eight had been dramas and only one, *Platoon*, was focused on war. Spielberg himself had made the highest-grossing movie ever about World War II—*Schindler's List*, which had reaped $96 million in the U.S.

The entire strategy of a July launch for the movie was also being second-guessed. Movies of this sort normally were grist for December, when audiences seemed more hospitable to weighty dramas and when Oscar season loomed.

One reason that Spielberg went out on a five-city tour—a highly unusual venture for him—was to legitimize the movie historically and fend off possible criticism about its level of violence. Spielberg was accompanied by Stephen E. Ambrose, an esteemed World War II historian and certainly a credible partner in the proceedings. Ambrose thus became a sort of unofficial adviser to the film, even though Spielberg did not approach him until after he had completed principal photography. This move struck skeptics as an effort to legitimize a fictional plot and also protect it against the usual array of litigious wannabe screenwriters who had developed a habit of suing Spielberg on most of his recent films.

There were several reasons for the summer release date. Dream-Works distribution executives were deeply worried about the crush of product scheduled for Christmas release—daunting competition even for a Spielberg picture. Then, too, Spielberg liked summer—even late summer. His movies always had performed strongly in the warm months and he clearly was of the belief that *Saving Private Ryan* would continue this phenomenon.

Despite all the pressure, the marketing of *Saving Private Ryan* had been a study in understatement. "The impact of the movie would be diluted by hype," explained Terry Press, DreamWorks' outspoken chief of advertising. "The experience of the film is stronger than any marketing material I can come up with."

She had a point.

WEEK TWELVE Monday, July 27

Saving Private Ryan commanded the attention of the film industry on this weekend with speculation focusing not only on its results but also on its lost results. In a rare glitch, the Technicolor company failed to deliver more than one hundred prints of the drama to theaters around the country in time for their Friday openings. One of the theaters missing a print was in East Hampton, Long Island, where Steven Spielberg was vacationing. As luck would have it, the director marched to the theater just before ten in the morning to see how it was playing, only to find an outraged manager standing out front, offering refunds. Not surprisingly, the normally even-tempered filmmaker blew a gasket.

The reason for the glitch apparently was that the lab simply had been overloaded, handling not only the Spielberg film but also such movies as *The Parent Trap* and *The Negotiator*, both of which had staged sneak previews over the weekend. Ironically, Spielberg had appeared in a recent video that was sent to exhibitors, emphasizing his almost paternalistic attitude toward the film and urging theater owners to give it special care. They might have—had they received it.

Despite all this, *Ryan* nonetheless defied skeptics by registering an impressive opening weekend of $30.1 million, well ahead of most forecasts. Once again, the grosses seemed to fly in the face of those doubters who had felt that *Saving Private Ryan* would never reach hit status because it was too grim and too intelligent for the young audience. On the opening weekend those moviegoers twenty-five and older outnumbered the younger crowd by 53 percent to 47 percent, but the male-female ratio was roughly fifty-fifty.

Also baffled were those who argued that *Ryan* was simply not summer fare because it was too serious. Jim Tharp, the distribution chief at DreamWorks, responded that summer offered the opportunity to reach the widest potential audience. "We expect the midweeks to be strong and to play well into the fall," he predicted.

Spielberg's decision to embark on his first media tour in forty-seven years, accompanied by Tom Hanks, significantly bolstered the promotion campaign. The interviews resulting from that tour were omnipresent on local TV stations.

Normally reserved film critics for once seemed willing to vent their emotions. "Spielberg has taken Hollywood's depiction of war to a new level," wrote David Ansen in *Newsweek*. "The truth is, this movie so wiped me out I have little taste for quibbling. When you emerge from Spielberg's cauldron, the world doesn't look quite the same."

Kenneth Turan of the *Los Angeles Times* was similarly moved. "A powerful and impressive milestone in the realistic depiction of combat, *Saving Private Ryan* is as much an experience we live through as a film we watch on screen." Mike Clark of *USA Today* took it even more personally. The movie, he wrote, "is a wakeup call for those oblivious to a generation's sacrifice, and for any government that would accede to war for less than imperative reasons." The combat footage, wrote Richard Schickel in *Time*, "is quite possibly the greatest combat sequence ever made."

Janet Maslin in *The New York Times* summed it up, writing, "Steven Spielberg's soberly magnificent new war film, the second such pinnacle in a career of magical versatility, is the ultimate devastating letter home."

Among other films, *The Mask of Zorro* won a close duel for second place, grossing $13.7 million. This nonetheless represented a substantial 39 percent drop for its second week, far greater than its studio had expected. "There's no doubt our adult audience took a hit from *Saving Private Ryan*, commented Jeff Blake, the Sony distribution chief. *Lethal Weapon IV* grossed $13.2 million, off 40 percent, while *Something About Mary* exhibited the best legs. It grossed $12.7 million, off a mere 8 percent, to confirm suspicions that this film, not *Dolittle*, would turn out to be the sleeper of summer.

Neither of the weekend's other newcomers had even passable debuts—not MGM's *Disturbing Behavior* nor Disney's Mafia parody, *Jane Austen's Mafia*. They would be gone before anyone noticed.

Overall totals for the weekend were again impressive, registering 13 percent ahead of last year, with business divided among several movies—a fact that most insiders regarded as healthy despite persistent reminders from the press that the summer still lacked a runaway blockbuster. And those same insiders chose not to talk about the cost of these movies.

The weekend newspapers were resplendent with exuberant quote-filled ads. "A movie of staggering virtuosity and raw lyric power; a masterpiece," wrote the normally restrained Owen Gleiberman of *Entertainment Weekly* about *Saving Private Ryan*. *Something About Mary* also took double-truck ads headlined: "Everyone's Talking About Mary" and featuring a wide array of positive quotes from major media. Equally aggressive were the ads for *Zorro*, which proclaimed it "America's Number One Movie." The last ad making that claim ran Friday night, when *Zorro*'s brief moment in the sun came to an end.

For this was clearly Steven Spielberg's moment and everyone knew it. The premiere in Westwood of *Saving Private Ryan*, unlike other such events this summer, had the pomp and excitement of a true celebration. This was a premiere that Hollywood insiders actually *wanted* to attend. All of the principal streets of Westwood were blocked off as hundreds of stargazers lined up for a glimpse of Tom Hanks, Sylvester Stallone, Rene Russo, Bill Paxton, and others. In a tribute to Spielberg's charisma, more filmmakers were in attendance than at any premiere within memory—the likes of James Brooks, Rob Reiner, Oliver Stone, and Penny Marshall.

Prior to the event, the principals and their guests were invited to a cocktail party at the elegant Geffen Theater, two blocks from the Westwood Theater, where *Saving Private Ryan* would be unveiled. Hanks stood to one side, admittedly a bit unnerved by the hoopla, but Spielberg, almost giddily upbeat, diligently worked the room, shaking hands and chatting with guests. Having placed himself on a rigorous fruit-and-vegetable diet, the director looked leaner and more youthful than at any time in recent years, as if to demonstrate to colleagues the benefits of his stringent work ethic. Having delivered one of the grimmest movies in the recent annals of Hollywood, Spielberg by contrast seemed ebullient. Whatever the shortcomings of his other summer movies like *Deep Impact* or *Zorro*, *Saving Private Ryan* bore his personal stamp. His other movies bespoke commerce, while this was a work of deep-felt passion.

His abiding concern, however, was one of historical context. Taking me aside at the party, he reiterated his fears that the young audience out there would simply not understand what World War II was all about. Could they even begin to understand what was at stake? he wondered aloud. His smile disappeared as he explained that this, indeed, was why he and Hanks had ventured on their tour. The two were eager to explain, even to educate, yet at the same time were well aware of the obstacles. "In the end, either they will get it or they won't," he shrugged, and then, changing the subject, began describing the intricacies of his new diet, which he claimed had exponentially increased his energy level. "The key to this thing is that you've got to squeeze and mix your own fruit juice," he warned. "You can't delegate that task to anyone else." And with that admonition, he sailed back into the crowd, eager to shake more hands.

Half an hour later, he and Hanks strolled along the proverbial red carpet, waving to onlookers and pausing only to serve up their TV sound bites. Prior to the screening, Spielberg yet again betrayed the apprehensions that he had expressed to me. He walked to the front of the huge theater to address his remarks to his expectant audience— something he had never before done at similar events. In viewing his movie, he advised, bear in mind that "D-Day was nothing less than the pivotal moment of the twentieth century." This was not just another campaign in the long history of warfare. This was about "saving Western civilization." It was as though the director was urging his audience to spread the word—this was, like *Schindler's List*, something more than just an action movie.

When he'd concluded, Spielberg took his seat to generous applause. The moment the theater grew dark, he and Hanks and their wives were on their feet, unobtrusively making their way out of the theater and into waiting limousines. They had made their pitch. They had done their tour. And now, as Spielberg liked to say, it was in the laps of the movie gods.

August

WEEK THIRTEEN Monday, August 3

Though summer was only half over, the weekend felt as though the curtain were coming down. All of the summer's major movies had now opened. The audience had cast its votes at the box office. The results were in and the Hollywood players were licking their wounds and working on their spins.

A few pricey projects had yet to appear, of course, but the advance buzz already had rendered them nonstarters. Insiders who had seen Warner Bros.' thriller *The Avengers* had called it "unwatchable." Brian De Palma's *Snake Eyes* also came with the stigma of a loser.

By contrast, the week's winner was *Saving Private Ryan* which, after surprising everyone with a $30 million opening, had followed up with an impressive $23.3 million, a drop of just 24 percent. This represented the best second week of any summer movie that ever had opened at the top of the charts. With $73 million already registered, the possibility loomed that this might become a challenger to *Armageddon* as the top grosser of the summer. The handicappers now put *Armageddon* topping out at $190 million.

Despite its length, grisly content, and R rating, *Saving Private Ryan* had generated more electricity than any film thus far in the year. It had been heralded in newspaper editorials and argued about on talk shows and, more important, had managed to penetrate the psyche of the youth culture.

Second place this week went to *The Parent Trap*, which finished a distant second at $11.5 million. Disney was convinced that this PG-rated movie would hold up well through August because of its appeal to young families. The raunchy *Something About Mary* finished in third place with $11 million, down just 12 percent, and now improbably seemed headed for the $100 million mark. Two other gross-out movies did far less well, however. Universal's *BASEketball* from the Zucker brothers and starring the creators of "South Park," Trey Parker and Matt Stone, opened to a limp $3 million. And *Jane Austen's Mafia* from Disney was barely holding its own.

The Negotiator, a suspense thriller released by Warner Bros. but financed by the New Regency company, opened with a solid $10.4 million, and Fox's remake of the Cinderella story, *Ever After* starring Drew Barrymore, emerged from the fray with $8.5 million. All in all it was a strong weekend, continuing the solid summer-long performance. Ticket sales for the three-day period totaled $118 million, an improvement of 8 percent from the previous year.

In terms of advertising support, the Sunday papers for the first time in many weeks were not bedecked with double-page movie ads. The only studio to buy two pages in major cities was not DreamWorks for *Saving Private Ryan*, but rather Warner Bros. for *The Negotiator*. "Summer's Best Surprise," proclaimed a huge headline, a quote by Joanna Langfield from something called "The Movie Minute." The studio's support for the film reflected its urgent need for another summer hit. The only other summer success from Warner Bros., *Lethal Weapon IV*, would cross the $100 million mark by the weekend.

WEEK FOURTEEN Monday, August 10

Articles about the impact of *Saving Private Ryan* continued to run in magazines and newspapers around the nation, examining the film's impact on veterans of that war and also exploring the reactions of younger audiences to the graphic combat scenes. Not surprisingly, the movie continued to dominate the charts as well. The film became the eighth release of summer '98 to pass the $100 million mark with an estimated three-day gross of $17.2 million, running up a strong per-theater average of $6,640 at 2,592 screens. For Steven Spielberg, this marked the tenth time that one of his movies had ranked in first place on *Variety*'s rankings. The only director to have topped him was Vincente Minnelli, whose sleek Hollywood musicals and comedies had registered eleven first-place finishes in the forties and fifties.

Snake Eyes, the Brian De Palma film starring Nicolas Cage, opened at $16.5 million despite mediocre reviews, and *Halloween: H2O*, a slasher movie from Miramax, reported a gross of $16 million. *Snake Eyes* was also laboring under the disadvantage of an R rating, despite repeated protests from its director.

Given the weak newcomers, the weekend's total numbers were down 5 percent from the previous week, but still a stalwart 18 percent ahead of the comparable period in 1997. Through Sunday the year's box office had reached $4.3 billion, or 10 percent ahead of 1997.

Among the holdovers, *Something About Mary* continued to show astonishing vitality, grossing $9.8 million and reaching a total of $76.8 million. *The Parent Trap* declined 26 percent to register $8.2 million in its second week. The Drew Barrymore movie, *Ever After*, grossed $7.8 million, a decline of just 9 percent, reflecting the fact that the fairy tale had found a loyal following among the teen crowd but had yet to cross over to an older audience. Despite heavy advertising, Warner Bros. was having little luck selling *The Negotiator*. The movie dropped 37 percent in its second week for a gross of $6.5 million.

The Mask of Zorro also seemed to be petering out ahead of expectations. The retro romance fell to $5.6 million, off 33 percent, and had made $71.7 million so far. The vaunted $100 million plateau seemed a distant hope for the pricey TriStar film. *Armageddon*, meanwhile, was still pulling in audiences and had passed $172 million, while *Lethal Weapon IV* had hit $116.3 million.

With three weeks remaining in August, these strongly performing blockbusters had a chance to add substantially to their tallies. Following a long-standing tradition the studios had no heavyweights left to unfurl in late summer, though Warner Bros. was spending heavily on *The Avengers*, attempting to combat weak tracking and hostile word of mouth. The ads, not surprisingly, depicted it as the hottest thriller of summer.

The dire forecasts for *The Avengers* came as no surprise to Warner Bros., which had financed it. The studio already had all but given up on the film, which was an extraordinary bit of defeatism considering the superstar cast, the $60 million cost, and the fact that it was once deemed the studio's prime summer prospect.

While it was shooting in London, *The Avengers*, which starred Sean Connery, Uma Thurman, and Ralph Fiennes, had received an unusual degree of favorable hype. Here was a romantic thriller with style, sophistication, and retro charm. Yet a week before its scheduled opening, Warner Bros., in response to press inquiries, let it be known that there would be no premiere, no media screenings, not even a press kit. If critics wanted to see it, they would have to pay their way on Friday mornings at their local theater—the studio would not show the movie to them, nor pay for their ticket.

It is not unheard of for a studio to duck critics' screenings in the case of an action or exploitation picture that clearly doesn't work. Critics' opinions were irrelevant on projects such as these; why go to the trouble of screening a movie when you know you're going to get killed? studios reason. With prestige movies such as *The Avengers*, however, such a refusal was extraordinary. Indeed, Warner Bros.' decision inspired an article by Bernard Weinraub in *The New York Times* suggesting skeptically that the studios "stealth opening" indicated that it "prefers to delay critical appraisals until after the movie opens rather than face the customary Friday reviews."

Faced with the *Times'* admonition, Charlotte Kandel, executive vice president of publicity at Warner Bros., was compelled to issue a convoluted rationalization. "We're dealing with a cultural icon, not just in America but around the world," she explained. "We've always been concerned that reviews of the film will have comparisons to the original "Avengers." We feel confident in the movie and we feel it will deliver big-time to the audience. We think it's a very hip and cool movie."

Well, maybe. What she didn't say was that Warner co-CEOs Bob Daly and Terry Semel positively hated the movie. Hence, when Jerry Weintraub, the producer, and Jeremiah Chechik, the director, begged them to hold critics' screenings, they refused even to discuss the issue.

To Warner's watchers, the big mystery surrounding *The Avengers*, however, was not why they hated it but why they ever agreed to make it. Said one Warner hand who was close to the production, "The only tenable explanation is that neither Daly nor Semel ever read the script. They had no idea what sort of movie they were making. They knew it had a $60 million budget and three big stars and they needed a summer movie so they went with it, and when they saw it they realized it was not close to what they expected."

The question as to whether Daly or Semel customarily read scripts was a favorite subject of debate at the studio. Since the two executives had been doing their job for almost two decades and were responsible for several other divisions as well, such as TV, music, and Warner retail stores, it was theorized that they relied heavily on their aides to read the screenplays and pass along their recommendations. In the case of *The Avengers*, this process apparently had broken down.

According to one executive who has worked with Chechik, the reason the Montreal-born filmmaker was attracted to the project to begin with was because it was "highly stylized, somewhat surreal, and distinctly nonlinear." Indeed, this was the way he viewed the TV series, which he'd watched as a kid. This was also the reason three major stars had committed to the screenplay (written by Don McPherson), in Chechik's view. "Why else would Sean Connery agree to play a heavy for $8 million, less than his usual salary, if it wasn't because his was a surreal role in an arty, nonlinear movie?" Chechik had once asked his producer.

The director himself had been skeptical about the project when it was first brought to him by Lucy Fisher, then an executive vice president at Warner Bros. who later moved on to Sony before the film was shot. Chechik had just finished shooting a remake of *Diabolique* starring Sharon Stone for Warner Bros. and the studio apparently liked his work even though his film proved to be a box office failure, grossing only $16.5 million domestically. "I thought *The Avengers* could be made as a quirky movie that maybe Gaumont or some art house distributor could release, but it wasn't a studio movie by any means," Chechik told a friend at the time.

Oddly, the studio persisted even after Fisher's exit. Billy Gerber, who had shared the top production responsibilities, again urged Chechik to take it on despite the vehement opposition of his coequal, Lorenzo DiBonaventura. Another proponent was Jerry Weintraub, a swaggering, tough-talking, onetime manager of John Denver and others, who had had a colorful and checkered career, at one time heading United Artists and later running Weintraub Entertainment, an independently financed production company that had disintegrated amid a rain of controversy and lawsuits. A man who liked hard-edged movies, it was puzzling to many at the studio why Weintraub had long been fixated on *The Avengers*—especially on Chechik's take on *The Avengers*. To be sure, Weintraub had admired the Canadian's first film, the very commercial *National Lampoon's Christmas Vacation*, released in 1989. Since then, however, Chechik had revealed his more serious streak, directing *Benny and Joon*—a critically well-received film dealing with mental illness—and, of course, *Diabolique*.

In its original incarnation, "The Avengers" was very cool, very British, and rather arcane. John Steed and Emma Peel, played by Patrick Macnee and Diana Rigg, were sometimes pitted against a malevolent Scot, Sir August De Wynter (later to become Sean Connery), who had managed to gain control of the weather and thus blackmail civilization. Steed carried an umbrella, not a gun, and the relationship between him and Peel was flirtatious but platonic—they were just too cool for it to be hot.

The series had its cult following, but that was, after all, the 1960s. After *Batman*, however, Warner Bros. began to look kindly upon TV series and offbeat heroes. Tim Burton had done some pretty strange things with *Batman* and had gotten away with it. Why not let Jeremiah Chechik try his luck?

Though DiBonaventura's antagonism for *The Avengers* continued to be so intense that on at least one occasion Semel publicly chastised him to keep silent, Chechik and Weintraub managed to get through their shoot without major problems. The first omen of what lay ahead came in the form of a notification that the studio had locked in a summer date. This was not exactly a prototypical summer movie, the filmmakers protested. Even as they argued, however, they knew that, other than *Lethal Weapon IV*, Warner Bros. had no summer movies. *The Avengers* had star power and the studio was not given to subtle strategies.

Not long thereafter, a proposed ad campaign arrived from the studio. Again, it was a thoroughly professional campaign, but it seemed to the producer and director like a campaign for a summer action movie, which their film certainly was not.

Then came the most ominous news. Warner Bros.' researchers had decreed that the initial test screening for *The Avengers* would be held in Phoenix, Arizona, so that the studio could determine how the movie would play before a "typical" crowd. "The moment Chechik and Weintraub walked into that theater, they knew they were cooked," said an associate. "This was a working-class audience, perhaps a third Hispanic. You could tell they didn't understand the movie, and didn't understand the Englishisms. It was a disaster." The atmosphere on the Warner corporate jet heading back to Burbank was icy. Little was said. The sides had clearly been drawn.

The next morning the producer and director met in Terry Semel's office with ten Warner executives and research personnel, and the ordeal of the night before was reviewed. The audience had hated the movie; the cards they'd filled out reinforced that impression. Major changes would have to be made in the cut. The musical score also would have to be redone.

"Many of Chechik's favorite scenes were the first to go," one Warner Bros. executive recalled. "The studio was determined to reshape this movie as a summer action picture, even though it hadn't been shot that way."

"Chechik felt he was in the hands of these faceless, nameless research people," said one associate. "They were dictating the changes. He knew now that his movie would not just be a failure, it would be a debacle."

"The Warner Bros. studio was having something like a psychotic breakdown," said another filmmaker on the lot who knew about the project. "Nothing was turning out right for them. They had greenlighted a movie they never wanted to make, and now they were trying to re-create it into something that wasn't there. It was craziness."

When the release date finally arrived, it seemed more like an end than a beginning. The studio refused to underwrite a premiere either in London or New York. A party was held in London, ostensibly for those who created the soundtrack album, but the movie was not shown and none of the stars were there.

The reviews were predictably scabrous. A surprising number of critics seemed not only irritated at the movie, but also at having to pay their way into the theater. Janet Maslin of *The New York Times* called it "a film to gall fans of the old television series and perplex anyone else. I can't remember another Friday-morning show where I heard actual cries of 'Ugh' on the way out the door."

Not only did the *Los Angeles Times* movie critic, Ken Turan, deplore the movie, but even the paper's TV critic, Howard Rosenberg, chimed in. Having been a fan of the old TV series, Rosenberg called the movie "a sorry monotone of a movie . . . a bad seed."

Jerry Weintraub, for one, was devastated. It had been his intention to make the "coolest" movie of the summer. Its reception, however, was beyond cool; it was downright frigid.

WEEK FIFTEEN Monday, August 17

For many families around the world, the last half of August represented the heart of the vacation season, a time when they paused to catch their breath. To Hollywood distributors, however, August was a dumping ground, an occasion to release those films that were deemed hopeless or those produced by filmmakers the studios wanted to punish, mixed in with an assortment of genre or exploitation films aimed at hard-core action fans.

One exception this week was *How Stella Got Her Groove Back*, which represented another specifically targeted movie from Twentieth Century Fox, along the lines of *Waiting to Exhale*. *Stella*, which starred Angela Bassett, grossed an impressive $11.8 million on its first weekend. The demographics were true to form, with 80 percent of the moviegoers black, 70 percent female, and 70 percent over the age of twenty-five.

The Fox strategy, of course, was to start with a targeted audience and try to break out from there. Whether *Stella* would achieve that remained to be seen, but in the first week, at least, the movie impacted slightly on *Saving Private Ryan*. The Spielberg picture clung to first place, though, posting a $12.9 million weekend and a still-solid $4,861 per-screen average, leading the fray for its fourth successive weekend. Third place belonged to *The Avengers* from Warner Bros., which grossed a dismal $10.7 million for the weekend.

Despite its display of stage fright in canceling media screenings and premieres of *The Avengers*, Warner Bros. spent liberally on ads, putting the emphasis on style over content. "Saving the world in style," proclaimed the copy line. The critics didn't seem to appreciate either the "style" or the snub, and the studio made no effort to manufacture quotes for ads, not even calling upon the quote-on-demand blurbmeisters for instant effusion.

The two other films making their debut the previous weekend failed to catch on. Polygram's *Return to Paradise* effectively vanished with a gross of $2.4 million in 965 theaters, and a rare Miramax children's movie, *Air Bud: Golden Retriever*, posted a mere $2.5 million on 1,669 screens. Two holdovers suffered major erosion. Paramount's *Snake Eyes*, the Brian De Palma thriller, sank 47 percent during its second weekend while *Halloween: H20* dropped 48 percent.

Something About Mary, meanwhile, continued its remarkable hold, dropping just 6 percent. The movie grossed $9.1 million, bringing its total to $91.6 million. A movie catchily titled *The Slums of Beverly Hills* opened in seven theaters, grossing a hearty $130,000 with an $18,571 average.

As evidence that the fall doldrums were at hand, no film grossed over $15 million during the weekend for the first time since early May, but ticket sales were 19 percent higher than the comparable weekend of 1997. With many schools starting the following week, midweek ticket sales soon would start to tumble. Bucking this trend, four movies were scheduled to open with wide releases on Friday: *Blade* from New Line, *Dance with Me* from Sony, *Wrongfully Accused* from Warner Bros., and *Dead Man on Campus* from Paramount and MTV. Not surprisingly, two of the four fell into the gross-out category.

WEEK SIXTEEN Monday, August 24

The opportunity for exploitation movies to make a quick strike in late August was ably demonstrated by *Blade*, starring Wesley Snipes as a vampire slayer. Inspired by a Marvel Comics hero, the Snipes character has both extraordinary strength and a lifelong lust for blood, but opts instead to become a sort of black Robocop, wreaking harm upon his fellow bloodsuckers. The movie lapped up an opening weekend gross of $17 million, catering to a substantial black audience. Among holdovers, *Saving Private Ryan* still held pretty well at $10 million and *Something About Mary* at $7.6 million.

In a way the most intriguing news from the weekend was the astonishing dismissal of *The Avengers* by the moviegoing public. After opening to a lame $10.7 million, the film plummeted 66 percent in its second week to $3.6 million, one of the steepest declines for a major release in recent memory.

Also doing disappointing business were *Dead Man on Campus* at $4.3 million for the weekend and *Wrongfully Accused* at $3.4 million. Following the disappointing results of *Jane Austen's Mafia* and *BASEketball*, the once-rich franchise for gross-out comedies pioneered by the Zucker brothers and Jim Abrahams seemed now to have become both unfocused and rickety.

Another surprise weekend loser was *Dance with Me*, directed by Randa Haines and once thought to have a shot at becoming another *Saturday Night Fever* or *Flashdance*. No such luck. The Hispanic-themed picture didn't catch the public eye, opening with a dull $4.5 million weekend.

Indeed, the only late-summer movie still deemed to have a shot at earning a sleeper label was *54*, which would open later in the week. This disco movie starring Mike Myers would be released by Miramax, which, in the past, had found good luck in this late-August slot. But the promotional fusillade for *54* had yet to begin.

WEEK SEVENTEEN Monday, August 31

After all the cosmic plans and lavish campaigns, summer '98 seemed to be ending with a dull murmur rather than a triumphant roar. The nation's attention was shifting to school, football, a new TV season, and other distractions. Movies no longer were near the top of anyone's agenda.

The new movies in the marketplace were attracting scant notice. *54*, from Miramax, and *Why Do Fools Fall in Love*, from Warner Bros., opened to meager grosses of $6.6 million and $4.2 million respectively, while *Blade*, the Wesley Snipes vampire movie, held well at

$11.1 million, down a moderate 35 percent. The absence of exciting new films seemed to be catapulting *Something About Mary* to a whole new life at the box office—an extraordinarily rare phenomenon in the annals of summer movies. The Fox comedy actually gained strength over the weekend, posting $8.8 million for a gain of 14 percent. This was sufficient to vault *Mary* ahead of *Saving Private Ryan* for the first time since its July 17 opening and bring its cumulative gross to $116.7 million.

Two forces were propelling *Mary*, according to Tom Sherak, Fox's distribution guru. Filmgoers were going back for a second visit, a practice that is not unusual with dramas or sci-fi epics, but is rare for a comedy. At the same time, the movie had increasingly penetrated the subculture of small-town America. "Films with an R rating take much longer to reach the smaller markets," Sherak observed. "There's a bit more resistance in booking them and in the audience accepting them. The good news is that moviegoers in small-town America seem to know all about the film and are ready to embrace it. It's gotten into the movie culture."

In response to this, the studio was actually adding 154 new theaters to its mix rather than pulling back, and also was going wide with a revised TV campaign. The assumption was that *Mary* could well move into first place once again with continued support. Its only imminent competition next week would come from yet another exploitation picture, *Knock Off*, starring Jean-Claude Van Damme.

The failure of Miramax's *54* to make its mark came as no surprise to those who saw the film. It had the choppy look of a movie that was re-edited under duress. The gossip about *54* was that Miramax had objected to scenes it deemed distractingly homoerotic and had demanded reshooting as well as eleventh-hour alterations in the editing room. As a result several scenes in the film seemed to double back on themselves, starting in one direction, then abruptly shifting to another.

In fact, none of the three retro movies about disco that opened in 1998 seemed to stir either nostalgia or an awakening of interest among younger audiences. Further visits to the disco scene might best be reserved for another generation.

WEEK EIGHTEEN Tuesday, September 8

And so, the denouement. After all the bombast of summer, the season's final weekend ended with a triumphant gross-out comedy leading a tattered and forlorn parade. In the end, *Godzilla* was long since forgotten, but here was *Something About Mary* capturing a far wider audience than had ever been imagined. Working its way up the box office charts for more than seven weeks, the movie emerged as number one with a four-day take of $11.5 million, a feat unheard of for a wide-release movie. In finally leading the field, *Mary* surged past *Blade*, which was off 25 percent to $10.4 million. All other movies effectively tumbled off the radar screen.

Indeed, the only footnote to the weekend was the revelation that *Titanic*, having finally run its course in discount theaters, had actually managed to cross the $600 million mark in its domestic release. It achieved this milestone one day before its long-waited video release. *Titanic* originally was heralded as the big release of summer '97, but, one summer later, the ghost of *Titanic* still loomed large.

The FALLOUT

If mixed messages emerged from summer '97, the lessons of summer '98 were delivered with alarming clarity. Even as the anticlimactic releases of late August came and went, the studios already were reshaping their strategies for the future. "This summer seemed downright brutal," Joe Roth acknowledged, running his hand through an ample mane of hair that seemed more liberally laced with silver than when we'd last met in June. "I knew this business was becoming more competitive—that's true of every business—but now it's getting crazy."

All across Hollywood, Roth's peers were inclined to agree. While the surface numbers made summer '98 seem more bountiful than previous seasons, insiders at the studios knew otherwise. The good news was that moviegoers spent $2.6 billion to see the films of summer, which was 16 percent more than in 1997, the first period of significant growth in over five years. And though no megahit emerged from the pack, business was spread generously among more movies from more studios. The range of choice offered the moviegoing public also showed a marked improvement during summer '98, with serious adult movies successfully challenging the frenzied assault of action fare.

All that was good news, but balanced against it were some troubling realities. At a time when nearly all sectors of American business were successfully keeping costs under control and inflation had all but disappeared, the movie industry found itself gripped by its own private inflationary spiral. Production and marketing costs for summer '98 sustained double-digit increases, despite concerted efforts to control them. Nine movies costing over $100 million were released during the summer, compared with six a year earlier, and a few, like *Godzilla* and *Armageddon*, had even entered the perilous $150 million zone. The summer also yielded more than its share of expensive mistakes, like *Quest for Camelot* and *The Avengers*, without huge breakout projects to compensate for them. Indeed, a few of those movies that seemed substantial winners on paper were, in fact, profitable principally to their superstar talent. *Saving Private Ryan* and *Lethal Weapon IV* were prize examples, with studios giving away over 35 to 40 percent of their gross receipts to Spielberg, Gibson, and others.

There were other numbers worries, albeit niggling ones. The 16 percent jump in box office receipts wasn't quite what it seemed. Admission prices had risen by about 5 percent, accounting for some of the increase. The box office numbers also for the first time included receipts from Imax special-format theaters, which experienced a 10 percent growth during the year. In addition, the calendar smiled on summer '98 with the configuration of the Memorial Day and Labor Day weekends adding a week to summer playing time.

Details aside, summer '98 had proven to be a superbly beneficent period for the superstars, their agents, managers, and assorted camp followers. Arguably it had also been a good season for the moviegoers—at least better than the previous two or three years.

But for the entities charged with the responsibility of creating, marketing, and distributing the product, and hopefully showing a return to their stockholders, summer '98 had proven a major disappointment. Permeating the executive suites was the sense that movies were now a lousy business, whose structure and practices were in desperate need of overhaul. If the men sitting atop the corporate pyramids had distrusted the business going into summer '98, their antipathy was only further inflamed by the time summer had run its course.

And it fell to the studio chiefs and their minions to work out a new set of strategies to cope with this mood. The process would prove a painful one. Studio chiefs, like most corporate apparatchiks, tended to like the status quo. They all had grown up within the system. It had made them wealthy beyond their wildest dreams. They well understood the inequities and disproportionate rewards of the system, but they'd made it work for them. They had not, however, made it work for the multinational moguls who now ruled their destinies.

There, indeed, was the rub. Movies never constituted a "business," as defined by the new post-eighties lexicon—at least not since Hollywood's golden era of the thirties and forties. In that short window of time, the near-fanatical devotion of an enormous "habit" audience of moviegoers had made it possible to predict an annual return on investment. The studios effectively owned the talent, thanks to an intricate system of contract players. They also owned the mechanism of distribution, thanks to their control over theaters. In making fifty or sixty movies a year at controllable prices, they could bury their losers in a maze of creative accounting.

That, to be sure, was a "business" that the M.B.A.'s would understand. MGM's profits were sufficient for Louis B. Mayer to become the highest-paid executive in America just before World War II. But it was hubris for the media mavens of the nineties to imagine that they could reinvent that structure and implant it amid a nineties media environment.

In striving for that, they'd misread several barometers. The advent of the global blockbuster led them to believe that movies of this sort could be produced on an assembly line. The advent of video led them to conclude that technology would open up an endless array of new revenue streams to serve as an economic underpinning for their increasingly expensive movies. The growth of the global audience for American films led them to hypothesize that a proliferation of overseas moviegoers would more than compensate for the static U.S. audience. In establishing worldwide oligopolies in distribution, they believed these mechanisms would force-feed their movies to cable and satellite audiences across Europe, Latin America, and Asia.

The leaders of the new entertainment leviathans were so arrogant about their ability to achieve these scenarios that they publicly forecast extraordinary levels of growth. In re-creating Disney, Michael Eisner set himself the goal of 20 percent annual growth. Gobbling up movie, TV, cable, and satellite companies as well as sports teams, Rupert Murdoch pumped up revenues in just five years from slightly over $7 billion to almost $13 billion in 1998, burying much of his profits in Australian and Caribbean tax havens (his rivals guessed Murdoch's corporate tax rate averaged 5.7 percent, less than a fifth of that paid by Viacom, Time Warner, or other U.S. competitors).

These forecasts for growth, however, overlooked some important issues. For one thing, the sheer ego-driven competitiveness of the global media moguls had driven up acquisition costs to such an extent that profit prospects were pushed further and further into the future. As Rupert Murdoch headed into his late sixties, his voracious appetite seemed virtually out of control. It was one thing to spend $575 million for Twentieth Century Fox in 1985 and $1.9 billion for six big-city TV stations that formed the basis for the Fox network, but by the late nineties, he seemed to be spinning off into outer space, paying $1.9 billion for the Family Channel, $4.6 billion for NFL broadcast rights, and $1.4 billion for the Manchester United Soccer Club in England. As a result, while revenues kept climbing, his actual profits remained flat and shares of his company traded at lower multiples than those of rival companies. As his cost of borrowing soared, Murdoch confessed he'd been remiss in his thinking, explaining, "It's very expensive to have a lowly rated stock, but we've never been frightened to take a long-term view."

His competitors may have looked askance at his strategies, but they admired his ferocity. "Rupert wants to rule the world and he seems to be doing it," said Viacom's Sumner Redstone.

Michael Eisner at Disney was no less ambitious than Murdoch. It was Eisner's dream that the typical consumer would patronize Disney movies, watch Disney TV shows, buy Disney videos, spend money at Disney stores, vacation on Disney cruise lines, take his or her kids to Disney theme parks—all the while becoming completely enveloped in the Disney subculture.

In pumping billions into these acquisitions, however, the nineties moguls had inadvertently promulgated a blur of leisure-time choices

that were exacerbating problems for their movie studios. In the Hollywood business model of the thirties and forties, movies held sway as
the prime leisure-time activity for Americans. With a new millennium
dawning, a veritable frenzy of options now confronted virtually every
consumer.

Which would be fine for the media giants if they continued
to control all the options. But it was not turning out that way. Ever-
increasing numbers of people were devoting their time to the Internet,
which had remained substantially out of the reach of the Murdochs
and Eisners. Indeed many of the most persuasive postmillennium
models showed the Internet becoming the primary delivery system for
TV, music, and other forms of information and entertainment, a direct
challenge to the established distribution patterns of the entertainment
industry.

There were also indications that the movie and TV industries were
following the trend of the music business, where local repertoire had
increasingly pushed aside American exports. The indigenous cinema
cultures of Germany, Italy, the United Kingdom, and other countries,
having been all but obliterated in the eighties by the Hollywood onslaught, were showing signs of recovery, offering idiosyncratic film
fare—financed by local entrepreneurs—to ever-expanding audiences.

In short, a distinct possibility was emerging that the media and
entertainment universe might not become the exclusive domain of the
media barons—a fact that further fueled their frustration with Hollywood.

Having allocated billions of dollars to establishing global delivery
systems, the media moguls had to be able to depend on a steady flow
of financially viable software to feed their distribution machines.
Cable and satellite networks could not function without movies. The
theme parks and company stores were dependent on new toys, styles,
and ideas created by movies.

Mindful of this, the corporate titans were determined not to let
Hollywood become an expensive philanthropy. In the rigid calculus
of corporate thinking, movies had to show a substantial return, just

like any other product line. If the assembly line could not meet corporate projections, it had to be retooled and realigned.

That's where the problem started. The Hollywood of the thirties and forties was led by an uneasy amalgam of entrepreneurs and filmmakers who were dedicated not just to money but also to movies. Their decisions were unilateral, not framed by committees of suits. Personal whim took precedence over business plans. Talent relationships were more important than ties to Wall Street. Rather than chasing quarterly earnings, Hollywood chased stars and directors.

And though big studios like MGM, Fox, Columbia, and Warner Bros. were the key players in town, much of the true innovation of that period stemmed from feisty entrepreneurs like David O. Selznick and Samuel Goldwyn, who were largely self-financed and zealously autonomous.

Hollywood was never a true corporate culture. Its fortunes went up and down cyclically, according to the success of individual films and the resiliency of their financing. The multinationals understood cycles. They realized that what the lawyers called "intellectual property" was subject to unpredictable upswings and downswings. When they heard filmmakers talk fatalistically about the movie gods, they empathized.

On the other hand, they demanded results. They required the trappings mandated by their gospel of growth: precise earnings projections, persuasive business models, quantified strategic objectives, and other statistical crutches that M.B.A.'s lean on.

When Warner Bros. was actually ruled by the Warner brothers, they would shrug off a bad summer, albeit irritably and with a tirade of foul language. The Warner Bros. that was now owned by Time Warner had no such tolerance. The studio's tumbling fortunes happily came at a time when the parent company's shares were soaring thanks to optimistically revisionist calculations about the future of cable. The $13 million per episode paid by NBC for the renewal of the studio's prize TV show, "ER," also distracted from the movie losses. Nonetheless, there were dark rumblings emanating from Time Warner's New

York headquarters, along with hints that continued losses from movies could not be tolerated.

But what to do? Corporate headquarters could dispatch battalions of consultants, such as those unleashed by Edgar Bronfman, Jr. upon Universal, but their thick reports would hardly ensure improved results. Indeed, Universal's fortunes fell sharply following the onslaught of consultants.

Clearly this was not the appropriate economic or regulatory climate in which to tear down the existing structure and try to reinvent it along the lines of the old Hollywood. On the other hand, a series of palliatives could be introduced—measures designed to cushion the impact of the hits and misses. The cycles would still prevail, but at least they would be tempered by the following measures:

- Reduce the number of releases and demand that producers supply co-financing from outside sources. By the end of summer '98, all the studios were significantly curtailing their 1999 output. Disney was taking the lead, planning to release only fifteen or so films in 1999 compared to the over thirty releases distributed by Disney a few years ago. Only Sony insisted it would maintain its present level of output, arguing that, unlike the other majors, it controlled no networks or theme parks, but rather counted on filmed entertainment as its core business.

- Cut back sharply on pricey event movies. "The trend is away from the expensive techno-movies," observed Larry Gleason, MGM's distribution chief. Given the fact that the big effects movies of 1998—*Armageddon* and *Godzilla*—were both problem projects, this retrenchment was hardly a surprise. This mandate did not portend that the genre had run its course. Indeed, the expectations were high for two big special-effects extravaganzas scheduled for release in summer '99: George Lucas's prequel, *Star Wars: Episode One—The Phantom Menace*, and a bloated sci-fi western coming from Warner Bros. called *The Wild Wild West*, directed by

Barry Sonnenfeld, the man responsible for *Men in Black*. But these tentpole epics had virtually a clear field for summer '99.

• Step up the output of relatively inexpensive comedies and genre pictures geared to young filmgoers. With fewer big-budget movies destined for the pipeline, comedies modeled after *There's Something About Mary* inevitably would emerge as the leading contenders. The studios were acutely conscious of the steady shift in the nation's demos that sharply favored the teenage crowd. The success of Fox's *Ever After*, the Drew Barrymore vehicle that recycled Cinderella, was interpreted as a model for the youth demographic. The movie opened to modest business, but thanks to the loyalty of teenage girls, it sustained its run for over three months, grossing nearly $70 million in the U.S. alone.

Another genre aimed at teens and increasingly coming into favor will most certainly be slasher movies like *I Know What You Did Last Summer*. It is not surprising that Sony, the company that gave us *Godzilla* in 1998, will focus in summer '99 not on big effects movies, but on slasher sequels, an Adam Sandler comedy, and a children's effects movie titled *Muppets in Space*.

By successfully releasing serious movies like *The Truman Show* and *Saving Private Ryan* during summer '98, distributors reinforced their theory that, as Warner Bros.' Terry Semel declared, "good movies will play any time of year." This was no small lesson to an industry that, more and more, has tended to make summer a ghetto of action fare.

Indeed, action films, especially sequels, may become an endangered species by next summer. Even Warner Bros., which had habitually depended on sequels as its summer tentpoles, probably would have none on its agenda. The explanations were more pragmatic than strategic. Aware of the sky-high salaries Warner Bros. had paid on *Lethal Weapon IV*, stars involved in other sequels had pumped up prices as never before. As a result, studios desperate to hammer out sequels to hits like *Men in Black*, *Jumanji*, and even *Rush Hour* found themselves coming up empty-handed.

At each individual studio, the business of mobilizing new strategies took on different nuances as a result of the politics of the parent company and its relative performance during summer '98.

For Universal, summer '98 was a study in utter exasperation, with corporate troubles piling atop those of the studio. Wherever he turned, Edgar Bronfman, Jr., found himself whipsawed. The economic malaise sweeping Asia pummeled sales of alcoholic beverages, sharply reducing profits of his parent company, Seagram, and hurting the price of its shares. By late September, Seagram stock had plunged 35 percent in three short months. While the much-heralded $10.4 billion acquisition of Polygram stayed on track despite the dollar weakening against the Dutch guilder, Edgar Jr.'s plan to deal away Polygram's movie business for as much as $1 billion hit the wall. There were no takers. By early fall, it was apparent that his best option was to split off the Polygram film library and peddle it to the highest bidder, which turned out to be MGM, while retaining some of its production units within Universal. Several elements were scaring off prospective buyers. Whoever acquired Polygram's film business would have to pump in over $300 million to fund new films and pay off debt. The mediocre opening in late September of *What Dreams May Come*, Polygram's $85 million tear-jerker starring Robin Williams, hardly increased confidence about the other projects in Polygram's pipeline.

For Edgar Jr., there was little left to do but to keep stressing that music represented a solid growth industry that fortunately lacked the daunting cycles of the film business. It was also a business he understood and could manage, his aides reiterated.

As for the film side, there was no denying the studio's utter failure in creating a summer slate, but, again, better times lay ahead. Releases for fall and Christmas and beyond had looked solid on paper, buttressed by a sequel to *Babe* called *Pig in the City*, *Patch Adams* starring Robin Williams as a middle-aged medical student, and *Meet Joe Black*, the very long and very expensive Brad Pitt–Anthony Hopkins remake of *Death Takes a Holiday* that originally was to be the summer centerpiece of 1998. Early in September Casey Silver, Universal's production chief, arranged a private screening for me as part of his effort to counter the industry skepticism over the long-delayed project. This was well before the media screenings; indeed, final credits were not yet in place. As I sat with Silver in his cavernous office prior to the screening, I sensed his bemused fatalism. He had been at Universal for eleven years in various capacities, he explained, and it had been a good run. Now it was make-or-break time. "Everything's riding on these next several films," he said with a pained smile. "It all comes down to this."

Fatalism aside, there was clearly a subtext of urgency in Silver's manner. Not only did he care about his job, he also cared deeply about movies in general. Though more reserved and distant than most of his counterparts at other studios, Silver, who started as a writer and production assistant, was fiercely dedicated to the filmmaking process.

For the next three hours I was alone in Silver's screening room. Soon I found myself pacing the room as the rhythms of the movie became glacial. Martin Brest was a meticulous filmmaker, but this was clearly a case where the style of the filmmaker was at odds with the content of the movie.

My first call the next morning was from Casey Silver. "What did you think?" came the question.

"It just didn't work for me," I replied. "It's a slight tale and it should be a moving one, but its sheer weight worked against it. Instead of a soufflé, you've got yourself a cheese omelet."

There was a slight pause at the other end of the line. "Listen, I asked for your candid opinion and you gave it to me. I disagree with you, of course. I happen to think it's great."

Silver reiterated the terms of our deal. I had agreed not to tell anyone that I had seen the movie. It was the same deal as I had made on *The Truman Show*. The only difference was that I'd admired that movie, which was not the case with *Meet Joe Black*. If this was to be the cornerstone of Silver's future slate, then he might soon be confronting some problems.

In any case, Silver's films were in the can, and several of them, such as *Meet Joe Black* and the sequel to *Babe*, were expensive projects indeed, and both had run dangerously behind schedule. Once those films had run their course, Edgar Jr. and his top team, including Ron Meyer, would make their determination about Universal's future commitment to movies. Several key decisions already had been handed down. In the future, Universal would adhere to Paramount's policy of passing the hat on most of its projects. Before the green light started flashing, some form of cofinancing would have to be available. It would not be enough for producers to come with a script and a cast; now they would also have to come up with an investor. At the same time, Universal had no intention of living up to the pledge made by Casey Silver at the 1997 Cannes Film Festival that his company would release as many as thirty to thirty-five films a year. Indeed, if the studio released half as many, that number would be considered sufficient.

Universal was scaling back, that much was vividly apparent. Edgar Jr. may have started out producing films as well as writing songs, but, in the end, movies were no longer music to his ears. By the Thanksgiving holidays, his worst fears were realized. *Meet Joe Black* opened to dismal business and, despite predictions that it would soon find its audience, that following never materialized. After stressful delays owing to problems with special effects, an eleventh-hour test screening of *Babe* was similarly alarming. For many children, the movie seemed too dark, and there was little time to modify the film if the release dates were to be met. While the "mix" was toned down to reduce the shrill music and harsh sound effects, the word somehow had gotten out that *Babe* was not as appealing as such competitive films as *Rugrats* and *A Bug's Life*. By the end of the five-day Thanksgiving weekend, the numbers told a grim story. *Babe* had grossed $8.5

million compared with $46.5 million for *Bug's Life* and $27.6 million for *Rugrats*. As for *Meet Joe Black*, after 17 days it still had barely edged past $35.8 million.

Insiders were not surprised when the golden parachutes started opening all around Universal City. Frank Biondi, Bronfman's chief at Universal, was out with a $30 million settlement. And shortly thereafter Casey Silver also was history, with a lavish production deal. It would now be up to Ron Meyer, the ex-agent, to reinvent Universal in a consistent with the new corporate strategy, the details of which still remained vague.

At Sony, the postsummer reassessment was equally opaque. This was the summer that was to establish John Calley's regime as Sony's new driving force. Once considered too elitist for a post like this, Calley had chosen to enter the fray armed not just with a solidly commercial project, but with a franchise—*Godzilla*. As summer moved along, however, he became exasperated by the chorus from the press and Wall Street securities analysts that *Godzilla* was a flop.

Clearly *Godzilla* was not a flop. What it was, however, was a supreme frustration bordering on an affront. By any rational judgment, *Godzilla* represented an appalling example of dumb filmmaking—"a cold-hearted mechanistic vision," as Roger Ebert put it. The performances were lame but so was the script. Even the effects seemed misbegotten, an out-of-scale creature romping around rainy, gloomy exteriors. As a rival producer of special-effects movies put it, "These guys kept telling us they would bring this franchise into the nineties, get rid of the man in the rubber suit and all the miniatures, but they gave us a picture that was less satisfying than the original."

At the outset of their project, Dean Devlin and Roland Emmerich agreed to brief me at various stages of the production, reviewing both the good and bad news. Once the film opened and the critical catcalls were being heard, however, Devlin and I had the following phone conversation.

"It's been a long summer for you, Dean," I said, "but I wanted to sit down with you for that final look back we'd talked about in April."

There was a pause. "I don't want to participate," Devlin replied. "I feel we've been treated badly by the press. We don't want to talk anymore." An outgoing, ebullient man, Devlin's voice usually has a mirthful timbre, as though he was about to tell you a terrific joke. Now he seemed both confused and angry, his voice shaking as he talked.

I tried to assuage his concerns. "Everyone feels like he's been mistreated by the press," I said. "Filmmakers think all their interviews are going to turn out like their sound bites on 'Entertainment Tonight' or 'Access Hollywood.' It doesn't work that way anymore, Dean. Reporters want to do stories about the budget, about the effects, about production problems. It's the way things are in the nineties."

"I know what you're saying, but the whole thing kind of took the wind out of us. We just don't want to talk." He paused for a beat, then: "Let me just repeat what I told you before, I will never again make a movie under this much pressure when a release date is staring us in the face and there's no time for a test screening, when I have to fly blind. Never again."

I understood Devlin's reticence, but I nonetheless decided to put the same money questions to John Calley, from whom I'd extracted a roughly similar commitment. "John, back in April, you generously offered to lead me though the economics of *Godzilla* when the whole thing was over, so I could get a grasp on this thing. We seem to be at that point now."

Calley's response was immediate: "I can't do that. It's all proprietary information. Look, *Godzilla*'s going to make money. That's all I care to say."

"Let me remind you how pissed off you were. Even the *Wall Street Journal* was calling it a turkey. You told me at the time that you would lay out the numbers."

"I changed my mind," Calley replied. "Besides, what's the point? Why should I give out proprietary information just to help you make money on your book?"

"It was your idea, John. Your way of setting the record straight."

"Let me talk to Dean [Devlin] and Roland [Emmerich]," Calley said. "They're my partners on this picture. I can't do anything like that without consulting them."

"Fine," I replied. "I'd appreciate it."

I never heard back from Calley.

So how much money did *Godzilla* make? By summer's end, its domestic gross had plateaued at $135 million. By early fall, however, the movie was eliciting a warm reception overseas, opening to near-record numbers in Spain and even surpassing the numbers for *Men in Black* in Sweden. While it opened strongly in Japan, a curious counterreaction occurred, with audiences apparently resenting the fact that a Japanese franchise had been so boldly Americanized. Before long, *Saving Private Ryan* and *Deep Impact* had eclipsed it.

Though Sony executives were being evasive, their estimates for overseas business approached $250 million, bringing the total world gross to roughly $385 million. Given the $200 million cost of producing and launching the movie in the U.S., Sony would clearly elicit a profit from its remake, albeit an unspectacular one and nowhere the $80 million that Disney claimed it had earned on *Armageddon*.

Sony's summer did not begin and end with *Godzilla*, of course. Despite all its preproduction tribulations, *The Mask of Zorro* also turned out to be a solid success for Sony's TriStar unit. It grossed $90 million in the U.S. and a like number abroad. Given the healthy share designated for Spielberg's company, however, *Zorro* hardly seemed destined to be a major profit center for Sony.

The plan at Sony was to surround its tentpoles with an array of inexpensive movies, most of them aimed at that beckoning youth audience. But while this plan worked for Fox, it didn't for Sony. A succession of films like *Can't Hardly Wait* simply didn't perform, though *Madeline* was a modest success. As a result, the company's vaunted claim on market share leadership, which Calley ardently hoped to retain, was surrendered ignominiously. Disney and Fox finished in a virtual tie, claiming 20.9 percent and 20.3 percent of the summer market, respectively, while Sony languished in fifth place with a mere 11.8 percent, down 48 percent from 1997.

To an outsider, the import of these numbers may seem trifling, but in the executive suites, market share was not only a measure of success but of macho. Some studios build their bonus plans around market share. Plunging from first to fifth represented one more irritant not only to Calley but to his corporate overseers in Japan.

Indeed, in my several encounters with Calley toward the end of summer, I found him a changed man. The quick jest, the ready smile had vanished. He seemed irritable, even defensive. His face was creased with lines of worry, and he seemed to have aged several years in the course of the summer.

Back in April he'd talked excitedly about the projects he was preparing, but now he talked about his intention to turn over most of the decision-making at the studio to Amy Pascal. It would be Pascal, he explained, who would assume the main responsibility for picking the pictures and assembling their elements, while Calley focused on his other executive duties. When asked about the future of Devlin and Emmerich, he replied that they were working on important projects, but that a sequel to *Godzilla* was not immediately among them.

The transfer of power to Pascal triggered gossip on the Sony lot that Calley would retire from his post some time during the next several months, perhaps joining his longtime friend Sidney Pollack in establishing a new production entity. According to the rumors, lawyers were already at work putting together the deal and securing the financing. Not surprisingly, Calley denied any of this was happening. "I'm here and I will be here until I decide not to be here" was all he chose to say. But not everyone was to remain in place in Calley's tight little hierarchy. Chris Lee, the Yale-educated Asian American who had risen to president of TriStar and then became part of the Columbia production team, would no longer be part of management. It was a suitable coda to the summer: Lee's claim to fame was that he was the executive who kept advocating Devlin and Emmerich for *Godzilla*. He was their chief loyalist, and now he was history.

If Sony presented a rather dour face to the community, the atmosphere at Warner Bros. was hardly more robust. That studio had managed to finish ahead of Sony with a 12.3 percent market share, but that was still 6 percent below 1997, which also had been a weak year—discouraging results for a company that had accustomed itself to being either number one or two. Though *Lethal Weapon IV* was principally responsible for its market share position, the project still carried an aura of corporate desperation—a movie they were compelled to make, not one they had wanted to make.

Hollywood loves rumors, and again they were swirling around Warner Bros. Terry Semel would go to Universal to be succeeded by Joe Roth, who would leave Disney, was one rumor late in the summer. Ted Turner had grown impatient with the studio's profligacy and lack of results, it was whispered, and would imminently swoop down to make drastic changes.

The Turner gossip was especially pervasive if impossible to prove. As the biggest stockholder in Time Warner, the mercurial "Mouth of the South" was known to be impatient with the Daly-Semel team. Though mainly identified with cable television, Turner, five years earlier, had exhibited a sudden interest in the movie business. He had paid well over half a billion dollars to acquire two sharp independents, Castle Rock and New Line, and had then established yet another company, Turner Pictures, ostensibly to produce quality films. The reason for this sudden surge of activity related in part to the needs of his cable channels, TNT and TBS among them, for fresh film output. On the other hand, Turner was now married to Jane Fonda, an actress and occasional producer, and was dropping some rather idealistic lines at dinner parties about his growing interest in making what he considered to be "quality movies."

But Turner's film forays had uniformly turned sour. Shortly after their acquisition, both Castle Rock and New Line went into severe slumps, their once exemplary records suddenly tarnished by a series of losers. Castle Rock had looked as if it couldn't miss, making films like *When Harry Met Sally*, but now it was mired in projects like *Mississippi Burning* and *North*. New Line's output ranged from genre hits like the *Nightmare on Elm Street* series to daring films like *Seven* and *The Mask*. Suddenly, under Turner ownership, it was making *The Island of Dr. Moreau*, *Last Man Standing*, and *The Long Kiss Goodnight*.

After Turner's empire was gobbled up by Time Warner, his movie agenda shifted once again. Turner Pictures was abruptly folded, Castle Rock continued to flounder, cofinanced now by Warner Bros. and Polygram, while New Line managed not only to retain substantial autonomy but also to resume its winning streak. Despite Turner's obvious disdain for the policies of the Daly-Semel regime, a tacit hands-off treaty was negotiated by Gerald Levin, chairman of Time Warner, to keep the corporate peace. And though rumors persisted that Turner was bridling under this agreement, he nonetheless was abiding by it.

Meanwhile Daly and Semel, pinched by new budgetary constraints, were busily looking for cofinanciers for their movies. Where in the past the studio had moved on its own, co-venturing a few films each year only with New Regency, which had now moved to Fox, a whole new array of financing entities suddenly were opening offices on the lot. And, as at Paramount and Universal, the drill for a producer was not only to assemble the package but also the funding.

The town still asked: Could Daly and Semel successfully retool their strategy? Were they so locked into their big-budget, star-driven thinking that change was impossible?

By the end of summer '98, both men were saying all the right things. They continued to talk about modestly budgeted movies, pledging never again to start a movie until the script was right. The audience was changing, they said, and so must the studio.

Many agents and producers doing business day to day with the studio, however, dismissed this as mere spin. "All they really talk about is *Wild Wild West*, which takes them right back into the $100 million league," said one producer with long-term ties to the regime. "The studio's thinking will never change. But their luck better change."

By early fall, however, yet another expensive Warner Bros. action picture, *Soldier*, starring Kurt Russell, landed with that familiar dull thud in the marketplace. Its producer was Jerry Weintraub, the close friend of Semel whose last effort for the studio was *The Avengers*, a similar debacle. The scenario seemed to be repeating itself.

There was no such ambivalence at Fox. Having felt like the town's whipping boys through much of 1997, the studio's managers suddenly were sitting atop the heap. They had survived *Titanic*. They had assembled a highly credible summer slate within prudent budget parameters. They had even come up with the year's biggest sleeper, *There's Something About Mary*. The debacles of *Speed 2* and *Volcano* and the nightmare of Jim Cameron were behind them. Even Rupert Murdoch, who had never believed in the economics of the movie business, suddenly was hinting that maybe it was tolerable after all.

By summer's end it looked like *Dr. Dolittle* would do $145 million in the U.S., *The X-Files* would come in at $84 million, and *There's Something About Mary* would end up near $175 million in the U.S. and $200 million overseas. Meanwhile, the studio had done remarkably well with its smaller films: Though *Bulworth* failed to crack $26 million and had little impact overseas, the domestic gross on *Hope Floats* totaled $60 million, on *Ever After* $70 million, and on *How Stella Got Her Groove Back* $38 million.

The tendency of Fox executives to brag about their superior strategy annoyed rivals. Fox's success at the box office had nothing to do with combining low-budgeted, demographically targeted movies with so-called multiquadrant fare, as management kept crowing. Rather, it was all about luck—the "movie gods" again, they said. In point of fact, both sides had a point. Fox management had been shrewd in fast-tracking *Dr. Dolittle* based on concept alone. On the other hand, Eddie Murphy's very next release, *Holy Man*, which Disney brought out in October, opened to a pathetic $5.1 million. So why was *Dolittle* greeted so warmly from the start? Could it have been, in part, the *Dolittle* name, which Fox's ad team had ridiculed?

Similar arguments could be mustered on *There's Something About Mary*. MGM had gambled on the Farrelly brothers' previous movie, *Kingpin*, and had failed. But it was Fox, not MGM, that had courted the brothers and later, after seeing a very rough cut, had promptly moved the movie to summer—surely one of the year's smartest decisions. The distribution team also looked good in moving *How Stella Got Her Groove Back* to summer from fall.

Clearly, among all the studio managements, Fox's stood out in summer '98 as the luckiest, most resilient, and most agile. Despite the battering they took during the days of *Speed 2* and *Titanic*, the team managed to maintain its appearance of unity and equanimity. Bill Mechanic, the plain-spoken, monotoned former video executive; Tom Rothman, a nerdish but fiercely aggressive and hardworking former New York attorney; and Tom Sherak, a modest and magnanimous studio veteran who doubled as one of the town's prominent charitable fund-raisers, combined to present a forceful corporate team. Nonetheless, as Sherak summed up, "The same talented people who make and market the movies that work are the same talented people who make and market the movies that don't work."

The studio's approval rating was far from unanimous, however. Many felt Fox's decision to structure itself into four distinct divisions had turned out to be both confusing and redundant. The divisions were Twentieth Century Fox, led by Tom Rothman; Fox 2000, run by former producer Laura Ziskin; Fox Animation, headed by Chris Meledandri; and Fox Searchlight, whose president was Lindsay Law. The grand design was for each division to produce its own distinctive brand of film. It had worked, to a degree. Fox Searchlight, for example, distributed *The Full Monty*, but its four other 1998 releases were disappointments, including *Shoot Fish* and *Two Girls and a Guy*. Fox Animation got off to a dicey start with *Anastasia* but was determined to continue its battle against Disney. The Ziskin-led Fox 2000 remained relatively inactive in 1998 but promised a vigorous slate the following year. That left Rothman's wing with the bulk of the responsibility for filling out the slate. And given this responsibility, it was Rothman, aided by Sherak, who led the inspired charge on the Farrelly brothers. And in doing so, they managed to more than compensate for the missteps and redundancies that had been committed at the studio.

While Fox was standing by its multidivisional structure despite the overall mood of belt-tightening, Disney was headed in quite the opposite direction. Joe Roth had never been comfortable with the several units arrayed around the lot and by the end of summer '98 he had shut down the biggest, Touchstone Pictures, and terminated its production chief, Donald DeLine, consolidating all filmmaking activity under David Vogel, who reported to Roth.

Indeed, he was more than ready to back off further *Armageddon*-style adventures. Though that project had never incurred the risks of a *Titanic*, it nonetheless was a high-wire act. And while Roth had argued against cofinancing partners on that megafilm, he was now more than ready to find partners for his future big films—with the exception of animation. On that franchise, Disney now and forever would go it alone.

At summer's end, Roth felt he had accomplished his primary mission. He was, yet again, number one in market share. On the other hand, by early fall Disney stock was again plunging, the ABC Network was having another disappointing TV season, and rumors were rife of imminent executive changes, including those involving Roth. The Disney chief denied all this, pointing to his expectations that his lineup for winter '98 would be the company's strongest ever and that he was in no mood to start from scratch elsewhere. But as one close friend noted, "Disney is a tough place, no matter how you define it. The pressures are extreme. Joe has a good working relationship with Eisner, but Michael tends to have his fingers in everything. I think Joe is wearing down."

In retrospect, Roth's summer slate had proven to be a hairy but productive ride. He had bet the store on *Armageddon* and, despite all the static, it had been a winning bet. The movie turned out to be the only $200 million movie of summer (although a strong post-Oscar campaign for *Saving Private Ryan* should close the gap between the two films). In terms of worldwide gross, *Armageddon* had a good chance to pass the $500 million mark, which only six other Hollywood films have achieved.

None of Roth's other films came close to that mark, to be sure. *Mulan* grossed $120 million in the U.S. and roughly $200 million worldwide, putting it ahead of *Hercules* but still well behind *The Lion King* at $760 million. *Six Days, Seven Nights* ended up grossing $75 million in the U.S. and a like number overseas, reminding insiders both of Harrison Ford's star appeal and of Disney's marketing prowess. Paradoxically, these numbers were matched by Robert Redford's ponderously self-important movie, *The Horse Whisperer*. *The Parent Trap* grossed a respectable $70 million in the U.S. while *Jane Austen's Mafia* ended up at $19.8 million.

Roth's bottom line was that he had emerged from summer with two solid moneymakers in *Armageddon* and *Mulan*, which would ultimately provide grist for Disney's hugely profitable video arm, its retail outlets, and other ancillary streams. His other two pricey films, *The Horse Whisperer* and *Six Days, Seven Nights*, managed to satisfy Hollywood's rule-of-thumb criterion that if a film's domestic gross equals its negative cost, it will ultimately finish in the black.

What Roth hadn't delivered, to be sure, was a movie that the studio could take special pride in—a *Saving Private Ryan*. Even on the animation front, Disney's principals were looking over their shoulder uneasily to see what DreamWorks might be coming up with. The supreme irony at the Disney empire was that its brightest achievement artistically had come from its newest endeavor—theater. On Broadway, *The Lion King* was still the hottest ticket in town, nightly stunning its audiences and serving as lasting testimony to Disney's creative energy and risk-taking. But by December, Joe Roth, true to his forecasts, seemed to have a virtual lock on the box office yet again, with hits like *The Waterboy*, *A Bug's Life*, and *Enemy of the State*. The naysayers had been quieted yet again.

Of all the principal companies, the most unsettled by summer '98 was surely MGM. Undercapitalized and demoralized, MGM had managed to mobilize only two movies for summer '98—*Dirty Work*, and *Disturbing Behavior* starring Norm McDonald (its disastrous sequel to *Species*, its 1997 sci-fi hit, had opened at the start of May).

Between them, the once-proud studio had managed to achieve a pathetic 1.1 percent market share, lower even than Universal's 2.4 percent. Frank Mancuso, MGM's cagey chairman, said he had been troubled by the summer crush and so had delayed playing his "ace," *Ronin*, a $75 million thriller, until fall. In an effort to buy itself some star value, MGM had paid $14 million to Robert De Niro, by far his highest salary ever, to star in the movie and also had assigned sixty-eight-year-old John Frankenheimer to direct. Though it picked up some reasonably good reviews, the noirish thriller couldn't nudge past the $40 million mark in the U.S. and finished badly in the red.

None of this seemed to faze Kirk Kerkorian. This was the third time the eighty-two-year-old entrepreneur had found himself owning MGM, and he had billions at risk with well over 90 percent of the shares. Would he stay the course?

In the past, Kerkorian's behavior always had been to wait until things looked blackest, then magically extricate himself with a Houdini-like maneuver. By early fall, the ideal conditions for this sort of caper seemed to be at hand. MGM reported it had lost $113.9 million for the first nine months of 1998. The company was preparing to market a $700 million stock offering to the public, with the old Armenian acknowledging that he would invest another $630 million in the company.

Kerkorian also calmly agreed to pay an additional $235 million to Seagram to acquire the Polygram film library, which had become available after Edgar Bronfman Jr. had unsuccessfully tried to sell the entire Polygram film arm. According to experts in evaluating transactions of this sort, Kerkorian had made an excellent deal for himself. In so doing, the library of old films he now controlled totaled some six thousand features, second in size only to Warner Bros.

Thus Kerkorian was diligently building up his core asset, which would be a key pawn in any future negotiations to merge MGM with a more substantial distribution organization, a scenario that clearly enticed him. To further signal that MGM was still a going concern, the company announced its intention to release twelve to fourteen movies during 1999 and also to continue building its TV operation. "Kerkorian always has a strategy," one MGM insider observed. "And he always plays with a strong hand."

In sharp contrast to Kerkorian, DreamWorks, the fresh-faced newcomer, was cheerfully counting its winnings for the first time in summer '98. Four years after proclaiming themselves the new Dream Team, Spielberg, Katzenberg, and Geffen had finally made a major dent in the marketplace. Two DreamWorks projects, *Saving Private Ryan* and *Deep Impact*, had finished among the top five summer films and in early fall *Antz*, a smartly crafted animation movie, also became a genuine hit. As if this was not enough, the company's long-frustrated efforts to start construction of a new studio facility at Playa Vista, not far from Los Angeles International Airport, also looked to be back on track.

From the moment they first announced they were forming DreamWorks, two of the company's three partners had seemed frustrated by their reception. Geffen and Katzenberg, two of the town's most gifted spinmeisters, had expected their new venture to be greeted by deafening applause (Spielberg was, as usual, off in his own little universe, far removed from the barbs of the press). This was to be Hollywood's first major new studio in at least three generations. They had the capital, the proven management experience, and, most important, the big dream.

Things didn't quite turn out as they had expected. The response in the press was more curmudgeonly than grateful. Geffen and Katzenberg had long been accused of playing favorites in the press, planting scoops with favored reporters who could be depended upon to toe the official line. Nonloyalists tended to be snubbed. Geffen's unstinting campaign against Michael Ovitz, whom he loathed, provided an ongoing reminder of this phenomenon. "David was interested in *Vanity Fair* and maybe *Time* magazine, *The New York Times*, and the *Wall Street Journal*, and the rest of the press could get lost," said one reporter with long-standing Hollywood credentials. In part as a result of all this, reporters, instead of writing paeans to the new triumvirate, questioned whether DreamWorks had sufficient working capital, whether Spielberg would deliver films to the company or would wander off, or indeed, whether there was a real need at all for a new company. When DreamWorks TV shows hit some speed bumps, the press made much of it. "Ink," "High Incident," and "Champs" all tanked, leaving "Spin City" with Michael J. Fox as the company's lone success.

Similarly, the DreamWorks music subsidiary under Mo Ostin and Lenny Waronker could claim no multiplatinums as yet, but nonetheless had released about a dozen albums, one of which, the cast album of *Rent*, had sold seven hundred thousand copies.

Though things had not gone badly for the neophyte company, many of the town's power players had helped fan the nasty rumors. Investors were getting antsy, went one report. As a result, DreamWorks would supposedly be forced to merge into Universal Pictures, with Spielberg perhaps reducing his commitment to the company.

All of these rumors proved apocryphal, but they were irritants nonetheless. Said the outspoken Geffen: "We've had to listen to more shit, to more people saying, 'Do these guys know what they're doing?' At the end of the day, it's all bullshit. At the end of the day, the product speaks for itself."

That Geffen or Katzenberg would be surprised by the static was in itself surprising. They were, after all, going into competition with established companies in an increasingly troubled business. Katzenberg had had his prior conflicts with Disney management and now was systematically hiring away animators from Disney, vastly raising the market for salaries in the field. The old axiom about competition in Hollywood states: People don't just want to succeed, they want you to fail. And that certainly included Messrs. Spielberg, Katzenberg, and Geffen.

Even those working for the new company found it not only a different work environment, but in many ways an utterly confusing one. In a New Age–type stab at corporate democracy, no one at DreamWorks was awarded a title, yet it was assumed that each colleague knew for whom he or she was working. Confounding at the lower levels, this policy proved truly baffling atop the pyramid, where a group of high-paid, titleless executives served Steven Spielberg. They included Robert Cooper, who functioned as a chief of production, and the husband-and-wife team of Walter Parkes and Laurie McDonald, who did somewhat the same thing, but also served Spielberg's needs at his personal production company, Amblin, producing some of his high-profile sequels. Given this idiosyncratic structure, no one quite knew whether to submit a new project to Parkes, McDonald, Cooper, or even Spielberg. In fact, when Spielberg was working day to day at DreamWorks, the system worked one way, but when he was off directing a movie, it worked in quite another.

Parkes, for one, insisted that, out of the apparent chaos, an order had finally evolved. As a result, DreamWorks had quietly built up an estimable list of future productions encompassing directors like Robert Zemeckis, Ridley Scott, Jan De Bont, and Cameron Crowe, and such stars as Harrison Ford, Michelle Pfeiffer, Tom Hanks, and Kevin Spacey.

To finance these and similar projects, DreamWorks managed to string together some hefty bank financing, private investments from the likes of Microsoft cofounder Paul Allen, and major output deals with distributors and TV networks here and abroad. All of this assured DreamWorks a capitalization of roughly $4.5 billion, more than enough to sustain the company in the coming years.

Still unanswered was the question of whether DreamWorks would utilize these resources merely to replicate the output of established Hollywood companies or rather to strike out on its own, creating its own distinctive personality and putting its own stamp on its product.

When questioned about this, the partners all had given oblique answers or simply shrugged it off as irrelevant. Yet back in Hollywood's golden era, each of the studios had its own distinct personality, MGM with its opulent musicals and lavish corporate style (white telephones at the time were deemed the ultimate status symbol, and only MGM had white phones). Warner was more down-and-dirty, but its genre gangster films were a memorable signature.

In the Hollywood of the eighties and nineties, however, all the studios were essentially indistinguishable. Warner Bros. focused on its stars and Disney had its animation franchise, but, other than that, each receded into a corporate blur. Would DreamWorks break the mold?

Certainly Geffen and Katzenberg were, at their core, tough-minded businessmen who were bent on creating a viable enterprise, but each had his own private agenda. It was Katzenberg's desire to prove that he could improve on Disney's animation factory, and he felt that *Prince of Egypt*, headed for release at year's end, would realize this aim. Geffen, behind his game-playing and incendiary rhetoric, was a sophisticated man who loved art and theater and who, in some of his early films such as *Risky Business* and *Beetlejuice*, had tried to break with convention.

And finally there was the enigma of Spielberg, a man who had shown a gift at veering from the blatantly commercial to the artistically ambitious. Some of his critics argued, however, that when Spielberg became "arty," he tended to pull his material down to the simplistic or even saccharine. *The Color Purple* and *Amistad* were most often held up as examples. Moreover, when Spielberg chatted about his new company, he tended to fixate on technical or architectural novelties. The old-fashioned studios had never allowed enough room between stages so that trucks could comfortably unload their scenery and other material, he would point out. The sound stages never had provided room for directors to rehearse their actors for upcoming scenes. At the new Playa Vista stages, not only would there be rehearsal space, but provision also would be made to include at least two actual theaters to facilitate live performance, some of which might be tied in to movies in development.

All this augured well for the new studio, but didn't speak to the product or policies that would evolve from DreamWorks. Either none of the principals had thought much about it, or they were keeping their ideas close to the chest as though not to invite further ridicule from competitors or a feral press.

But one thing emerged loud and clear from summer '98: Dream-Works was here to stay. Admittedly the profits on its pictures, like *Saving Private Ryan* and *Deep Impact*, would have to be divided with cofinanciers and codistributors. And there would be a massive payout to their *auteur* partner, Spielberg, a man who, despite his goodwill and enthusiasm, also had the gift for emerging with extraordinary largesse from any transaction. The skepticism and the rumors had now been put to rest. As David Geffen put it rather bluntly, "We don't have to take any shit for a while."

The Dream Team could rejoice about *Saving Private Ryan*, but it was Paramount that developed the movie and shared in its bountiful revenue streams. The same held true for *Deep Impact*. The shotgun marriage with DreamWorks clearly had been good for the studio.

Aside from these triumphs, however, and from the glowing success of *The Truman Show*, the remainder of Paramount's summer program had failed to generate excitement. Brian De Palma's *Snake Eyes* received poor-to-mixed reviews and lost steam at $55 million in the U.S. Paramount's vaunted alliances with other Viacom divisions such as MTV and Nickelodeon yielded little for the summer, a further reminder of the myth of corporate synergy, though Nickelodeon's Rug-rats would emerge as a major winter hit. While Lorne Michaels maintained his viselike grip on "Saturday Night Live," despite a steady descent into mediocrity, the latest of his dumbed-down movie spin-offs, *A Night at the Roxbury*, came and went with haste (only *Wayne's World* in recent years had worked for him on the feature level). *Dead Man on Campus* from Viacom's MTV division also failed to make a dent. But Paramount could still crow about *Titanic*, surely one of the shrewdest, or luckiest, dealmaking parlays of recent movie history. Having capped its investment at a modest $65 million, the studio nonetheless was a generous and eager participant in its $1.8 billion worldwide gross.

Though nitpicking over the balky policies of Sherry Lansing and Jonathan Dolgen had become a favorite sport among agents and producers, the reality was that over six years, the unlikely team had built a remarkably durable regime. With his Mephistophelian demeanor and darkly sardonic humor, Dolgen posed a fearsome figure on the lot, but his policies were consistent and respected. And Sherry Lansing's firm hand on projects like *Deep Impact* and *The Truman Show* had further reinforced her reputation as perhaps the most effective, tough-minded woman executive in show business. Warmly empathetic one moment, then fiercely combative the next, she never let herself become a media punching bag as had Jamie Tarses, the young programming executive at ABC. Unlike Gerry Laybourne, who'd walked away from Disney, or Lucy Salhany, who'd resigned as head of UPN, or Kay Koplovitz, who'd let herself get pushed out at USA Networks, Lansing had displayed a ferocious aptitude for outdueling bureaucratic foes and outlasting corporate enemies. "I kiss her, she kisses me, I hug her, she hugs me, I call her honey and she calls me sweetie, but she's without doubt the toughest person I know in or out of show business," says one producer who has been dealing with Lansing for years.

To be sure, Lansing often gave the impression of backing into projects. She was dubious about *Forrest Gump*, especially about its cost, but she let her enthusiastic aides such as Michelle Manning push it through, albeit with sharply compromised deals. She was similarly skeptical about *The Truman Show* and disliked its first cut, but, once again, she came forth with constructive proposals and remained supportive. "Sometimes Sherry will love something from day one, like *The First Wives Club*, but more often she senses something will work and will let herself be eased along by her staff," says one of her key executives. "She will nag us and natter at us and we think she may turn on us, but then she hangs in there and somehow it all comes out right."

Some Paramount critics, to be sure, took a "what-might-have-been" look at the studio and emerged with quite a different conclusion. Yes, the studio had had a solid summer, but if Sumner Redstone, the chief of Viacom, had not been so adamant about sharing the risk and had been more generous in allotting the studio a bigger budget, the results could have been astonishing. According to this what-if scenario, Paramount, with some shrewd negotiating, might have emerged as the sole financier of *Titanic*, *Saving Private Ryan*, and *Deep Impact*. Spielberg might have agreed to make *Ryan* away from DreamWorks if pressured to do so, it is argued. And Rupert Murdoch was sufficiently queasy about *Titanic* to have backed out had he received a good enough offer. Had all this come to pass, Paramount could have had not a good summer, but a cosmic one.

But that was not to be. This was a time for prudence, and Paramount had proven itself once again to be a shrewdly prudent player.

More and more the studios, like the television networks, were presenting a corporate face to the creative community. The turnaround at Twentieth Century Fox was engineered by a corporate team acting on a corporate game plan. Some of the studios still were being led by strong individuals like Joe Roth and Sherry Lansing, but they, too, were industriously executing policies designed to appease their corporate superiors as well as their boards of directors. Indeed both, in their quiet moments, would readily concede how rare, if ever, they got to make films they personally looked forward to seeing.

By and large, Roth, Lansing, and other studio heads emerged from summer '98 utterly fatigued and vaguely dispirited. It was a season to survive, and they had done so not with a rush of triumph but with a sigh of relief. They were grateful for their successes but fretful about the cost of that success, both in terms of money and morale. "Sure, *Armageddon* reached $200 million domestic, but that was a tough $200 million to get to," said Jeff Blake, the distribution chief at Sony. "We reached our $135 million domestic on *Godzilla*, but it was a tough $135 million." A tough guy, Blake wasn't whining, just observing.

In reality it was not the suits but rather several of the individual stars and filmmakers who were the true winners of summer '98. Some, like Steven Spielberg and Mel Gibson, had been to the well before. For the Farrelly brothers, however, the spoils of victory represented a new experience and a delicious one. *Dumb and Dumber*, which they wrote and directed, was deemed a triumph for Jim Carrey, not the Farrellys. Their participation got them a payday, but not a career. Indeed, their next project, *Kingpin*, proved a failure and the studio that financed it, MGM, had slammed the door on any further movies, nor were other studios lining up for their services. By summer's end, however, with *There's Something About Mary*, they were the darlings of Hollywood with executives literally pressing money into their hot hands.

When I talked to the brothers in early fall, they were still stunned by the chain of events. Though outgoing and genial as ever, they nonetheless were finding it necessary to become increasingly self-protective.

"Our lives have been getting complicated," Peter Farrelly acknowledged. Though still living on the south shore of Massachusetts, far removed from the Hollywood hustle, the brothers now faced scripts pouring in, friends asking for help with their projects, offers accumulating, and agents making sly overtures. "It's so easy to end up wasting most of your time in meetings," Peter Farrelly said. "What we really want most to do is to focus on our next picture and make it happen."

On the surface, little had changed in their lives, he said. They had no intention of moving west and had not built palatial new homes, though Peter had bought some land in West Tisbury on Martha's Vineyard and hoped to build there someday. They had not switched agents, nor had they solicited or received a richer deal from Fox.

"We count ourselves lucky to have avoided all the static," Peter Farrelly reiterated. He'd heard all the horror stories of filmmakers desperately trying to collect on their points from studios. Under their deal, the brothers would receive a gross participation if and when the film reached break-even. Their confidence was bolstered, he said, when just before their movie opened they were invited to a small dinner in Los Angeles hosted by one of their producers. Says Peter: "We were surprised to find four guys from Fox at the dinner. I mean, it was an unpretentious evening in this guy's little house, but suddenly there was Bill Mechanic, Tom Sherak, Tom Rothman, and Hutch Parker [the production executive assigned to the project] crowded into the place. Before dinner Mechanic pulled us aside and handed us each an envelope. Inside was a check for $1 million. I had never seen a check for $1 million. Let's put it this way: It was quite a gesture."

The gestures continued. Though some studios would have delayed additional payments for as much as a year, Fox dispatched further advances within two months after the opening.

"Needless to say, we feel very good about Fox," Peter Farrelly explained. "There are enough other things to figure out without having to worry about that stuff."

One of the things the brothers were trying to figure out related to their newfound craft. To most filmmakers, directing represented the ultimate prize at the end of the rainbow. To the Farrellys, it was something they came upon almost by accident. They were writers, jokesmiths, who suddenly had a new gig. As such, it became part of their shtick to put down directing, or at least their directing skills—hence their line about being the "anti-Coens," referring to the rather austere and self-important Coen brothers.

Now the Farrellys were worried that their self-effacing jests had been misunderstood, that they had seemed somehow disrespectful. "The only point we were trying to make was that we were not trained as directors," Peter Farrelly explained. "We had never done a video or a commercial. When Jim Carrey turned to us and said, 'Okay, you guys direct *Dumb and Dumber*, we were as surprised as anyone else. He was coming off *Ace Ventura* and he liked his director on that picture, a first-timer [Tom Shadyac], so I guess he figured, Let's try it again. I mean, we were a bunch of guys trying to get over a few good jokes."

The brothers made no effort to conceal the fact that they'd like to work with Carrey again. And despite their down-home modesty, they

said they would also like to work with Tom Hanks, whom they regarded as a comic actor without peer.

To accomplish all this, of course, they would have to be taken
seriously, or at least convince the town that they were serious about
their craft. "Look, we don't pretend to know everything about the camera, but we work with an excellent and experienced crew, and our set
functions like a democracy," said Peter Farrelly. "We don't just say,
'Here's the shot we want,' we say, 'What's the best way to get this
shot?' and then we listen. Sure, we'd like to think like Jonathan
Demme, where one shot transitions into another and you watch it and
you think, 'That's amazing.' We'd like to get there, but we're
learning."

Whatever their level of skill, the Farrellys insisted they had no
intention of veering away from their idiosyncratic subject matter.
"Movies have been taken off course by special effects," says Peter
Farrelly. "They're all about big explosions and big noise, but they're
not story-related. We're obsessed with story. It's like, we want to get
back to basic rock 'n' roll. We want to get a laugh, not blast some poor
bastard out of his seat."

At summer's end, it was clear that the Farrelly brothers could do
whatever they wanted. And though they were understandably reticent
about revealing their personal stake in *Mary*, insiders estimate their
cut at between $8 million and $10 million—certainly one of the biggest bounties ever for neophyte filmmakers.

Their take was modest, to be sure, when compared with that of
Spielberg, who had been involved in four summer films as a director
or producer. With each project carrying its own arcane deal, it was
difficult to estimate precisely how much the nation's wealthiest filmmaker earned from his 1998 endeavors. On projects that Spielberg
produced, he customarily received 10 percent of the gross receipts.
On ones he directed, his percentage increased as the revenues keep
rolling in to his distributor, rising ultimately to a fifty-fifty split. He
also earned a healthier share of video revenues than any other filmmaker. Taking all this into consideration, a reasonable estimate of his

earnings from summer '98 would be in the neighborhood of $130 million, half of it from *Saving Private Ryan*.

By any definition, that represented a solid summer's work.

Among the stars of summer '98, the three biggest winners were Tom Hanks, Mel Gibson, and Eddie Murphy. It was Hanks, of course, who first read the script of *Saving Private Ryan* and who helped recruit Spielberg to direct. Like Spielberg, he received no up-front compensation for his role, but a 20 percent share of the gross receipts. As such, his reward for his two-month acting chore totaled about $30 million.

Gibson's agent, the wily Ed Limato, did not want him to do another *Lethal Weapon*, feeling that the series was old news. Gibson accepted out of his personal fondness for Dick Donner, the stimulation he derived from improvising his role, and the fact that no other project had captured his interest. Thanks to the success of the fourth iteration of *Lethal Weapon*, Gibson should ultimately take home an additional $22 million above and beyond his $20 million base salary.

After the end of principal photography, however, Gibson found himself in the same dilemma over future projects. Though every studio was offering him scripts to read accompanied by firm offers, he was having difficulty making a decision. "He's too rich and there are too many things to choose from," observed one Warner Bros. executive. "You've got to envy him and at the same time feel sorry for him." From time to time in early fall, various producers declared they had interested Gibson in a variety of projects. He was supposed to star in a remake of the Charles Dickens classic *A Tale of Two Cities*, but Warner Bros. couldn't devise a deal that was satisfactory to the star. A similar flirtation took place involving a movie based on the old TV show "Hogan's Heroes." Gibson considered playing a role in a movie called *The Million Dollar Hotel*, to be directed by Wim Wenders. But the star remained frustrated in his efforts to trigger the one project that remained his primary interest, a remake of *Fahrenheit 451*, the old François Truffaut movie. Several drafts had failed to meet expectations. Gibson tried to woo Brad Pitt to play the lead but couldn't elicit a firm commitment. Warner Bros. had expressed its willingness to finance the film provided Gibson star in it, but Gibson wanted to direct and not act, unlike his dual role in *Braveheart*. The fact that Mel Gibson, perhaps Hollywood's most sought-after star, was having such difficulty casting his own picture brought a measure of joy to the hearts of the many producers and directors who had tried to pin him down for their own projects. Gibson, at least, now knew what it was like.

For at least two directors, the experience of summer '98 had been less than felicitous. Even before tackling *Jane Austen's Mafia*, Jim Abrahams had felt that he was nearing the end of a cycle with his *Airplane*-like parodies. His partnership with the Zucker brothers had ended several years earlier, but Abrahams had persisted with his laugh-a-minute formula. This time it simply didn't work: Some of the gags clicked; the majority were duds. Abrahams had the added misfortune of opening his movie barely ten days after *There's Something About Mary*. "Tom Rothman of Fox put it best," Abrahams recalls. "He pointed out that some movies create such an impact that they kind of change the landscape. That was the case with *Mary*; it changed the landscape for comedy.

"I'd been wanting to pull away from these flat-out parodies," he continued, "but Hollywood is always willing to pay you more than you're worth to do something they want you to do, and so I ended up trying it one more time. Now it's done. I want to do a picture that can touch people, a laugh-and-cry movie. I know I can do it. I did a TV movie with Meryl Streep that demonstrated as much. That's what I'm looking for."

As of late fall, he still hadn't found it.

For Jeremiah Chechik, who had the misfortune to direct *The Avengers*, the experience reinforced his conviction that the big studios now were simply a black hole for any filmmaker who was serious about his work. With *The Avengers* he had clearly stated his intention to make a stylized, nonlinear thriller and Warner Bros. had decided to sell it as a James Bond movie. Having sworn off studios, Chechik said he had put together the financing for an edgy independent film but he declined to give the specifics.

Uma Thurman, Ralph Fiennes, and certainly Sean Connery remained established stars, and *The Avengers* doubtless would disappear from their filmographies in due time. But for the career of Jerry Weintraub, the wizened producer and driving force behind *The Avengers*, it represented a major setback. A friend and ally of Terry Semel, Weintraub had followed that movie with yet another flop in October, the ill-conceived sci-fi epic *The Soldier*, starring Kurt Russell. "Semel has a reputation for standing by his friends, but Semel's own position isn't exactly super-solid," noted a long-term Warner executive who worked outside the production arena. Weintraub himself declined to speculate. "The whole experience involving *The Avengers* wounded me deeply," he told me. "I find it excruciating to even think about."

The impact of *Bulworth* on Warren Beatty's career also was difficult to gauge. Even before *Bulworth*, his superstar shine had begun to tarnish. Beatty saw *Bulworth* as his chance to endear himself to a younger audience. He was the cool albeit long-in-the-tooth rapper who was coming on to a beautiful young African American woman—how hip can you get?

The movie worked for the older audience—or at least a narrow segment of it—but it didn't for young filmgoers or for blacks. A survivor first and foremost, Beatty leaped into a new role almost immediately upon *Bulworth*'s release. It was a romantic comedy called *Town and Country* with Beatty playing a philandering husband yet again.

The new movie was funded by New Line, which had been anything but happy with its star. "He behaved badly, plain and simple," said one senior New Line executive. "He claimed that the script had been changed from the version he had approved and, since his contract provided him with script approval, he insisted that Buck Henry be on the set to rewrite the movie. It's been a nightmare."

Bob Shaye, the feisty chairman of New Line, told friends that he was not even sure how the movie got the green light at his company. "One day we were considering it, then suddenly we were making it," he said. If true, this represented an interesting parallel to Beatty's *Bulworth* deal at Fox, where no executive ever admitted to having green-lighted the project.

Though Ivan Reitman's picture *Six Days, Seven Nights* had done vastly more business than Jim Abrahams's, his mood at summer's end was far from euphoric. The movie seemed to reinforce the criticism of Reitman's work as formulaic. An intensely industrious man, Reitman was eager to prepare a diverse program of films that would erase this stereotype. Joining forces with Tom Pollock, an astute attorney who had served as chairman of Universal in the pre-Bronfman epoch, Reitman closed an opulent deal with Polygram to develop and produce a slate of movies. Upon putting twelve projects into development, however, the Reitman-Pollock deal was abruptly put on hold. Polygram had been acquired by Universal and the chances of Universal picking up their deal were remote indeed. Only a year earlier that studio had abruptly terminated its overall deal with Reitman, and Bronfman, of course, had previously dispensed with Pollock. Hence both were scurrying to find a new base.

Other directors, too, were having difficulty zeroing in on their next project. Delighted with the reception to *The Truman Show*, Peter Weir, a notoriously indecisive man, was reading and pondering. Dick Donner, too, was happy with his summer's labors on *Lethal Weapon IV*, but acknowledged, "I would never do it again." The frenzied thirty-seven-day postproduction ordeal had left him debilitated and, in late fall, he was still recovering his energy and reading scripts in search of a new project.

Stung by the harshness of some of his reviews, Robert Redford had traveled extensively overseas to promote *The Horse Whisperer*, then devoted himself to the Sundance Institute. High on his agenda was a drive to expand the Sundance TV channel and also open a small chain of Sundance theaters that would exhibit independent films. Redford flirted with a script set against a golfing background and another about spies, but was taking his time before making a commitment.

Chris Carter renewed his deal at Fox to continue producing "The

X-Files" TV series and also closed a deal with Bantam Books to write a novel with a supernatural background. There were no precise plans, however, to create a new *X-Files* feature motion picture. Nor was there any announcement from Sony about a sequel to *Godzilla*. Dean Devlin and Roland Emmerich, it was said, were intensely busy on a new project about the American Revolution by Robert Rodat, but no one seemed to know what it was.

While many of the directors of the films of summer '98 had the luxury of sifting and sorting, the writers were all back at work earning their next paycheck. Having written the ultimate screenplay about paranoia in *The Truman Show*, Andrew Niccol admitted he was too paranoid to reveal the subject of his next opus—"I'm not even trusting my own mother." The success of an unconventional movie like *The Truman Show* might prompt other studios to reach out for similarly unusual topics, he said, but, more likely, "The studios may also regard it as a complete aberration and go back to business as usual."

Though not happy with the way *Six Days, Seven Nights* turned out, Michael Browning nonetheless found that it earned him several healthy paychecks writing scripts on assignment. Like Niccol, Browning was intent on directing and was optimistic that the financing could be raised to shoot his original script, entitled *More Dogs and Bones*. It would not become a big studio picture, Browning said.

Robert Rodat's career also received a major boost from *Saving Private Ryan*, with the afterglow of that hit lasting for months. Spielberg invited Rodat to join his entourage at both the Venice and Deauville Film Festivals. "I had been to Venice six months earlier as a tourist with my wife and young kids," he said. "Now I was back, but in a world of police escorts and black-tie dinners."

What *Ryan* had given him was the opportunity to write big-canvas movies—the genre that most intrigued him. One script was about the fall of Rome; another, which had attracted the interest of the *Godzilla* producers, was about the American Revolution. "I think in terms of epic movies," Rodat reflected. "Thanks to *Private Ryan*, I now get paid to write them."

For Jonathan Hensleigh, *Armageddon*, despite all its pitched battles, was an unmitigated boon. The moment the film opened, his agent, David Lonner of the Endeavor Agency, trumpeted Hensleigh as "the can't-miss guy," pointing out that he had written *Die Hard, Jumanji, The Rock, The Saint, Con Air,* and now *Armageddon*. The implication: Hire Hensleigh and you'll get a "go" picture—a glowing commendation for a man who, only eight years earlier, was practicing law in Manhattan.

Within two weeks of the opening of *Armageddon*, Hensleigh was signed to write a sequel to *Jumanji* for a fee of $2.5 million for his initial draft against $4 million if the movie got made—perhaps the single richest writer's deal on record.

While Hensleigh was thrilled with the deal, he nonetheless felt thwarted in his ambition to move from writing to directing. Prior to the opening of *Armageddon* he had spent nine months in preproduction at Universal on a movie called *The Hulk*. He'd written a script and had also hired Industrial Light and Magic to work on the film. The studio seemed to like both the script and ILM's special effects, he said. Indeed, it had sunk $21 million into the project.

In late October, however, Hensleigh was summoned to the office of Casey Silver and informed that the studio had pulled the plug. There would be no directing job—indeed, no movie. Explanations were sparse. Hensleigh's hope that the success of *Armageddon* would help his chances as a director were dashed. The "can't-miss guy" had indeed missed, but was determined to keep trying.

Having survived the rigors of a high-tech movie, Mimi Leder was eager to establish herself in other genres. She signed to do a thriller starring Michael Douglas called *Still Life*, was talking with Universal about a romantic comedy called *Saving Grace*, and was also pursuing a more personal project appropriately titled *Sentimental Journey*. This was a true story of Leder's father, Paul, who, as an enlisted man in World War II, became involved with and later married a prisoner in a Nazi death camp.

Producer Jerry Bruckheimer also was determined to expand his

turf after *Armageddon*. His next film, *Enemy of the State*, a political
thriller starring Will Smith, opened around Thanksgiving to strong
box office response. He also started a low-budget division of his company with a movie called *Rock Star* as its first entry. Bruckheimer said
the film would be directed by a twenty-three-year-old tyro named
James Cox, recently out of NYU film school.

Jersey Films, run by Danny DeVito and his two partners, Stacey
Sher and Michael Shamberg, produced an edgy romance, *Living Out
Loud*, the first directing effort of screenwriter Richard LaGravanese,
and also planned to foster the directing debut of Scott Frank, who
wrote the two Elmore Leonard movies *Get Shorty* and *Out of Sight*.
Frank's movie would be called *The Dangerous Husband*, a dark ro-
mantic comedy. DeVito also hoped to direct his own film, a remake of
The Man Who Came to Dinner, under the auspices of the two Amblin/
DreamWorks executives, Laurie McDonald and Walter Parkes.

As for Steven Spielberg, his plate for 1999 was predictably as
diverse as it was overflowing. In development was a movie based on
the best-selling biography of Charles A. Lindbergh by A. Scott Berg,
with Paul Attanasio writing the screenplay, and a sci-fi thriller called
Minority Report to star Tom Cruise. Also on his slate was another
popular novel, *Memoirs of a Geisha*, which he hoped to shoot in Japan
in the spring. He later delayed the start date, explaining that he
didn't want his movie opening amid the millennium madness of
Christmas '99.

While his directing life remained busy, however, Spielberg's
agenda as a producer was suddenly all but empty. For the first time
in years there would be no Spielberg-produced project headed for
summer '99, with the possible exception of a sequel to *Casper*. "It was
my decision to focus on getting DreamWorks up to speed," Spielberg
explained. Some six films were put into production at DreamWorks in
November and December, all of them nurtured by Spielberg but none
emblazoned with his credit.

Releasing films without the Spielberg brand name might turn out
to be a mixed blessing. On the one hand, his DreamWorks partners

were delighted to have the filmmaker's focused input on their future projects. On the other, the Spielberg imprimatur arguably carried considerable weight in the marketplace—certainly it meant more than the DreamWorks logo at this stage in its development. Yet in all likelihood, the Spielberg producing credit might not again appear until sequels to such films as *The Mask of Zorro* and *Men in Black* rolled out in a year or two.

Spielberg's decision to focus on his DreamWorks commitment was rewarded in late fall by one important development. After what seemed like interminable negotiations with political and environmental groups, DreamWorks finally received the green light to start construction of its long-delayed studio at Playa Vista. Some speculated that 2002 or even 2003 might be a realistic date when they would be open for business. Always the optimist, Spielberg guessed two years earlier. That it would open at all was a minor miracle in view of the many obstacles. It was also vivid testimony to the stubbornness of Spielberg as well as the tenacity and solid connections of his colleagues.

Even as the studios carved up the largesse of summer '98, they pondered the legacies. Big bucks had been made, but there had been some big scares.

The biggest was the hype scare. Allied with its fast-food partners, toy makers, and other marketing zealots, Hollywood felt prepared to rewrite the textbooks on mass marketing. That is, until the customers started their revolt.

The great *Godzilla* rebellion sent shock waves through the ranks of the hypemeisters. The noise level of the hard sell had been turned up too high, and suddenly moviegoers seemed to be saying, "You'd better deliver the goods or we'll turn on you." The weapons of mass marketing had produced a countervailing force—mass disdain—and the studios as well as the filmmakers had to run for cover.

Yet in the end the audiences kept coming back for more. Movies were regaining their grip on the pop culture. Weekly admissions, having plummeted from 78.2 million in 1946 to 15.8 million in 1971, suddenly were sharply on the rise yet again. The fact that both *Saving Private Ryan* and *There's Something About Mary* were runaway hits vividly illustrated the range of taste globally. There was room both for an *Armageddon* and for a *Truman Show*.

To be sure, the Great Divide in moviedom seemed to widen. The art movie all but went into hiding during summer '98. More and more, the blockbusters dominated the marketplace. The fond hope of a decade ago that the modern megaplex would offer a glint of light for art movies had been dashed. Older moviegoers looked back fondly to that brief moment in the early seventies when innovative movies like *The Godfather* led the way at the box office and when the "top ten" list actually was dominated by serious filmmakers.

Those filmmakers responsible for the serious fare of summer '98 sadly did not represent a bold new generation of cutting-edge artists. Steven Spielberg, who made *Saving Private Ryan*; Peter Weir, who directed *The Truman Show*; and Warren Beatty, who created the brilliant but short-lived *Bulworth*, were brave survivors of that earlier epoch. The bright young comers like Kevin Smith (*Chasing Amy*) or Atom Egoyan (*The Sweet Hereafter*) were all huddled together in the art house cellar. And their share of market, if anything, seemed to be shrinking.

As Hollywood kept raising the stakes of the blockbuster game, risk-taking would become all the rarer. And the stakes would keep rising: The number of $150 million escapades may diminish, the special-effects megamovies may be somewhat curtailed, but the overall costs of producing and marketing movies showed no signs of retrenchment. Making movies had become a global game of chicken, with the new oligarchs of mass entertainment rewriting the rules as they went along.

Summer '98 flashed some signals of caution, and they were noticed, but the beat goes on. A new corporate culture was being planted in Hollywood. The vanities were firmly in place but there were as yet no flickers of a bonfire.

Epilogue: Summer 1999

One year after the battles of summer '98, the movie landscape had changed radically. The presummer slots that a year earlier were occupied uneasily by *Godzilla* and *Deep Impact* were now the province of George Lucas's *Star Wars* prequel. The box office numbers, though not as cosmic as some had predicted, were nonetheless remarkable, as was the sale of merchandise and all the other bric-a-brac turned out by the Lucas empire. Another sequel of quite a different sort, *Austin Powers,* had deftly infiltrated the gross-out market that a year earlier belonged to *There's Something About Mary.*

But while Hollywood was closely watching the numbers, its attention was also riveted on a real-life melodrama unfolding in a Century City conference room rigged as a surrogate courtroom. The stars were Michael Eisner and Jeffrey Katzenberg and the story line seemed a perfect metaphor for the basic condition in which Hollywood found itself.

The set-up: Katzenberg was suing Eisner and his company, Disney, in an effort to secure bonus monies owed him for his ten-year stint as Eisner's right-hand man. Disney honchos acknowledged they owed their former executive millions of dollars stemming from his 2 percent share of the profits—a cut the company had agreed to pay several years before—but the two parties fiercely disagreed on the precise amount. In fact they were roughly half a billion apart in their estimations.

To support his case, Katzenberg's high-priced legal team (his tab would ultimately approach $40 million) brought forth a blizzard of charts and graphs to demonstrate Disney's past profitability and future revenue streams. The Katzenberg view of the show-biz future was rosy: billions would flow from burgeoning new technologies as well as from vast, unexploited markets such as China and India. Though conceding that his live-action movies had proven unprofitable in the short term, Katzenberg foresaw billions in long-term profits. He even advanced the extraordinary argument that, during and after his reign, Disney had seriously undervalued its movies and TV shows, selling them to the ABC network (a Disney subsidiary) for less than they would fetch at rival networks. This amounted to an open admission that Disney had short-changed its partners in the creative community.

In response, Eisner's legal eagles found themselves in the awkward position of downplaying the company's profitability and minimizing the new vistas. Contradicting the glowing forecasts Disney had once provided to stock analysts, Eisner now painted a grim portrait of a stressed-out company struggling within a troubled industry.

These contradictory views effectively mirrored Hollywood's overall ambivalence about its future. For example, summer '99 was turning out to be a bountiful period, with audiences lining up to see the new movies and to buy the concomitant goodies. On the other hand, costs were too high, competition too feverish, and the margins too skimpy to justify the risk—at least not according to the criteria imposed by the multinational corporations that owned the studios. Theoretically it was a great business; it was just that the numbers weren't adding up.

The Eisner-Katzenberg battle was about more than business projections, however. Essentially it was also about greed. As far as most Hollywood denizens were concerned, it pitted a "suit" who demanded to be overpaid for past services, against a corporate mogul who—having made hundreds of millions for himself—was determined to underpay his former aide. And in mobilizing their respective cases, each had managed to undermine the basic integrity of the entertainment industry. Those entrusted to tally up the numbers apparently had been lying to those around them. All the past paranoia about the scorekeepers had been justified—the game was cooked.

As the trial began weakening Hollywood's self-confidence, so Washington seemed bent on eroding its credibility. In the months following the Columbine high school massacre, the anti-Hollywood drumbeat had steadily picked up in intensity. The culture warriors were on the warpath.

As far as Hollywood was concerned the cacophonous attacks from Washington represented a blatant effort to distract the public's attention from the real issue—guns. The politicians were unwilling to stand up to the gun lobby, which paradoxically was now headed by Charlton Heston, the one-time star of Bible epics. Speechifying about Hollywood carried with it little political risk. The huge audience that relished action films wasn't going to raise its voice in protest. When President Clinton joined in the chorus, there was a moment of stunned silence from his Hollywood constituency. Steven Spielberg, David Geffen, and others had given generously to the Clinton cause. Was the president now turning on his own supporters?

To be sure, Clinton's specific proposals proved to be tamer than his rhetoric. There would be a stepped-up effort to restrain kids under the age of seventeen from venturing into R-rated movies, which everyone could agree to. The problem of implementation was something else, however. When a kid bought a ticket to *Tarzan* at the multiplex, there was nothing to prevent him from darting into another auditorium to catch an R-rated movie like *The Matrix*. The owners of the big circuits had no intention of hiring squadrons of security guards to police their corridors. These were places for relaxation, after all, and uniformed guards would provide an unpleasant and alienating environment.

Still, Hollywood resented the chorus of criticism for several important reasons. There was, to begin with, a genuine concern about a new wave of censorship. Reactionary local censorship boards had been driven out of business by the industry's own machinery of self-regulation, which implanted ratings like G, PG-13, R, and NC-17 upon Hollywood's product. These ratings were far from perfect. Over the years members of the ratings board had seemed more concerned with sex than violence. A gore-fest with a heavy body count could squeak by with a PG-13, but subtle displays of sexual contact could relegate a movie to NC-17 hell. And while the Motion Picture Association of America argued that an NC-17 was by no means punitive, many newspapers around the country automatically rejected ads for movies carrying that rating and some big theater chains refused to even book them.

Whatever its flaws, however, the industry's self-administered "code" had been a huge success in achieving its prime objective: those nasty local censors had all but vanished. Given the rhetoric of the new "culture warriors," however, there was now concern that they might return, and the prospect of a movie having to pass muster with scores of local boards around the country sent chills through the Hollywood studios.

There was another reason why the politicians touched a raw nerve. Despite all the official position-taking, segments of Hollywood's creative community shared the conviction that movies and TV were indeed too violent and that self-restraints were simply not working. Washington stereotypes notwithstanding, the people who turned out the movies and TV shows—the writers, directors, artisans, and even the actors—by and large subscribed to "family values" similar to those espoused by the politicians. They, too, worried about the influences of the pop culture that they themselves had created. They, too, perceived how shrewdly and cynically movies were targeted to the youth market.

And some professed to be doing something about it. "We don't have the final control," one filmmaker told me, "and we can't decide what movies will get made." Nonetheless he, like many of his brethren, claimed to be doubling efforts to soften the action and to develop more films that reinforced positive values. Given this determination, the criticism from Washington seemed all the more empty and acrimonious.

If Hollywood's denizens were troubled by political backbiting, they were equally fretful about economic difficulties that were eating away at the superstructure. While the nation as a whole was experiencing a buoyant economy, Tinseltown's was far from robust. The number of movies being made per year was shrinking. The job market was getting tighter. In the midst of all the prosperity, Hollywood was teetering on the edge of a recession.

Part of the explanation was the old bogeyman of runaway production. According to one study cited in *Daily Variety*, Hollywood in 1998 had sustained a $10.3 billion loss in potential revenue from projects developed for TV or film that ultimately were shot overseas. To be sure, some of these shows were set in distant places and were more appropriately shot abroad. Nonetheless well over a quarter of them were being filmed outside Hollywood for purely financial reasons— it was cheaper to shoot in places like Toronto or Vancouver or even overseas. According to the unions, this translated into a loss of 20,000 jobs that year. And the two countries that seemed to gain the most from this trend were Canada and Australia. The quality and training of crews in those countries had improved considerably over the last decade while costs remained lower than those in Hollywood. Moreover, the relative value of Canadian and Australian currencies had declined between 15 percent and 23 percent over the past decade, adding further inducement.

The net effect of all this was that Hollywood was losing its swagger. The film capital had been savoring boom times for a couple of generations now, but suddenly the skies were darkening. And the very people who owned the town—the multinational corporations—seemed the most shaken. Though crowds were still lining up to see Hollywood product, the men at the controls did not seem to believe in the economic viability of their industry. And with employment declining,

Washington taking potshots, and men like Eisner and Katzenberg at each other's throats, Hollywood seemed trapped amid its own short-comings. These were indeed the best and the worst of times.

Given Hollywood's downbeat attitude, it was not surprising to find the studios reaching ever more eagerly to foreign partners to share the risk. Overseas distribution entities like Australia's Village Roadshow and pay-TV giants like France's Canal Plus now willingly accepted cofinancing deals that were vastly more felicitous than those offered them a few years earlier. Suddenly Hollywood was giving them a chance to share in the full spectrum of revenue streams, not merely those from TV or theater grosses in their specific territories. To be sure, this meant that a company like Warner Bros. now found itself forfeiting half the profits from a hit like *The Matrix*. That same studio, on the other hand, in a moment of hubris, had neglected to protect its downside on its dreadful comedy, *Wild Wild West*, starring Will Smith and Kevin Kline.

Hollywood's producing fraternity found itself in a curious di-lemma as a result of these fiscal maneuverings. Suddenly their prime responsibility was to produce money, not movies. Veterans like Alan Ladd, Jr., who had green-lit *Star Wars* while heading production at Fox, and Richard Zanuck, whose long list of hits included *Jaws* and *Driving Miss Daisy*, found themselves stripped of their once bountiful studio deals and of the overhead and development funds that those deals entailed. Some of the younger producers, like prolific forty-year-old Scott Rudin, managed to sustain their studio ties (Rudin's were at Paramount), but were nonetheless exasperated with their unwanted new responsibilities as financiers.

"My strength is finding outstanding material and packaging that material with the right filmmakers," said Rudin, whose credits in-cluded *Ransom* and *The Truman Show*, and who managed to produce six movies and five Broadway plays during 1999. "Yet now I find myself dealing with as many as twelve subdistributors around the world who are advancing much of the money for my films. I'm in the banking and distribution business, not the producing business. Producing movies this way is a burdensome occupation."

Though top filmmakers were frustrated by the studios' new posture, their omnivorous corporate parents looked on approvingly. As far as the multinationals were concerned, Hollywood was at last displaying some prudence. And though an occasional mega-movie like *Wild Wild West* still defied budgetary limits, much of the summer '99 product had been prudently produced as well as shrewdly targeted for a specific demographic. *Big Daddy*, starring Adam Sandler, *American Pie*, and the sequel to *Austin Powers* all were relatively inexpensive projects aimed at young males, those avid filmgoers who represented the closest Hollywood could find to its habit audience of the golden 1930s and '40s. It didn't require a multimillion-dollar spot on the Super Bowl to ignite their interest, nor were they swayed by the critics. The right buzz for a new movie could be created on the Internet together with properly placed ads on MTV and a shrewd publicity campaign. A giant *Godzilla*-like marketing budget was not required.

Despite those precautions, the studios' corporate parents were looking on with great apprehension as summer '99 unfolded. Though Fox prided itself in its marketing of George Lucas's *Star Wars* prequel, *The Phantom Menace*, its strategy had been meticulously set forth by Lucas's own organization and, since Lucas also financed his film, Fox received only a minimal distribution fee for its efforts. The rest of the studio's cautious program fell far short of its performance of a year earlier. "If Rupert Murdoch had it to do over again, he would never have bought the studio," said one of Murdoch's top lieutenants. "He would have been far happier buying movies on a picture-by-picture basis and not worrying about the overhead."

Michael Eisner's mood was easily as sour. Apart from the rigors of his litigation with Katzenberg, Eisner was far from thrilled by his studio's summer program, despite the success of *Tarzan*, its latest animated feature. ABC was also continuing to have its troubles and revenues from the Disney stores, a longtime gold mine, suddenly hit the wall. Even more daunting, the studio's seemingly limitless inventory of animated features, which had long sustained the profits of its video division, was now exhausted. Wall Street wondered whether the Disney miracle had abruptly ended.

Having survived a traumatic '98, Edgar Bronfman, Jr. could breathe a sigh of relief as his Universal Studio churned out surprise hits like *The Mummy, Notting Hill* (a semisequel to *Four Weddings and a Funeral*), and *American Pie.* To be sure, the executive who had nurtured Universal's winning slate, Casey Silver, had long since been removed from office—a repeat of what had happened several years earlier to Sony's Guber-Canton regime. Working under the close scrutiny of Bronfman and Ron Meyer, the new team at Universal faced tight budgetary constraints. Edgar Jr. had dealt away the studio's TV assets and remained highly skeptical of his movie operations. His focus remained on music but, even there, the results as yet were mixed.

DreamWorks sent forth yet another negative signal when it unexpectedly scuttled plans to build its long-heralded studio at Playa Vista. The new facility had long been a centerpiece of its strategy and Steven Spielberg had talked glowingly of his futuristic design. The new studio was going to house not only state-of-the-art sound stages, but also as many as three small theaters to try out live productions. In calling off these ambitious plans, the Spielberg-Katzenberg-Geffen team cited problems in arranging the financing, but friends in the industry observed that, if the "Dream Team" really wanted that piece of real estate, they would have simply written a check. Rather, the real bone of contention at Playa Vista stemmed from personality conflicts with developers who were tied to the project combined with the nagging worry that there were geological surprises buried underneath the land—surprises for which the DreamWorks partners might be personally liable. No one wished to discuss the specifics—whether the concern was methane gas, an earthquake fault, or the possibility that associates of Howard Hughes had allegedly buried arcane chemicals on the premises.

Perhaps mindful of the negative message sent forth by the cancellation of Playa Vista, DreamWorks surprised the town in midsummer by unveiling an ambitious program of productions involving such filmmakers as Robert Redford, Cameron Crowe, Bob Zemeckis, Ivan Reitman, and, of course, Spielberg himself. And Katzenberg promptly anointed himself as interim head of production, presiding over this expanded program, thus adding to his existing duties in overseeing television and animation. There were two provisos, however. One was that the post be termed "interim," meaning that someone else might take his place at some later stage. The second was that, despite his new position, Katzenberg would not consider himself to be a member of the triumvirate at DreamWorks that made the final decision on what movies to produce. That triumvirate consisted of Spielberg, Walter Parkes, and his wife, Laurie McDonald. Some at the company expressed skepticism that Katzenberg, a man of strong opinions, could actually resist an involvement in any decision-making process, but the key players concerned were adamant. When it came to movies, they said, Katzenberg would administer but he would not be a key decision-maker.

In assuming his new position, Katzenberg was supplanting a man named Robert Cooper, who had once headed production of in-house movies at HBO but who had not been able to click in his DreamWorks post. The departure of Cooper caused few ripples in Hollywood. Not many had felt he would be effective amid the forceful personalities at DreamWorks.

Indeed, as rumors of his imminent departure began to spread, they were dwarfed by changes of a far greater magnitude at Warner Bros.: the surprise departure of Robert Daly and Terry Semel, the two moguls who had seemed to be an island of stability in the movie business. Couched in the usual corporate euphemisms, the announcement stated the two had decided of their own volition that the time had come to move on to "other opportunities." No one in the film community bought that, however—at least not in the case of Semel. According to one widely-held theory, Gerald Levin, the CEO of Time Warner, had simply declared his unwillingness to renew Semel's bountiful contract when his current one expired in the fall of 1999. Both he and Daly also realized that the enormous autonomy they had exercised would now be impinged upon. Levin, Ted Turner, and their allies in New York had become impatient with moguldom—with the salaries, the lavish expenditures, the mind-blowing perks. "The way the New York suits saw it, the studio and the music company should be divisions of the corporation, not private fiefdoms," was the way one senior Time Warner executive explained it.

The customary praise was heaped on the two Warners hierarchs. Daly issued a quote emphasizing that he was departing at a time when the studio was in excellent shape. There was a degree of truth in this assessment, but in point of fact Warners had lately hit some bumps. *Wild Wild West*, its $180 million comedy-western, had been greeted by dismal reviews and catcalls from audiences. And while it opened to big numbers, the box office total fell precipitously as word got out that it failed to deliver laughs. *Eyes Wide Shut*, the Stanley Kubrick picture starring Tom Cruise and Nicole Kidman, by contrast was treated to ecstatic praise by major critics—Kubrick fans to the end—but, again, the public wasn't going along. To younger audiences, the movie was over-long, uniquely unerotic and curiously anachronistic.

Somehow the two films, *Eyes Wide Shut* and *Wild Wild West*, both seemed appropriate signals that the regime had run out of steam. It was time for a fresh point of view.

All in all, summer '99 was exhibiting the same sort of confused trends that marked the previous year. On the surface, business was strong, yet confidence shaky. The demand was on the rise, but the suppliers seemed faint of heart.

And adding to the malaise was yet another grim realization: By the end of the July 4 weekend it had become clear that, though the kids were lining up for the movies, the adults, by and large, were disappointed with what they were seeing. Movies like *Big Daddy* and the *Austin Powers* sequel simply didn't work for older audiences, and the appeal of Lucas's *Phantom Menace* also seemed focused on the subteen set. *Wild Wild West,* blasted by critics and disdained by most adults, also managed to work for the very young audience.

Those few films that seemed tailored for the older crowd also proved disappointing. *The General's Daughter,* starring John Travolta, seemed ordinary and *Notting Hill* was pallid compared with *Four Weddings and a Funeral.* The only director who was bent on making a statement was Spike Lee with *Summer of Sam,* but this, too, disappointed many of his fans because of its shrill excesses.

The questions raised by all this were inevitable: Was the new corporate Hollywood struggling so feverishly to please its multinational masters that quality and innovation were being compromised? In their quest for "numbers," were the studios surrendering to the tyranny of the kids' demo?

To further exacerbate their self-doubt, along came the bizarre little "mockumentary" called *The Blair Witch Project* that defied all the laws of summer movie-making. Made by a couple of total outsiders, the film cost—not $50 million—but $50,000. Its audience learned about the movie, not from a massive TV campaign, but from some shrewd manipulation of the Internet. In fact, Web-heads around the country somehow felt they had participated in the making of *The Blair Witch Project.* The result: A staggering $28.5 million opening weekend, putting it on course to become the most profitable movie in the history of the industry. Its two young directors, Eduardo Sanchez and Daniel Myrick, would end up earning over $12 million apiece even as Hollywood's established filmmakers scratched their heads in complete bewilderment.

Clearly the game had changed and Hollywood was struggling feverishly to figure out the new rules.

Acknowledgments

Thirty years ago my friend William Goldman wrote an incisive book called *The Season*, in which he scrutinized the shows and showmen who occupied center stage during one season on Broadway. Peter Gethers, the author and editor, suggested applying that precept to a season in Hollywood, and I am indebted to him for his insights, as I am to Goldman, who also was immensely helpful along the way. Robert Wallace of St. Martin's Press supplied the guile and guidance to help bring this idea to reality.

I would like to acknowledge the many people who worked on the specific films examined in this book and who were helpful to me, some on the record and some off. My thanks also to David Held, a former industry executive, for his insights; to Gerry Byrne for his support and forbearance; to my ever-diligent agent, Kathy Robbins; to my talented assistant, Bashirah Muttalib; and to my wife, Blackie, for her keen intelligence and for her patience.

Index